The Quotable Paul Johnson

THE QUOTABLE
PAUL JOHNSON

A Topical Compilation of His Wit,
Wisdom and Satire

EDITED BY
GEORGE J. MARLIN,
RICHARD P. RABATIN
AND
HEATHER RICHARDSON HIGGINS

WITH AN INTRODUCTION BY
WILLIAM F. BUCKLEY, JR.

FARRAR, STRAUS AND GIROUX
NEW YORK

LIBRARY OF CONGRESS CATALOGING-IN-PUBLICATION DATA
Johnson, Paul
The quotable Paul Johnson : a topical compilation of his wit,
wisdom, and satire / edited by George J. Marlin, Richard P. Rabatin,
and Heather S. Richardson ; with a foreword by William F. Buckley,
Jr. — 1st ed.
p.   cm.
Includes index.
1. Johnson, Paul—Quotations. 2. History—Quotations,
maxims, etc.   I. Marlin, George J.   II. Rabatin, Richard
P.   III. Higgins, Heather R.   IV. Title.
D15.J64A25 1994   909—dc20   94-18893   CIP

Our efforts are dedicated to

PATRICIA RICHARDSON
(1930–1990)

JACK SWAN

EILEEN M. LONG

Contents

Introduction

Many years ago somebody wrote to me apropos the public neglect of I forget who, complaining that his subject suffered from his absolutely predictable excellence. As so often happens on hearing an insight that comes to you with aphoristic distinctiveness, this one settled quickly in my mind as a cliché: Why hadn't *I* realized this, this . . . truism?

Well, I hadn't, and very soon after I began to wonder what would have been the reaction to Shakespeare if one of his sonnets were grievously disordered, or Bach if one or two cantatas had been just awful. The man who wrote to me (it was Alistair Cooke, as a matter of fact) used Trollope as his example. After a while, Trollope lost the attention of much of his public because he was too regularly wonderful. You will have guessed that I am putting Paul Johnson in this category, which is correct. His performances are unvaryingly (boringly?) extraordinary.

I forget when I first came upon his name. It was very long ago, not long after he began the most fecund journey to Damascus of our time. Obviously he was welcomed by all those who lament the hold that socialism in all its forms, and skepticism in all its forms, have on so many minds wonderfully fine except in the matter of reaching correct conclusions. It was a bright day for sound doctrine when Paul Johnson drew away from the beguiling, wrongheaded world that had captivated him.

But what happened wasn't merely a redisposition to right reason. It was the beginning of as productive a literary-analytical career as any in modern times; yes, the title of his best-known work, which many people keep within reach as the most useful reference book devoted, not to the meaning of words, but to the meaning of causes to which a perverse ordering of words have been committed. It is an encyclopedia of brief takes on just about everything of interest to those who are concerned about modern history and political philosophy. It is a book, by the way, that merits, indeed demands, updating, not so much because more fruitful thought on political questions is likely, as because history continues to bestow on us practical demonstrations of the results, ranging from unfortunate to disastrous, of the neglect of right reason. There are Hitlers ahead of us in history, mini-Hitlers let's hope, and *Modern Times II*, and *Modern Times VI*, should note them, and demonstrate how the lessons learned conform so well with the preachments of Paul Johnson. I end with a fruitless dilemma. On the one hand, I'd hope that Mr. Johnson would be the man who updated such books. On the other hand, I'd hope he'd have left the scene before we experience all that many mini-Hitlers.

I have had a few personal experiences with him, the most memorable an hour's TV exchange with him and Trevor Huddleston. The auspices were wonderfully venerable, St. James's Church in Piccadilly, and the question was South Africa. Bishop Huddleston preached the "inevitability" of civil war, while Johnson insisted that evolutionary progress from apartheid was possible and in fact predictable. Bishop Huddleston was a first-rate polemicist, but in making a case readily made to the extent that the South African government derived its very existence from apartheid, as also the South African economy, he had a problem. Everywhere he scurried in pursuit of his point, Johnson was waiting for him to urge sound economic arguments and to warn of the historic perils of revolutionary solutions.

One got quickly from exchanges with Mr. Johnson the impression that here was a truly well-stocked mind, and in the years since that broadcast he has published a half-dozen volumes documenting the great reaches of his knowledge and understanding. Why not forage over his work? Arrange sentences and paragraphs under topic headings? Facilitate the researches of Johnson-lovers—and indeed even of those not thoroughly familiar with his work—people disposed to search for, make use of, and take pleasure from the satisfactions one gets from the congruity of artfully arranged words and finely reasoned thought? When word came that such an enterprise was underway under the guiding hand of George Marlin there was rejoicing in that circle. We are familiar with his splendid and meticulous work on G. K. Chesterton, and it merely recertifies his jeweler's eye for fine thought and fine language that now he should be giving us Paul Johnson. This book will sit perfectly alongside *Modern Times.*

WILLIAM F. BUCKLEY, JR.

Preface

Since the publication of *Modern Times*, Paul Johnson has been recognized as one of the world's most distinguished and popular historian/journalists. That *Modern Times* has been translated into over twenty languages attests to the high esteem in which Johnson is held worldwide. The breadth of his knowledge and insights is amazing, and he has the remarkable ability to transform complex topics into wonderfully lucid prose. The many sides of his versatile mind are exemplified by the wide range of his writings.

His incisive commentaries on the continuing dehumanization of man, on the arts, politics, social sciences, and on the idealistic movements and the intellectual fads of the day are exceptional. In the United States his books such as *Intellectuals, A History of the Jews*, and *Birth of the Modern* command wide audiences. His forthcoming *History of the American People* is eagerly awaited. Magazines like *National Review, The New Republic, The American Spectator, Commentary*, and *Crisis* frequently publish his essays and book reviews.

We have edited this book as a tribute to Paul Johnson, whom we admire greatly. As his avid readers we found ourselves at times frustrated at not having one of his insights at our fingertips. At other times, it was difficult to instill our enthusiasm in others in order to introduce them to his efforts. This book is an attempt to address those desires by providing both a handy reference and a delightful read. Additionally, for Johnson initiates, we hope it will prove a valuable addition to any collection of his writings.

We are grateful to all of those who kindly helped us in our efforts, but any inaccuracies herein must rest on the shoulders of the editors. Special thanks to Larry and Pat Azar, Jerry Bertwell, Michael G. Crofton, Jack Griffin, Alan and Chris Jones, Michael Long, Barbara

D. Marlin, Joe Mysak, Thomas Walsh, and Charles G. Woram.

The editors would like to thank, in particular, Roger Straus for his enthusiasm about the project, and Lisa DePasquale for her many hours of assisting with the production of the manuscript.

GEORGE J. MARLIN
RICHARD P. RABATIN
HEATHER RICHARDSON HIGGINS
NEW YORK CITY
FEBRUARY 1994

The Quotable Paul Johnson

A

ABOLITION

On 22 June 1772, an important date in world history, Lord Chief Justice Mansfield effectively ended the legal status of slavery in England by ruling that it was "so odious that nothing can be suffered to support it but positive law" . . . [But] the French Revolution paradoxically delayed abolition because it allowed slave-trading interests to associate abolitionists with Jacobinism.

B.M., P. 322

ABORTION INDUSTRY

The abortion industry has been given a green light to do, in effect, what it wills. A fully formed child can be ripped from its mother's womb, screaming and gasping for breath, and then coldly butchered on the waiting slab by men and women—"specialists"—whose sole job in life is performing such lawful operations.

S., JUNE 23, 1990

ABSOLUTES

When absolute or fundamental values, resting on a sacral notion of natural moral law, are abandoned in favour of moral relativism, or even the complete suspension of moral law represented by modern "permissiveness," there is a danger, as [John Paul II] puts it, of "a purely utilitarian relationship between individual and individual."

[3]

It is at this point that de-humanization occurs, because each individual tends increasingly to see the other not as a person but as an object, to be made use of or exploited. Altruism disappears, the humanity of the other is no longer considered, a quasi-animal relationship develops, and as it does so the humanity of the exploiter diminishes too. We end with two exceptionally ingenious animals which are, because ingenious, exceptionally destructive.

P.J., PP. 108–9

ACADEMIA

. . . that traditional home of lost causes . . .

M.T., P. 698

ACADEMIC DESPOTS

Unfortunately, as in the past, those who run universities itch for a wider role. Pedagogues indulge in a recurrent fantasy in which they . . . rule the world; inside most dons a benevolent despot is struggling to get out . . . academic triumphalism takes many forms: in the Middle Ages and the Renaissance, the triumphalists proclaimed that their caste alone could authoritatively interpret the law of God and nations; now the emphasis has switched to the university as the progenitor of power and wealth—the brain behind the GNP. This new phase was born in the great Allied research programmes of the Second World War (notably the Manhattan Project), gathered pace during the 1950s and came to a resounding climax in the 1960s. It was adumbrated a generation earlier by the late-Victorian scientific professoriate, imbued with Darwinian survival-of-the-fittest nationalism, who saw in embryonic university technology the key to world power.

E.S., P. 162

ACADEMIC FASCISM

. . . one of the tactics of the Fascist Left is to mount campaigns of virulent personal abuse, in leaflets, student magazines, posters and so forth, against any members of the staff who offer them the slightest opposition. In nearly every case the accusations they hurl are complete fabrications; but, as with the Goebbels "big lie," they are often half-believed, and a distinguished academic can have his reputation permanently muddied in consequence.

E.S., P. 171

ACADEMIC TRIUMPHALISM

The rise of academic triumphalism damaged the university ethic because it devalued its sense of intellectual individualism, and flew in the face of Newman's wise observation: "A university is an *alma mater*, knowing her children one by one, not a foundry, or a mint, or a treadmill." Unfortuantely, the new and malignant forces which triumphalism conjured up outlived its downfall, and the damage threatens to be permanent. Despite the demonstration during the last decade that the universities cannot help governments, to anything like the degree that had been claimed, in their pursuit of economic and political objectives, the "heathen politicians" show no inclination to abandon their attempt to control academic strategies.

E.S., PP. 166–67

ADENAUER, KONRAD

Adenauer was one of the most gifted statesmen of modern times; certainly the most wholly successful in recent German history. . . . He [had] a strong streak of genuine idealism and ample reserves of cynical cunning. Erhard thought he had *Menschenverachtung*, a contempt for mankind. It was, rather, a vivid awareness of human weakness, and especially of German vices. . . . Collectively, he felt the Germans could only be trusted within the iron framework of the absolute rule of law, overawing even the state; his establishment

[5]

of this framework will in the long run prove, perhaps, his chief contribution to German political culture.

M.T., PP. 584–85

[Adenauer] tied the West Germans, economically, militarily and politically, to Western culture and legitimacy as tightly and as permanently as human ingenuity could devise. Therein lay the real idealism which balanced his Realpolitik. He was the first German statesman to put European before German interests.

M.T., P. 586

ADENAUER, KONRAD, AND ALCIDE DE GASPERI

At the end of the war in 1945, Alcide de Gasperi was sixty-five, Adenauer sixty-nine. Both were men from the borders, devout Catholics, anti-nationalists, men who revered the family as the social unit, hated the state (except as a minimal, regrettable necessity), and believed the most important characteristic of organized society to be the rule of law, which must reflect Natural Law, that is the ascendancy of absolute values. In short they set their faces against many of the salient features of the twentieth century.

M.T., PP. 577–78

AIDS

Thanks to the exertions of the homosexual lobbies, AIDS is the first epidemic to be politicised and information about it is correspondingly muddled. Homosexual activists have a clear motive: they want spending on AIDS research to increase astronomically, in the hope—probably vain—that a miracle "cure" can be found, so that they can resume their hyper-promiscuous activities. To increase public spending, they need to convince electorates that AIDS is not confined to sexual deviants and drug-addicts, but is spreading with terrifying speed among the normal population. They have enjoyed enviable success in getting this fantasy accepted by governments, international agencies, medical establishments and the media. Indeed, it should be a lesson to all of us how easily such supposedly intelligent and well-informed people are conned. As a result, statistical assertions about AIDS, often from exalted quarters, are an inextricable mixture of . . . tendentious projections, propaganda and downright falsehoods.

S., DECEMBER 7, 1991

AIDS LOBBY

. . . it is not so much the state itself which impinges on freedom but the lobby, particularly when it penetrates state organs. It is now becoming increasingly difficult, for example, to discuss homosexuality or the related problem of AIDS, except in terms approved by the homosexual lobby. It is worrying, for instance, that government advertising on AIDS, paid for by taxpayers, should be propagandistic rather than objective; worrying, too, that a book like *The Myth of Heterosexual AIDS* should have found such difficulty in securing a publisher here. Although a good deal of pro-homosexual material appears on the duopoly it is now almost inconceivable that a programme critical of such activities could be broadcast. That is censorship, and all the more objectionable in that it is imposed by controlling elements in the media, rather than by law and Parliament.

S., APRIL 21, 1990

AMERICA

. . . a nation of big spenders . . .

B.M., P. 315

. . . the United States evolved only through trial and error. The entity brought into existence by the Continental Congress, which declared its independence and fought and won a long war with Great Britain, was no more than a loose confederation. Like today's European union, it was a device to avoid internecine war. But it could not function indefinitely in that form—it would go either backward to individual sovereignty, or forward to true union. Even Thomas Jefferson, a lifelong upholder of limited government, states' rights, and strict construction, recognized that the dangers of falling apart were greater than the dangers presented by the dynamic of centralism.

C., AUGUST 1992

America was born Protestant, and did not have to become so through revolt and struggle. It was not built on the remains of a Catholic Church, or an Establishment; it had no clericalism or anti-clericalism. In all these respects it differed profoundly from a world shaped by Augustinian principles. It had a traditionless tradition; starting afresh with a set of Protestant assumptions, taken for granted, self-evident, as the basis for a common national creed. . . . This was the first commonwealth in modern history to make religious freedom, as opposed to a mere degree of toleration, the principle of its existence, and to make this a reason for separating Church and State.

H.C., PP. 422–23

. . . for the first time since the Dark Ages, a society came into existence in which institutional Christianity was associated with progress and freedom, rather than against them. The United States was Erasmian in its tolerance, Erasmian in its anti-doctrinal animus, above all Erasmian in its desire to explore, within a Christian context, the uttermost limits of human possibilities. It was Christianity presented not as a total society, but as an unlimited society.

H.C., P. 428

America's entrepreneurial market system was itself an effective homogenizer, binding together and adjudicating between ethnic and racial groups without regard to colour or national origins. The way in which the enormous German and Polish immigrations, for instance, had been absorbed within an Anglo-Saxon framework, was astounding: the market had done it. Mitchell Palmer was mistaken in thinking that aliens in the mass brought radical politics. On the

[8]

contrary: they were fleeing closed systems to embrace the free one. They were voting with their feet for the entrepreneurial economy.

M.T., P. 212

America was and is a millenarian society where overweening expectations can easily oscillate into catastrophic loss of faith.

M.T., P. 260

America's federal experience, it is true, was bedeviled by slavery and race, two factors which do not divide the Europeans. As against this, however, Americans had overwhelming compensatory advantages in building a continental federation: a common language and literature; a common political culture and law; for the most part a common religion; even shared inspirational texts, such as Locke's *Second Treatise on Civil Government*; and, not least, a common Anglo-Saxon tradition of pragmatism and compromise. They also had, in Great Britain, a common enemy, and no bitter memories of fratricidal conflict.

C., AUGUST 1992

America will never be an ordinary country; it's always going to be extraordinary. Every time I visit—and I must have been in the U.S. 100 times or more—I'm continually astonished by its diversity. When people in England attack America, which they often do, I say: "If you are anti-American, you're anti the human race, because that's what America is about. You don't need the United Nations; you've already got it there."

U.S.N., JUNE 22, 1987

Anyone who travels to every part of the United States, as I do, becomes aware that the notion of America oppressing humanity is absurd. To a great extent, America *is* humanity.

U.S.N., DECEMBER 30, 1985

In the 1770s, surveying the immensity and diversity of London, Dr. Samuel Johnson laid down: "Sir, a man who is tired of London is tired of life." The saying could be rephrased today. A man who hates America hates humanity.

U.S.N., DECEMBER 30, 1985

AMERICA (ANTI-)

Anti-Americanism is ubiquitous, a direct consequence of America doing her duty, the resentment of followers, not leaders. To be sure, anti-Americanism is an ignoble and irrational emotion. Like anti-Semitism, which in some ways it has replaced, it is impervious to facts or logic.

U.S.N., DECEMBER 30, 1985

The attacks on America during the 1970s were so venomous and for the most part so irrational as to merit the description of an international witch-hunt. One might say that the most ubiquitous form of racism during this decade was anti-Americanism. The adage "to know all is to forgive all" does not work in international affairs. One reason why America was attacked so much was because so much was known about her, chiefly thanks to the American media and academia, which poured forth a ceaseless torrent of self-critical material. But a more fundamental reason was that America as a great power and still more Americanism as a concept stood for the principle of individualism as opposed to collectivism, for free will as opposed to determinism.

M.T., P. 694

AMERICAN FANATICISM

It was there from the start, among the New England Calvinist pioneers, who settled there precisely to preserve their Biblical fundamentalism from the worldly-wise Erastianism of the Stuart court, and who have been joined, over the years, by successive waves of fanatics, one-issue immigrants, who came to America to practise their peculiar forms of intolerance in its tolerant climate. The Puritan New Englanders . . . enforced the earliest form of Political Correctness. Led by their divines, the 17th-century equivalent of the modern don, they ran their inquisitions into people's opinions and behaviour. The appalling witch-hunt at Salem, far from being an aberration, is in a way the quintessential event of New England history.

S., OCTOBER 1, 1991

Indeed, in the sense that it manifests this saturnine strain in America's composition, it is also a characteristic event in American history as a whole. Let no one think that the witch-hunt has died out in the United States. It has become politicised but it remains endemic. Sometimes it is launched from one end of the ideological spectrum, sometimes from the other, but its characteristics remain the same: fanaticism, self-righteousness, abuse of the legal forms, contempt for justice. The anti-aliens purge run by the Attorney General Mitchell Palmer immediately after the first world war, which claimed countless victims, Senator McCarthy's witch-hunt after the second world war, the Watergate and Iran-Contra hunts, the trial of Judge Bork before the Senate and now the electronic lynching of Judge Thomas, are all instances of what happens when the fanatic strain gets the upper hand in American society.

S., OCTOBER 1, 1991

AMERICA AND LIBERALISM

The agony of the United States—the stage on which the crisis of the twentieth-century liberal conscience is played—is the agony of a society corrupted and discoloured from within by the very process of repelling corruption from without. But is this a failure of liberalism? On the contrary, it is a failure of societies insufficiently liberal. It demonstrates not the limitations of liberal ideas, but the lack of courage, or numbers, of those who hold them. . . . The conclusion to be drawn is not to reject liberalism, and seek alternatives—there are, indeed, no rational alternatives—but to reinforce the liberal elements which survive, and build new ones. Liberalism is weak not because it is itself inadequate, but because it is starved of enthusiasm, conviction, intellectual nourishment, above all of followers.

H.E., P. 416

AMERICANS

I was, frankly, amazed that, on a fine spring evening, four or five hundred New Yorkers, including many who form and lead opinion, were prepared to cram into an overheated room to hear me discourse on "Is there a substitute for God?" And Americans, while disagreeing strenuously among themselves about how George Bush should handle the Kurdish problem, do at least debate the topic on its merits, not as an intriguing insight into their president's personality, social background and educational record. In New York nowadays I am made to feel how lightweight a country Britain is becoming.

S., APRIL 27, 1991

AMIN, IDI

. . . [as] notorious as a mass murderer of conspicuous savagery; he had not only dispatched some of his victims personally, but dismembered them and preserved parts of their anatomy for future consumption—the first refrigerator-cannibal.

C., MARCH 1984

THE ANCIENT WORLD

. . . the history of the ancient world is to a great extent the history of lost opportunities. Once the Neolithic breakthrough had been achieved there was no invincible reason why man should not have progessed fairly rapidly towards an advanced industrial society. Yet archaic societies are notable not only for stagnation but retrogression. . . . centuries rolled by without specific progress; often technology deteriorated, as the adventurism behind its discovery was lost to sight. Archaic technology was empirical: that is, discovered by trial and error rather than by analytical reasoning. Granted the enormous natural curiosity of man, or rather some men, it is hard to escape the conclusion that the wisdom of the individual was suppressed by the conservative folly of the collective.

E.S., P. 3

ANGLICAN

. . . the parson could not electrify his congregation and produce that emotional alternative to political passion which, since the French Revolution, was felt to be needed and which other churches—the Roman Catholic, with its theatrical glitter and appeal to the senses, and the Nonconformist with its thunder and terror —so abundantly provided. It was against this background of emotional starvation that the Evangelical movement found an increasingly important place in Anglicanism.

B.M., P. 381

ANGLICAN CHURCH AND QUEEN ELIZABETH I

As she was a woman concerned by the externals, rather than the inner beliefs, of religion, her interest focused very largely on liturgy. . . . There can be no doubt that she preferred services to be conducted mainly, if not exclusively, in English. That, at a stroke, set her apart from the Catholics, or at least the Romanists. Second, she was strongly opposed to the more superstitious aspects of Catholicism: the cult of the Virgin (her rival), miracles, saints, indulgences and so forth. . . . as a professional monarch, she was willing to exploit the spiritual apparatus of kingship. She revived the practice of touching for the King's Evil, and was robust enough actually to put her hands on the diseased places. Among ordinary folks this was a highly popular gesture; but it is significant that she made it only after the Pope excommunicated her in 1570—as it were, to prove his impotence—and that she had the text of the ritual translated into English, omitting all references to the Virgin.

E., PP. 88–89

ANGLICANISM

Anglicanism continues to have importance by virtue of two things: its property and its privileges. Without its cathedrals and houses, its estates and income, without its constitutional and legal status at almost every level of our official life, it would rapidly shrink into an insignificant sect, unable to offer careers for talent or to attract the high proportion of its followers who like its trappings as the Church By Law Established.

S., SEPTEMBER 14, 1991

Anglicanism has been based on compromise, illogicalities, unresolved contradictions and a mutual willingness not to push issues too far.

S., SEPTEMBER 14, 1991

ANGLO-IRISH RELATIONS

Despite all the clashes between the English and the Irish . . . we must remember there is also a great unwritten and largely unrecorded story of Anglo-Irish relations: a story of countless friendships and innumerable intermarriages, of shared enthusiasms and dangers, mutual interests and common objectives. We have the same language and literature, the same legal tradition and parliamentary matrix. Whatever happens in the future, we can be sure that Irish and English will always have more to unite than to divide them.

Id., P. 236

ANIMAL

Why do we respect some creatures and hate others (even vegetarians, in panic, have been known to kill harmless grass-snakes)? Our eclecticism is governed purely by instincts, however we seek to rationalize them. Snakes have no more and no less moral rights than foxes. Indeed one of the curators at the Butanta Institute in Brazil, where all kinds of poisonous creatures are bred and studied, told me that it was perfectly possible to have an affectionate relationship with a boa-constrictor, and that he had warm feelings towards even some of his tarantulas.

S.N., P. 43

ANIMAL EXPERIMENTATION

The eco-lobby . . . embraces those campaigning against the use of animals in medical research and what is termed "surgical adventurism" (transplants). This hostility denies or ignores the fact that, for instance, experiments with rats and monkeys are essential to elucidate the mechanism of the cyclical recurrence of malaria. Malaria is still, in terms of sheer numbers, the world's most serious disease, since it kills 2.5 million a year and debilitates at any one time over 250 million. Leprosy, thanks to work on mice, is now at last in process of elimination. Transplantation, which of course requires animal experiments, involves the whole science of immunology, one of the great keys in clinical medicine.

E.S., P. 94

ANTICHRIST

Joachim [of Flora] calculated that Antichrist would arise within the Church and hold high office—a new and riveting idea. On the basis of historical analysis and projection, he deduced that the "last age" would be enacted within history (not, that is, after the Four Last Things) and would be marked by universal peace, in which the institutions necessary for a turbulent world would wither away. For Marxists the parallels are disturbingly close.

H.C., P. 257

ANTI-CULTURE INDUSTRY

Today, thanks to crass publicity techniques, television and the hoo-ha of literary prizes, novels are not so much selected by readers as hyped by literary power-brokers working hand in hand with the money-bags. It is not a pretty picture and it is in danger of becoming downright ugly. Readers are conned into buying trash or into thinking mediocre stuff is a masterpiece by methods not wholly unlike the marketing of high-return investment trusts and similar risky ventures.

S., JANUARY 20, 1990

Leaving a TV studio recently, I stumbled into the exodus from one of these sessions. How pathetic and listless they seemed: young girls, hardly any more than sixteen, dressed as adults and already lined up as fodder for exploitation. Their eyes came to life only when one of their grotesque idols—scarcely older than they—made a brief appearance, before a man in a camel-hair coat hustled him into a car. Behind this image of "youth," there are, evidently, some shrewd older folk at work.

S.N., P. 47

ANTI-SEMITISM

. . . its theoretical basis has always been the work of intellectuals.

C., APRIL 1984

The works of Voltaire and his colleagues were the title-deeds, the foundation documents, of the modern European intelligentsia, and it was a tragedy for the Jews that they contained a virulently anti-

[16]

Semitic clause. Thus yet another layer was added to the historical accumulation of anti-Jewish polemic. On top of the pagan plinth and the Christian main storey there was now placed a secular superstructure. In a sense this was the most serious of all, for it ensured that hatred of the Jews, so long kept alive by Christian fanaticism, would now survive the decline of the religious spirit.

H.J., P. 309

The sexual-medical aspect of Hitler's anti-Semitism was probably the most important, especially among his own followers. It turned the merely prejudiced into fanatics, capable of any course of action, however irrational and cruel. Rather as the medieval anti-Semite saw the Jew as non-human, a devil or a sort of animal (hence the *Judensau*), the Nazi extremist absorbed Hitler's sub-scientific phraseology and came to regard Jews as bacilli or a particularly dangerous kind of vermin. Apart from anything else, this approach enabled all Jews to be lumped together, irrespective of their circumstances or views. A Jew who held a professional chair, who wrote impeccable German, who had served throughout the war and won the Iron Cross, was just as dangerous a racial polluter as a Jewish-Bolshevik commissar. An assimilated Jew carried the bacillus just as certainly as an old rabbi in a kaftan and was more of a threat, since he was more likely to infect, or "desecrate" as Hitler put it, an Aryan woman.

H.J., P. 473

There had long been a pornographic side to anti-Semitism, especially in Germany and Austria; the *Judensau* theme itself was often a symptom of it. But Hitler's stress on the sexual, race-defilement issue combined with Weimar permissiveness to produce a peculiarly vicious form of anti-Semitic propaganda epitomized by the weekly *Der Stürmer*, run by the Nazi boss . . . Julius Streicher. It helped to spread and intensify one of the chief, perennial sources of anti-Semitic violence: the notion that Jews are not part of humanity and therefore not entitled to the protection we instinctively accord a human being.

H.J., P. 475

[17]

Until the [Weimar] Republic, anti-Semitism was not a disease to which Germany was thought to be especially prone. Russia was the land of the pogrom; Paris was the city of the anti-Semitic intelligentsia. Anti-Semitism seems to have made its appearance in Germany in the 1870s and 1880s, at a time when the determinist type of social philosopher was using Darwin's principle of Natural Selection to evolve "laws" to explain the colossal changes brought about by industrialism, the rise of megalopolis and the alienation of huge, rootless proletariats. Christianity was content with a solitary hate-figure to explain evil: Satan. But modern secular faiths needed human devils, and whole categories of them. The enemy, to be plausible, had to be an entire class or race.

M.T., P. 117

Even the sunbathing movement, under the impulse of Aryan and Nordic symbols, acquired an anti-Semitic flavour. Indeed in 1920s Germany there were two distinct types of nudism: "Jewish" nudism, symbolized by the black dancer Josephine Baker, which was heterosexual, commercial, cosmopolitan, erotic and immoral; and anti-Semitic nudism, which was German, *Völkisch*, Nordic, non-sexual (sometimes homosexual), pure and virtuous.

M.T., P. 119

APOCALYPTIC

It is a curious fact about human nature that many people actually seem to want to believe in an approaching catastrophe. In the Dark and Middle Ages—indeed right up to the seventeenth century —religious seers would always collect a substantial following if they predicted the end of the world, especially if they gave a specific date for it. When the date came and went, and nothing happened, human credulity did not disappear. It re-emerged promptly when the next persuasive prophet mounted his soapbox. The ecological panic of our times is driven by exactly the same emotional needs.

another example of how, during the twentieth ... ining religious impulse has been replaced by . . . s, which are more often far more irrational and

N.R., JUNE 29, 1984

ARAB

The Arabs . . . were a conquering race whose sacred writings both inspired and reflected a maximalist position towards other peoples, the despised *dhimmi*. The very concept of negotiation towards a final settlement was to them a betrayal of principle. A truce, an armistice might be necessary and was acceptable because it preserved the option of force for use later. A treaty, on the other hand, appeared to them a kind of surrender.

H.J., P. 530

ARCHITECTURE

What is interesting about the age of dislocation in which we live is that all the arts contribute to [a] sense of homelessness, but each does so in its own way. Architecture, for instance, sometimes disorientates us in a physical, as well as metaphorical, sense. There must be many travellers who have had the uneasy experience of waking, after a doze in an international airport, forgetting where they are, and being totally unable for some moments to identify the place and country from their surroundings. The sheer geographical anonymity of many functional constructions, airports . . . hotels, and so forth . . . betrays a poverty of ideas, an absence of regional emotions, and a dominant cost accounting which knows no frontiers.

E.S., P. 225

ART

Art is a source not only of pleasure but of reassurance; it is not a luxury of civilization but a necessity. If art undermines the common certitudes, it lowers morale and makes external assault more deadly.

E.S., P. 226

The beneficence of great art consists in the way in which it builds up from the individual illumination to generality.

I., P. 268

ART (MODERN)

Most people regard contemporary art as a remote phenomenon which has lost contact with social reality, something for "them" (vaguely believed to be a cosmopolitan stew of pseuds and sodomites).

S., JUNE 28, 1988

ATHEISM

. . . by cutting the umbilical cord with God, our source of ethical vitality would be gone. Morally, we would become nothing better than a species of fantastically clever monkeys. Our ultimate fate would be too horrible to contemplate. For the truth is that we humans are all Jekyll and Hyde creatures, and the monster within each of us is always striving to take over.

R.D., JUNE 1985

ATOM BOMB

From the very beginning applied atomic physics had its ideological and moral dimensions. The concept of the bomb was born among the mainly Jewish refugee scientific community, who were terrified that Hitler might get it first. It was one of them, Leo Szilard, who proposed a self-imposed censorship of scientific publication. The bomb was created by (among others) men who put ideological considerations before national self-interest, just as it was betrayed by such men. . . . Robert Oppenheimer, a Jew, built the first A-bomb because he feared Hitler would do it first; Edward Teller, a Hungarian, built the first H-bomb because he was terrified of a Soviet monopoly. Hence the real father of the atomic bomb was Hitler and the spectres his horrifying will conjured up.

M.T., P. 407

The project was under the direction of an army engineer general, Leslie Groves, who shared to the full the giganticist philosophy of the new Forties phase of American capitalism. Given a clear and attainable objective, he was impervious to qualitative or quantitative difficulties. . . . But . . . [the] Americans were compressing perhaps three decades of scientific engineering progress into four years. There was no other way of being sure to get the bomb. There was no other country or system which could have produced this certainty. It was Hitler's bomb; it was also and above all a capitalist bomb.

M.T., PP. 408–9

It is ironic that totalitarianism, having generated the fear which made the bomb possible, made only feeble efforts of its own to justify the righteous terror of the legitimate powers. . . . According to Nikita Khrushchev it was not until the day after the Hiroshima explosion that Stalin put his secret police head, Beria, in charge of a crash project with absolute priority over all else in the state. . . . But to Hitler, the nuclear field was identified with Einstein and "Jewish physics." . . . In its colossal destructive power, it was an archetypal Hitler weapon: the destroyer-state incarnate. Even before the war he had grimly outlined to Hermann Rauschning the price of Nazi failure: "Even as we go down to destruction we will carry half the world into destruction with us." The atomic bomb could have brought this reckless boast closer to reality. But the bomb never possessed Hitler's mind as the rocket did. The failure in the imagination of this romantic nihilist rendered groundless the fears of the scientific exiles who caused the bomb to be made.

M.T., P. 409

Augustan Age

. . . rejoice that the Augustan age had spent the public's money on splendour rather than social workers.

P.P.J., P. 238

Augustine, St.

He was a tremendous egoist: it is characteristic of him that his spiritual autobiography should have been written in the form of a gigantic address to God.

H.C., P. 113

Authority

Most of the debates of principle in present-day society come down to the question of authority. In every sphere of life authority is being defied and often it does nothing to earn respect by its feebleness and pusillanimity. Broadcasting is an outstanding case.

S., MARCH 1, 1986

Autocracy (Leninist)

The stages by which Lenin created [the] autocracy are worth describing in a little detail because they became the grim model, in essentials, for so many other regimes in the six decades which have followed. His aims were fourfold. First, to destroy all opposition ouside the party; second, to place all power, including government, in party hands; third, to destroy all opposition within the party; fourth, to concentrate all power in the party in himself and those he chose to associate with him.

M.T., P. 78

B

BALDWIN, JAMES

His was a case of a man who might have led a happy and fulfilled life by virtue of his achievements, which were considerable. But instead he was rendered intensely miserable by the new intellectual climate of his time, which persuaded him that the message of his work must be hate—a message he delivered with angry enthusiasm. It is further evidence of the curious paradox that intellectuals, who ought to teach men and women to trust their reason, usually encourage them to follow their emotions; and, instead of urging debate and reconciliation on humanity, all too often spur it towards the arbitration of force.

I., P. 333

BEARDS

By one of those mysterious swings in fashion, the early decades of the 19th century were a time of marked prejudice against beards, at any rate in what were regarded as advanced societies. In England and France, beards were rare among the educated classes. . . . The fashion changed in the 1850s, and by 1874 only two out of 658 British members of Parliament were beardless; but during the years after Waterloo, however, beards were identified with radicalism in the West.

B.M., P. 298

BEATLES

The Beatles phenomenon, in fact, illustrates one of my favourite maxims: that if something becomes big enough and popular enough—and especially commercially profitable enough—solemn men will not be lacking to invest it with virtues. So long as the Beatles were just another successful showbiz team, the pillars of society could afford to ignore them, beyond bestowing the indulgent accolade of a slot in the Royal Variety Performance.

S.N., P. 45

BEAUVOIR, SIMONE DE

. . . this brilliant and strong-minded woman became Sartre's slave from almost their first meeting and remained such for all her adult life until he died. She served him as mistress, surrogate wife, cook and manager, female bodyguard and nurse, without at any time acquiring legal or financial status in his life. In all essentials, Sartre treated her no better than Rousseau did his Thérèse; worse, because he was notoriously unfaithful. In the annals of literature, there are few worse cases of a man exploiting a woman. This was all the more extraordinary because de Beauvoir was a lifelong feminist.

I., P. 235

BECKET, ST. THOMAS

The Becket affair changed English history in only one respect: it gave birth to English anti-clericalism, a smouldering national force which was to grow in depth and volume until it found expression in the Reformation.

H.E., P. 99

BECKETT, SAMUEL

The craftsmanship and ingenuity he displays are admirable, and some claim him to be the greatest writer of the twentieth century; but Beckett has reached the stage of aesthetic dominance when those who cannot understand what he is doing or why he is doing it are inclined to apologize for their own lack of comprehension rather than blame his failure to convey his meaning—an enviable position for an artist to secure for himself.

E.S., P. 230

BEETHOVEN, LUDWIG VAN

Beethoven was a key figure in the birth of the modern because he first established and popularized the notion of the artist as universal genius, as a moral figure in his own right—indeed, as a kind of intermediary between God and Man. . . . He seems to have felt that, by virtue of his creative powers, he had some kind of direct contact with the Deity. . . . He was the first to assert that the artist was the arbiter of public morals. . . . In 1821 Shelley . . . called the poet "the unacknowledged legislator of the world," but Beethoven was already making the claim twenty years before and, what is more, on behalf of the musician, then a lowly species.

B.M., P. 117

BEGIN, MENACHEM

Indeed, he must be the only politician in the history of democracy to lose seven elections in a row and still survive. But survive he did, thanks to the same power of will which Ben-Gurion had noted in Herzl and cultivated in himself.

C., OCTOBER 1987

[25]

BELLOC, HILAIRE

. . . this book [*The Path to Rome*] is more poignant today than when it was written: it catches for us the last flavours of pre-industrial Europe which were still perceptible to Belloc as he tramped along the narrow rutted roads, along which trundled only the farm carts and an occasional coach; peasants, dazzled by the sight of a rare stranger, and willing to give him a bed in the hayloft; the gleam in the eye of an innkeeper's wife when Belloc produced a gold coin from his purse; the strongly individual character of each village and region, expressed in dress, manners and speech; the solitude which descended abruptly as soon as the open road was gained—all features of a world that has gone for ever.

S.N., P. 242

BENJAMIN, WALTER

In his *Theses on the Philosophy of History* Benjamin argued that politics was not merely a fierce physical struggle to control the present, and so the future, but an intellectual battle to control the record of the past. In a striking phrase, he insisted that "even the dead will not be safe from the [fascist] enemy as he wins." Most forms of knowledge were relativistic, bourgeois creations, and had to be recast to ensure proletarian or classless truth. The irony of these brilliant but destructive insights was that, whereas Benjamin saw them as scientific historical materialism, they were really a product of Judaic irrationality—his was the old tale of how intensely spiritual people, who can no longer believe in God, find ingenious substitutes for religious dogmas.

H.J., P. 481

BIBLICAL SCHOLARSHIP

Analyzing the mass of evidence for the perfect [biblical] text is probably self-defeating. Beyond a certain point, scholarship tends to raise as many problems as it solves . . .

H.C., P. 26

BIGOTRY

. . . you cannot separate race, religion and culture. It will not work to say it is wrong and unlawful to insult a man's race but quite all right to spit on his god and insult the religious beliefs which form the biggest single element in his culture. In most societies the three are inextricably intermingled.

S., JUNE 17, 1988

BISHOP (MODERN)

There can be no body of men in the country whose moral and practical authority has declined so precipitously in recent decades. They no longer rule their dioceses and keep their clergy in duty and subjection. They do not dispense, *ex cathedra*, the moral and dogmatic theology of Christianity, at any rate with any degree of conviction. Indeed, they cannot agree on what it is.

S., JUNE 2, 1984

BISHOP (POLITICAL)

To many people the behaviour of the political bishops makes no sense at all. All they win by their outbursts is the grudging, temporary and fundamentally contemptuous approval of the atheist Left, people who have never set foot in a church in their lives and never intend to. At the same time, they distress and alienate the dwindling

[27]

band of regular churchgoers, who still accept the teachings of the Anglican communion . . .

s., APRIL 6, 1985

BOAT PEOPLE

China [in the 17th century] and indeed until the Opium Wars of the mid-19th century was, theoretically at least, a sealed country, the government having a monopoly on all transactions with the outside world. Chinese economic theory, which was highly irrational, even by the usual standards of economic theory, held that it was fatal to the well-being of the country to allow either silver or people to leave it. Nevertheless, Chinese people, for their own good reasons, wished to leave, as they still do—"Boat People" constitute an ancient phenomenon.

B.M., P. 773

BONAPARTE, NAPOLEON

. . . Bonaparte was in the 18th-century tradition of the Enlightened Despots. But in other respects his conduct looked forward to the horrifying totalitarian regimes of the 20th century. He was in no sense a democrat. To him, the people were a mob, *canaille*, to be dispersed, "by a whiff of grapeshot." . . . Nor did Bonaparte . . . stand for the principle of individual liberty. Indeed, he created the first modern police state, and exported it. Austria, Prussia, and Russia all learned from the methods of Joseph Fouché, Bonaparte's minister of police, and it is significant that when Jean-Baptiste Bernadotte, one of Bonaparte's marshals and trained in his system, became the effective ruler of Sweden from 1809, almost his first acts were to set up a secret police force and an espionage network, neither of which Sweden had ever possessed.

B.M., PP. 66–67

BOOKS

. . . books are not disembodied entities but come from the hearts and brains of living men and women, and . . . the key to their understanding lies in the interaction of theme and author.

I., P. 268

The book is a global product if ever there was one. As the world is homogenised by the confluent pressures of change, books will be directed increasingly at a world market of educated readers, built initially on the natural unity of the English-speaking communities, but taking into account the rapidly expanding Spanish and oriental language markets. I would now never dream of addressing a book primarily to a British readership. Publishers are right to set up commercial structures which take account of the new internationalism, and in particular to operate from both sides of the Atlantic.

S., JUNE 27, 1987

BOXING

There is one point to be made in favour of boxing. It has always offered one of the very few routes for members of deprived groups to achieve money and fame. A man with nothing but muscles and courage could effect a miraculous escape from the depths of poverty, thus supplying hopes, or at least dreams, to the millions he left behind.

S., OCTOBER 5, 1991

Most champions enjoy brief years of glory, then swiftly tumble into pathos. But we have to ask: which is better for a poor and valiant man, with few brains but great strength—a blinding, intoxicating flash of fame, followed by oblivion, or a lifetime in narrow obscurity? For that, to be honest, is the choice. Most men of spirit would pick the first, and that is the only argument I can find for prize-fighting. But it is a frail one and unlikely to prevail for long. The days when well-heeled mobs pay to watch two men inflict lawful assault and battery on each other are surely numbered.

s., OCTOBER 5, 1991

BRECHT, BERTOLT

He expressed the wish to be buried in a grey steel coffin, to keep out worms, and to have a steel stiletto put through his heart as soon as he was dead. This was done and published, the news being the first indication to many who knew him that he had a heart at all.

I., PP. 195–96

He is the only intellectual among those I have studied who appears to be without a sole redeeming feature.

I., P. 196

Brecht had always been anxious to give his work a "serious," even solid, dimension and attract the attention of academics, whom he shrewdly saw were excellent long-term promoters of a writer's reputation.

I., P. 182

BRITAIN

If I were asked to categorise Britain today, I think I would term it the Superstitious Society. Faith has gone, to the point that a policeman who utters the old Christian truism that he is an instrument of God is widely denounced as a nut-case and a menace, and forced to come to the Home Office to explain himself. And, since human beings feel they need to know more about existence than their puny reason can supply, the loss of faith has left a huge vacuum, which a variety of superstitions is filling.

s., FEBRUARY 14, 1987

BRITAIN AND BUSINESS

. . . in modern Britain [there] is [often] a kind of pathological suspicion towards any kind of business activity. Doing a deal, and above all making a profit, is regarded as constitutionally suspect, if not downright immoral: the onus of proof is automatically on the businessman to demonstrate his innocence. This anti-business ethic is deeply rooted in British schools, universities, churches and among opinion-formers and media pundits.

S., FEBRUARY 11, 1984

BRITISH BROADCASTING COMPANY

. . . the BBC enjoys the harlot's privilege of power without responsibility to anyone.

S., JULY 3, 1985

From its foundation in the 1920s to the 1960s it was in some respects the personification of Britain, its voice and image. It was open to the objection that it was too middle-class, too highbrow, stuffy and moralistic. But it was something; it stood for something; it was a recognisable, tangible entity, with a culture, a code of behaviour, a sense of decency of its own. All that has now gone. The BBC no longer has a personality. It is a decaying bit of nationalised property, run, insofar as it is run at all, in the interests of its employees. . . . It has no head, no heart and no soul, and above all no conscience. Religion and patriotism mean nothing to it. It would not lift a palsied finger to defend the British constitution or Parliament. Its attitude to the law is ambivalent. The only element of law enforcement it positively supports is the prosecution of those who evade the licence fee.

S., JULY 3, 1985

The BBC is devoid of any principle of authority, except on bureaucratic details: it is the Boneless Wonder.

S., JULY 12, 1986

Like the Church of England, it retains much of the furniture of its faith; but the spirit has long since flown.

s., JULY 12, 1986

Malcolm Muggeridge used to say of Anthony Eden: "He not only bores, he bores for England." The BBC not only rapes, it rapes for Russia.

s., SEPTEMBER 20, 1986

[This] is all we want from the BBC. We want it to get out of the propaganda business. We want it to abandon agitprop. We want it to resume its old and now largely forgotten practice of placing the truth before any other consideration.

s., OCTOBER 11, 1986

The reality is that the BBC has long been a fallen woman. At first, in the 1960s, it was just the odd bit of adultery on the side: a stealthy little porn sequence here, a sly left-wing twist to the facts there. Then the old girl started to drop her drawers more readily and soon she was doing it for money. Today, the BBC is a raddled old prostitute, a ratings-whore ready and hardened for any trick that will keep her on the trottoir.

s., OCTOBER 20, 1986

It is a curious institution. It calls itself "British," as though in some metaphysical way it embodies, stands for or represents Britain and her people. It lives entirely off our money, since it does not earn its own living and insists that every family in the country, including the poorest, pay a heavy tax merely for owning a television set. Yet it rarely misses an opportunity to spit in the face of the British people and denigrate the things we hold dear. It seems to swarm with people who feel it their public duty to kick Britain on every possible occasion.

s., FEBRUARY 6, 1988

It is a thoroughly political organisation with a Left-liberal slant, as is inevitable in a nationalised industry financed by taxpayers' money. I don't mind this as I am all in favour of a varied media. But it is wrong that the BBC should have the status and privileges of a national institution and that everyone should pay for it. Sooner or later a litigious fellow is going to go to court on the issue of whether he should be forced to pay a poll tax to support a body which habitually advocates not only political but moral views abhorrent to him. . . . If it truly values its independence and is not just fond of the soft, easy option (like most prostitutes), the BBC should go by the old slogan "Clean living is the only safeguard." And "clean," in this case, means earning it in the open market, just like all the rest of us in the media.

s., MARCH 3, 1990

BRITISH ECONOMY

One of the weaknesses of modern British society is the very wide-spread assumption that a compromise is always preferable, morally and intellectually, to a definite choice based upon conviction. Among the great and the good and the complacent it is generally agreed that Britain has a "mixed economy" and must at all costs continue to have one. They shrink from a socialist economy, knowing that it leads to poverty and totalitarianism. They recoil too from a genuine capitalist economy, believing it to be too brash and ruthless for refined British tastes. The result is our present hopeless compromise, which is not really a mixture at all but a political fraud whereby the private sector has, in practice, to carry on its back a large, expensive and constitutionally weak public sector. Virtually all our economic ills now spring from this sector. So do our strikes. It is an unrivalled squanderer of our wealth.

s., JULY 24, 1985

BRITISH EMPIRE

The British Empire reflected some of the salient characteristics of the domestic minimum-state. It was administered by a handful of people, backed by a tiny army and small, locally recruited police forces. It therefore involved a large degree of acquiescence, indeed consent, on the part of the governed. In some ways, the Empire resembled eighteenth-century England: power confined, in practice, to the political nation of the governing *élite*, but many important freedoms enjoyed by all. Freedom of movement and communication, freedom of speech and the press, free access to an impartial system of justice, freedom to enjoy life and property under the rule of law.

H.E., P. 345

. . . its imposition of western standards of public health led to a revolution in life-expectancy, an assault on tropical disease, and a sharp fall in the infantile death-rate. From 1898, Britain began to devote increasing sums to imperial schemes of economic development, beginning in the West Indies, but gradually spreading to all parts of the Empire. Thus Britain, in a high-minded manner, and from the most altruistic motives, is largely responsible for the three salient characteristics of the Third World today: interracial conflict, the population explosion, and the illusory panacea of "overseas aid"—what might be termed the International Poor Law.

H.E., PP. 345–46

Britain could be just to her colonial subjects so long as she was a comparatively wealthy nation. A rich power could run a prosperous and well-conducted empire. Poor nations, like Spain and Portugal, could not afford justice or forgo exploitation. But it follows from this, as many British statesmen had insisted throughout the nineteenth century, that colonies were not a source of strength but of weakness. They were a luxury, maintained for prestige and paid for by diverting real resources. The concept of a colonial superpower was largely fraudulent. As a military and economic colossus, the British Empire was made of lath and plaster, paint and gilding.

M.T., P. 161

BRYAN, WILLIAM JENNINGS

The hate-figure of the East Coast highbrows in the Twenties was William Jennings Bryan, the Illinois Democrat who had denounced the power of money ("You shall not crucify mankind upon a cross of gold"), opposed imperialism, resigned as Secretary of State in 1915 in protest against the drift to war and, in his old age, fought a desperate rearguard action against Darwinian evolution in the 1925 Scopes trial. . . . he was not seeking to ban the teaching of evolution but to prevent state schools from undermining religious belief: evolution should, he argued, be taught as theory not fact, parents and taxpayers should have a say in what went on in the schools, and teachers should abide by the law of the land. He saw himself as resisting the aggressive dictatorship of a self-appointed scholastic élite who were claiming a monopoly of authentic knowledge.

M.T., P. 208

BURKE, EDMUND

Burke brought originality to everything to which he set his pen. With his *Vindication of Natural Society* he invented sceptical conservatism; with his essay *On the Sublime and Beautiful* he adumbrated the aesthetic theory of the Romantic movement. He is the only eighteenth-century political philosopher whose reputation continues to grow, as modern anti-Utopians find and develop fresh Burkean flashes.

M.T., P. 116

BUSH, GEORGE

. . . the immediate origins of two world wars lay in the ethnic disputes of Eastern Europe, now rising to the surface again. But it also has its advantages, for George Bush in particular. He can set about building on Reagan's legacy with the reasonable certitude that the Soviet leadership, for the time being at least, has neither the time nor the energy—nor even, one suspects, the inclination—for acquisitive geopolitics. No American president in modern times has begun with such an advantage, and Europeans will judge Bush on the finesse with which he makes use of it.

F.A., JANUARY 1989

BYRON, GEORGE GORDON, LORD

He held it wrong to spend his patrimony inheritance on fornication, but money earned by poetry was another matter: "What I get by my brains I will spend on my bollocks, so long as I have a *tester* or a testicle remaining."

B.M., P. 505

C

CABINET

. . . the cabinet . . . was a nebulous concept. Foreigners conceded
that it must work, since Britain's position in the world was preeminent. They accordingly sought to imitate it, usually unsuccessfully.
As we have noted, it did not function well in Restoration France.
It existed in the United States, but at the end of the 1820s President
Jackson began to sidestep it. The British made it work partly because
it suited their inclination to have no formal rules. It was chaired
by a man often known as the prime minister . . . [who] had no
official existence.

B.M., P. 392

One of the most fascinating aspects of history is the way power
shifts from formal institutions to informal ones, where it is really
exercised. This happened in England, in the 17th and 18th centuries, when the decision-making process gradually moved from the
Royal Council to the cabinet, originally a furtive and rather disrep-
utable body.

B.M., P. 946

CALCUTTA

Calcutta's plight attracted many voluntary workers, who joined the
efforts of Mother Teresa and her Missionaries of Charity, who had
set up their stations in Calcutta in 1948. But often the Marxist
government seemed more anxious to drive out volunteer medical

bodies, who drew attention to its failures, than to tackle the problem at its root. Calcutta became the realized anti-Utopia of modern times, the city of shattered illusions, the dark not the light of Asia. It constituted an impressive warning that attempts to experiment on half the human race were more likely to produce Frankenstein monsters than social miracles.

M.T., P. 574

CALVIN, JEAN

Calvin, by contrast [to Luther], had never asserted that consciences should be free. How could the perfected society of the elect tolerate among it those who challenged its rules? The obvious answer to critics was to expel them from the city, following excommunication. If they attempted to remonstrate they were executed. But execution, Calvin found, was also useful to inspire terror and thus bring about compliance. One of his favourite ways of triumphing over an opponent was to make him burn his books publicly with his own hands—Valentin Gentilis saved his life by submitting to this indignity.

H.C., P. 289

CALVINISM

. . . strict Calvinism, as anyone who actually reads Calvin's *Institutes of Church Government* will find, not only does not promote commerce and the profit motive but militates against them. The entrepreneurial elements whose migrations, in the sixteenth and seventeenth centuries, helped to fix the pattern of future capitalist development, were not primarily Calvinist . . . Some were Lutherans, some Calvinist, some Catholic, some sectarians. What they had in common was their dislike of imposed religious uniformity, whether Roman Catholicism or anything else . . . they believed in a minimum creed, toleration and good works. They wanted religion to be private, not public; and, above all, they were profoundly anti-clerical. They settled in north-west Europe, and especially Britain . . . because there the religious background most conducive to their personal well-being and commercial bent was to be found.

E.S., P. 60

This terrifying doctrine of election, or damnation, was made palatable by the fact that election was proved by communion with Christ—that is, in practice, by membership in a Calvinist congregation: "Whoever finds himself in Jesus Christ and is a member of his body by faith, he is assured of his salvation." So long as a man avoided excommunication, he was secure. Here is both the strength and weakness of Calvinism: if you do not accept the horrific argument of double predestination, it is abhorrent; if you do accept it, it is almost irresistible.

H.C., P. 287

CALVINISM AND CAPITALISM

If Calvinism was the key to capitalism, then the Industrial Revolution should have taken place in the neighbourhood of Amsterdam, rather than in Lancashire and the English Midlands. . . . Scotland *was* predominantly Calvinist from the mid-sixteenth century on; but there, the characteristic medieval restrictions on trade, commerce and industry were retained much longer than in Anglican England. In fact, it was not until the theocratic grip of Calvinism was broken, following the union with England, in the mid-eighteenth century, that Scotland entered into a phase of commercial development, marked by religious toleration [and] intellectual adventurism.

E.S., P. 60

CAMBODIA

Angka Loeu consisted of about twenty professional political intellectuals. . . . All had studied in France in the 1950s, where they had absorbed the doctrines of "necessary violence" preached on the radical Left. They were Sartre's children. . . . while this group of ideologues preached the virtues of rural life, none had in fact ever engaged in

[39]

manual labour or had any experience at all of creating wealth. Like
Lenin, they were pure intellectuals. They epitomized the great destructive force of the twentieth century: the religious fanatic rein-
carnated as professional politician. What they did illustrated the
ultimate heartlessness of ideas. In any other age or place, the plans
of these savage pedants would have remained in their fevered imaginations. In Cambodia in 1975 it was possible to put them into
practice.

M.T., P. 655

CAPITALISM

Industrial capitalism, and the free market system, is presented as
destructive of human happiness, corrupt, immoral, wasteful, inefficient and above all, doomed. Collectivism is presented as the only
way out compatible with the dignity of the human spirit and the
future of our race. The expanded university threatens to become not
the powerhouse of Western individualism and enterprise, but its
graveyard.

R.F., P. 161

Capitalism is an unfortunate name; a misnomer indeed, whose wide-
spread use goes back only to about 1900. For what it describes is
not an "ism" at all. It is not an ideology dreamed up by an economic
philosopher and then put through parliament by political parties
and enforced by law and armies. Industrial capitalism simply
evolved, from the free and unco-ordinated transactions and un-
impeded movements of countless unknown individuals. It was not
a political creation at all.

P.P.J., P. 175

Industrial capitalism has done more to promote content among
mankind than any other man-made phenomenon in history.

P.P.J., P. 176

. . . measured in achievements over the last 200 years, judged in
terms of delivering the goods and fulfilling the promises explicit or

implicit in their births, the contrast is almost absolute: industrial capitalism has exceeded the most sanguine expectations of its founders, whereas political utopianism has proved a dismal and bloody failure.

P.P.J., P. 172

CAPITALISM AND GOVERNMENT

Industrial capitalism, or rather the free enterprise economy, and Big Government, are natural and probably irreconcilable enemies. It is no accident that the Industrial Revolution took place in late eighteenth century England. It was a period of minimum government. . . . As a matter of fact, the Industrial Revolution, perhaps the most important single event in human history, seems to have occurred without the English government even noticing. By the time they did, it was too late; happily—otherwise they would probably have stopped it.

R.F., PP. 163–64

CAPTION WRITING

The golden rule of caption writing, which I formulated for myself, is this. Never tell the reader what he can see for himself. That is the mark of the amateur writing in his snap album: "Myself and Signorina outside the Tower of Pisa." Tell the reader what he can't see and doesn't know and needs to know. Tell him who (if it isn't obvious), where and when and how (if it's relevant). You may have to tell him what's going on outside the picture or behind the photographer, or what happened immediately before or just after it was taken. One good test is to take away the photo and see how the caption reads standing by itself. If it enables you to imagine what the photo is like, it's no good. Ideally, by itself it should intrigue you and make you anxious to see the picture.

S., JUNE 22, 1985

[41]

CAROLINGIAN AGE

Augustinian theory saw Christian mankind and its institutions as a whole, fully integrated, almost organic. During this period a conscious effort was made to realize the conception, and genuine progress was made. Never before or since has any human society come close to operating as a unity, wholly committed to a perfectionist programme of conduct. Never again was Christianity to attempt so comprehensively to realize itself as a human institution, as well as a divine one. And of course the experiment had profound and lasting consequences. It laid the foundations for the complementary concepts of Christendom and Europe. It projected, in broad outline, the directions which European institutions and culture would take. And it determined in embryo many of the aspects of the world we live in now. We are right to regard the total Christianity of the Carolingian age as one of the great formative phases of human history.

H.C., PP. 177–78

CARTER, JIMMY

In European eyes, indeed, 1980 was the nadir of the post-war American Presidency.

F.A., JANUARY 1989

Policy under Carter was so confused . . . as to lack salient characteristics, other than a propensity to damage friends and allies.

M.T., P. 674

Jimmy Carter serves to remind us that leadership is in essence a combination of courage and judgment. Neither is much good without the other, and Mr. Carter seems to lack both. He has taken Adlai Stevenson's defeatist maxim a stage further: his conduct of office seems to suggest a belief that government not only cannot be more resolute than the people it serves but has no access to a superior knowledge, let alone foresight. This peculiar view of democratic leadership—or anti-leadership—as the lowest common denominator of a nation's wit and wisdom is illuminated by Mr. Carter's eccentric and sometimes desperate efforts to seek advice in America's highways and byways, as well as from the stream of cranks and busybodies who perambulate through his office. He calls irresistibly to mind Field Marshal Douglas Haig's caustic summation of his boss at the War Office, the Earl of Derby: "He is like a feather cushion—he bears the impression of the last person who has sat on him."

R.F., P. 225

CASTRO, FIDEL

At what point Castro became a Leninist is unclear. He had obviously studied carefully the methods both Lenin and Hitler had used to make themselves absolute masters. When he took over in January 1959 he had himself made Commander-in-Chief and, using as his excuse the necessity to prevent the re-emergence of gangsterism, secured for himself a monopoly of force. . . . within weeks of the take-over, the liberals and democrats had been effectively excluded from power. The cabinet was the Politburo; and, within it, thanks to his relations and cronies, Castro was dictator, exactly like Batista. But Batista had the saving grace of caring for money as well as power. Castro wanted power alone.

M.T., P. 622

. . . Cuba had, and has, a dependent economy. If America was unacceptable as a patron, another great power had to fill the role. And America was unacceptable, in the sense that Castro, like other Third World dictators, needed an enemy. After Batista went, it had to be America. And with America as enemy, he needed an ally; it had to be Soviet Russia. With Russia as ally and, from mid-1959, paymaster, Castro's ideology had to be Marxism, which fitted in well with his Left-fascist brand of domestic autocracy.

M.T., P. 623

CATHEDOCRACY

. . . that worst of all systems: a society run by its intelligentsia, a cathedocracy ruled from the scholar's chair. . . . The system was obnoxious because it placed scholars at the top, followed in descending order by farmers, artisans and merchants. What it meant in practice was that the country was ruled by those who were good at passing highly formalized examinations.

B.M., P. 780

CATHOLIC AUTHORITY AND CONTINUITY

No human institution in history has placed so much stress on continuity and authority as the Catholic Church. Some of the churches of Rome go back to the early fourth century, at which time the bishops of the city were already associated with a centralized, disciplined and magisterial presentation of Christianity. . . . the way the papacy sees the church and the world has not changed since the time of Pope Gregory the Great in the late sixth century. The tone of voice . . . in Gregory's 854 surviving letters—as . . . in his instruction to St. Augustine of Canterbury to . . . convert the English—is not very different from the Maundy Thursday letter which John Paul II addressed to his bishops in 1979. The atmosphere of stability and order radiated by the papal archives, which perhaps date as a concept from the time of Constantine when the popes first occupied the Lateran, is awesome. The prevailing sentiment of papal Rome has always been, for more than 1500 years, serenity of conviction. If security is to be found in any organ of earthly government, it is to be found there. And if that calm certitude affronts the mind of the twentieth century, it finds a grateful response in the twentieth-century heart.

P.J., PP. 24–25

CATHOLIC CERTAINTY

The people of the Catholic faith value it not because it is yielding but because it is inflexible; not because it is open-minded but because it is sure; not because it is adaptive and protean but because it is always, everywhere, the same. It is the one fixed point in a changing world; and if it changes itself (as from time to time it must), such transformations must be as imperceptible as a glacier's, moving with majestic gravity along a path preordained by its own nature. Catholicism has the time-scale not of fashion but of geology.

P.J., P. 137

CATHOLIC CHURCH AND FADS

Roman Catholicism is not a market-research religion. It is not in business to count heads or take votes. In its sacred economy, quantitative principles do not apply. Dogma and morals are not susceptible to guidance by opinion polls. The truth is paramount and it must be the naked truth, presented without cosmetics and exercises in public relations.

P.J., P. 185

CATHOLIC CHURCH AND HISTORY

. . . the Church possessed from the start a monopoly of the writing of history. This was absolutely central to its success in making so deep an impression on Dark Age society. For Christianity was essentially a "religion of the book"—that is, a historical religion. It taught that certain things had happened, and that certain things were going to happen. The first was a matter of record, in the shape of the Scriptures; the second a matter of prophecy, drawn from a variety of sources, not least the authority of the Church itself. The correct teaching and interpretation of history was thus central to the Church's evangelizing mission.

H.C., P. 136

[45]

Catholic Church (Irish)

The Irish Church was never consciously in rebellion against orthodoxy. It is remarkable that it Christianized the people without a single case of martyrdom, and without any recorded instance of heresy or internal persecution; there was no violence whatever.

H.C., P. 143

Catholic Church and Popularity

. . . the Catholic Church has not survived and flourished over two millennia by being popular. It has survived because what it taught was true. The quest for popularity, as opposed to the quest for truth, is bound to fail.

P.J., P. 185

Catholic Church and Truth

The church is not a secular body ruled by a government with material aims which can be secured by a choice between empirical means. That, indeed, lends itself to the notion of sovereign assemblies and direct representation, with all the apparatus of votes and majorities. But the church is quite different. It is concerned not with choices but with truth. There is only one truth, divinely revealed. Therefore the church is an autocracy tempered by consensus. The synod is not a parliament seeking a majority, but a mirror, as it were, in which the autocracy sees the consensus for which it speaks. Pope and synod interact. . . . They represent different aspects of the workings of the Holy Spirit. In their complementarity they are creative, and it is now difficult to see the church functioning without this partnership . . .

P.J., P. 128

Catholic Church and Tyranny

. . . the French revolution seemed to give it [the Church] new life, since it was a reminder that tyranny was multifarious—there could be tyrannies of reason and tyrannies of ideology, tyrannies of progress, and even tyrannies of liberty, equality and fraternity. [The Church] which upheld an international and timeless divine law was a necessary counterpoise to unbridled human assertion.

H.C., P. 385

Celebrities and Politics

There's no busybodies like showbusybodies. If a record is top of the pops, why should not the man who made it hold forth on the environment? Does not a stunning performance as Lady Macbeth entitle an actress to tell us about the rights and wrongs of the Gulf? If a man can force us to laugh till our guts ache, can't he tell us how to vote too? So they kid themselves. In fact the average dozen men and women you stop in the street are far more likely to produce political wisdom, or at least common sense, then showbiz personalities overburdened with self-importance, and soft touches for any kind of charlatanism around.

S., AUGUST 16, 1990

Censorship

It is true that the kind of press censorship a Labour government might impose, designed to restrict reporting and comment on certain groups—left-wing trade unionists, militant blacks, homosexual activists, Irish republicans and political extremists generally—would be unpopular and resented, but only for the reason that the people to be thus protected from the press are even more widely and deeply disliked than journalists themselves.

S., JULY 19, 1986

[47]

There are broadly two kinds of censorship: the censorship of ideas and opinions, and censorship to promote national security, both internal and external. Totalitarian states practise both but even democracies use the second to some degree; if they fail to do so, they do not remain democracies for long.

s., OCTOBER 17, 1987

We all censor things we do not approve of but we do not call our actions censorship. I exercise judgment; you suppress; he, she or it censors. Censorship is what the other fellow does.

s., OCTOBER 17, 1987

In recent years it has been fascinating, and also frightening, to watch the developing paradox whereby the era of permissiveness, introduced in the 1960s, has become in the 1980s the era of Permissive Censorship. The old taboos have been turned on their hands, rather as Marx upended Hegel's dialectic. Sections of society who once complained of injustice, like blacks, homosexuals, and militant women, now demand not just equality but privilege, including the right to censor their critics.

s., NOVEMBER 21, 1987

CHAPPAQUIDDICK

The alleged central crime of Watergate was the unsuccessful attempt to obstruct justice. But the worst example, during recent times, of justice-obstruction in America—successful, too—was the Chappaquiddick affair. This involved not a petty break-in but a dead woman. The beneficiary of this obstruction is still a prominent member of the U.S. Senate and frequently offers the world moralistic advice, notably on Ireland and South Africa.

c., OCTOBER 1988

[48]

CHARDIN, TEILHARD DE

Teilhard is a classic case not merely of a pseudo-intellectual, but of a French pseudo-intellectual. That is, he has no understanding of what makes a logical argument, or constitutes proof, but an impressive fluency of exposition which begins to disintegrate on second reading or when it is translated into English.

E.S., P. 124

Teilhardian phenomenology is a system which enables the more leisured class to accommodate scientific knowledge in a religious setting but which makes no intolerable demands on either flesh or intellect.

E.S., PP. 125–26

His most important work, *The Phenomenon of Man*, has been described by one of his fiercest critics, Sir Peter Medawar, as "philosophy-fiction" appealing to the "half-educated" or to people "educated far beyond their capacity to undertake analytical thought." On its first appearance it was hailed, however, by a number of leading French intellectuals as a remarkable synthesis of religious and scientific thought, and it arrived in Britain and the United States in English translation (1959) with distinguished credentials, including a fulsome introduction by Professor Julian Huxley. . . . [But] Teilhard tends to attract disciples with the same mental habits as the Flying Saucer worshippers, but from a significantly higher social background: he is the idol of upper-middle-class sub-intellectuals (especially ladies), among whom he has replaced such cults as Madame Blavatsky's Scientology.

E.S., P. 124

CHEKA

The Tsar's secret police, the Okhrana, had numbered 15,000, which made it by far the largest body of its kind in the old world. By contrast, the Cheka, within three years of its establishment, had a strength of 250,000 full-time agents. Its activities were on a correspondingly ample scale. While the last Tsars had executed an average of seventeen a year (for all crimes), by 1918–19 the Cheka was averaging 1,000 executions a month for political offences alone.

M.T., P. 68

CHIANG KAI-SHEK

The notion of Chiang as the architect of East Asian post-war stability was absurd. He never at any stage of his career effectively controlled more than half of China itself. He was a poor administrator; an indifferent general. As a politician he lacked the sense to grasp that what China needed was leadership which combined radicalism with patriotic fervour. Moreover, he knew little and cared less about the peasants.

M.T., P. 443

CHINA

In some ways 19th-century China was more archaic than was 6th-century Byzantium. To begin with, it had no effective state currency. One of the reasons that opium was so popular in China was that it became a highly effective substitute currency.

B.M., P. 777

CHINESE CIVIL WAR

Mao was an ambitious romantic who had had a good war and wanted to better himself in the peace. Chiang was the man in possession who could not bear the idea of an eventual successor, especially one with intellectual pretensions. Hence there was no historical inevitability about the Chinese Civil War. It was a personal conflict.

M.T., P. 444

CHOICE

The "right to choose" phrase, beloved of fierce women journalists and feminists generally, is peculiarly obnoxious because it associates having children (or not) with the notion of shopping and "consumer choice"; a child in the womb is "disposable," like panty-hose or plastic cartons.

s., DECEMBER 5, 1987

CHRISTIAN (ORTHODOX)

. . . they should . . . band together, compile lists of clergy who regularly subject captive congregations to Marxist claptrap, pacifist ideology and anti-British abuse, and ensure that, whenever they are scheduled to preach, a group of people are present to bring any political harangue to an abrupt end. Such systematic cleansing of the churches can be done without any breach of canon or secular law. It would be welcome to most bishops, Anglican or Catholic, . . . who would use the disturbances as an excellant and long overdue opportunity to discipline and if need be inhibit clerical extremists. Most of all, the vast majority of ordinary churchgoers, who attend for spiritual edification and comfort and precisely to get away from the lies and half-truths of party politics, would endorse such action. It would be the modern equivalent of Church driving the money-changers from the Temple.

s., FEBRUARY 16, 1991

CHRISTIANITY

For Luke, the Jerusalem Council is an ecclesiastical incident. For Paul, it is part of the greatest struggle ever waged. What lies behind it are two unresolved questions. Had Jesus Christ founded a new religion, the true one at last? Or, to put it another way, was he God or man? If Paul is vindicated, Christianity is born. If he is overruled, the teachings of Jesus become nothing more than the hallmarks of a Jewish sect, doomed to be submerged in the mainstream of an ancient creed.

H.C., P. 5

Christianity, by its nature, always ends by damaging its secular patrons.

H.C., P. 89

As an exercise in perfectionism, Christianity cannot succeed, even by its internal definitions; what it is designed to do is to set targets and standards, raise aspirations, to educate, stimulate and inspire. Its strength lies in its just estimate of man as a fallible creature with immortal longings. Its outstanding moral merit is to invest the individual with a conscience, and bid him follow it. This particular form of liberation is what St. Paul meant by the freedom men find in Christ. And, of course, it is the father of all other freedoms. For conscience is the enemy of tyranny and the compulsory society; and it is the Christian conscience which has destroyed the institutional tyrannies Christianity itself has created—the self-correcting mechanism at work.

H.C., P. 516

Christianity has not made man secure or happy or even dignified. But it supplies a hope. It is a civilizing agent. It helps to cage the beast. It offers glimpses of real freedom, intimations of a calm and reasonable existence. Even as we see it, distorted by the ravages of humanity, it is not without beauty.

H.C., P. 517

In the last generation, with public Christianity in headlong retreat, we have caught our first, distant view of a de-Christianized world, and it is not encouraging. We know that Christian insistence on man's potentiality for good is often disappointed; but we are also learning that man's capacity for evil is almost limitless. . . . Man is imperfect with God. Without God, what is he? As Francis Bacon put it: "They that deny God destroy man's nobility: for certainly man is of kin to the beasts by his body; and, if he be not kin to God by his spirit, he is a base and ignoble creature." We are less base and ignoble by virtue of divine example and by the desire for the form of apotheosis which Christianity offers. In the dual personality of Christ we are offered a perfected image of ourselves, an eternal pace-setter for our striving.

H.C., P. 517

. . . there is no flowering of civilization so rich in the financially-uncontaminated word as Christianity. When Christ spoke the Sermon on the Mount, no TV company fed him. St. Paul, writing his epistles, had no thought for the Roman serial rights. There was no film option on Pascal's *Pensées*. The four evangelists were not in desperate competition to get their Instant Biographies out first.

S.N., P. 70

CHRISTIANITY (AMERICAN)

The assumption of the voluntary principle . . . was that the personal religious convictions of individuals, freely gathered in churches and acting in voluntary associations, will gradually and necessarily permeate society by persuasion and example. It is . . . the agency of the good man, which will convert and reform the world. Thus the world was seen primarily in moral terms. This became a dominant factor whether America was rejecting the Old World and seeking to quarantine herself from it (a concept used as recently as 1962 during the Cuban Missile Crisis), or whether America was embracing the world, and seeking to reform it. It was characteristic of the American State, first to reject espionage on moral grounds, then to undertake it through the Central Intelligence Agency, a moralistic institution much more like the Society of Jesus than its Soviet equivalent.

H.C., P. 429

American religion, in its formative period . . . for essential purposes . . . had no theology at all . . . what mattered . . . was the deep Christian consensus on ethics and morality. So long as Americans agreed on morals, theology could take care of itself. Morals became the heart of religion, whether for Puritans or revivalists, orthodox or liberal, fundamentalist or moralist. . . . This was a consensus which even non-Christians, deists and rationalists, could share. . . . It could even (the argument is ironic) accommodate Roman Catholicism.

H.C., P. 430

Now here we come to an important stage in the argument around modern Christianity. The Augustinian total society had come into being in Carolingian times in great part because the Christian clergy operated a monopoly of education, which they only began to lose just before the Reformation. How could the total voluntary society of American Christianity come into being if Church and State were separated, and education were a secular concern? The Founding Fathers saw education and faith as inseparable.

H.C., P. 430

CHRISTIANITY (BYZANTINE)

Byzantine Christianity was the architect of its own destruction. It tried to define and particularize too much, and therefore became increasingly divided and acrimonious . . . [and] it was too authoritarian, seeking exact credal definitions of packed church councils, later enforced by imperial police . . . In the fifth and sixth centuries, it was increasingly disturbed by its efforts to suppress the monophysites, that is those Christians who held, in their desire to reconcile the concept of the Son of God with monotheism, that the divine and human elements in God made one nature, *monophusis*. The controversy created those Eastern Churches which are independent of both Rome and Greek Orthodoxy. Thus the Coptic Church of Egypt was monophysite . . . [and] so were most of the eastern provinces. In Persia, too, the Church was independent of Constantinople, and eventually became Nestorian, acknowledging the teaching of the ex-Patriarch of Constantinople, who distinguished between the divine and human natures in Christ, and held therefore

[54]

that Mary should be called "Mother of Christ" but not "Mother of God."

C.H.L., P. 165

CHRISTIANITY AND CULTURE

The stone crosses of the Celtic world symbolize the intense and complete identification between art and Christianity which was so striking and powerful a feature of these centuries. Christianity was not just a carrier of culture; through the agency of the monks it in effect became culture. . . . Monasticism, in fact, proved highly effective in persuading these emergent western societies to devote a dramatic part of their wealth and skills to cultural purposes.

H.C., PP. 158–59

CHRISTIANITY VERSUS MARXISM

It is characteristic of the accretive subtlety of Christianity that it ascribes evil in the world to a multiplicity of causes. Marx, by contrast, has a single-cause theory: all the evils of society arise from private property; abolish that, and they will disappear. But the result is not happiness. It is the Gulag . . .

E.S., P. 127

CHRISTIANITY AND THE ROMAN EMPIRE

The truth is that during the large-scale anti-Christian operations of the second half of the third century, the State was obliged to recognize that its enemy had changed and had made itself a potential ally. . . . Christianity had become in many striking ways a mirror-image of the empire itself. It was catholic, universal, ecumenical, orderly, international, multi-racial and increasingly legalistic. . . . Unlike Judaism, it had no national aspirations incompatible with

[55]

the empire's security; on the contrary, its ideology fitted neatly into the aims and needs of the universal state.

H.C., PP. 75–76

Christianity (Rational)

. . . the chief defect of rational Christianity was that it made no appeal to the emotions. It offered no incentive other than enlightened self-interest. The element of sacrifice and abnegation was eliminated. Morality was presented simply as a shrewd bargain. . . . Conscience had no role to play, since it was merely subjective opinion. Thus the element of personal responsibility was scrapped, and all a man needed to be saved was to stick to the rules. Now this was to sacrifice the whole point of the Reformation and to return, in effect, to the mechanical Christianity of canon law. And mechanical Christianity necessarily produced a corrupt Church, led by a secular-minded clergy. This is precisely what happened in the eighteenth century. In their anxiety to avoid fanaticism of any kind, the rational Christians tended to depersonalize religion, and to emphasize its forms and institutions at the expense of its spirit.

H.C., P. 343

Christianity and the Social Order

. . . if the Christian theory of the world, and its explanation of the miseries all of us undergo, no longer holds, then the Christian legitimation of social order, law and communal self-restraint cannot be maintained very long either, and the violent revolution, from being an aberrant interruption of customary stability, becomes the normal feature of life. As Albert Camus puts it in *The Rebel*, "man now launches the essential undertaking of rebellion, which is that of replacing the reign of grace by the reign of justice"—an even more futile undertaking, one might suppose.

E.S., P. 245

CHURCH OF ENGLAND AND THE MEDIA

There are, I think, two reasons for the media's obsession with our church by law established. The first is its entertainment value. I often complain about the lack of humour in newspapers, and editors reply that they cannot find funny writers. The Church of England at least supplies some good comic characters for the newspages. . . . The second reason for the media's interest is snobbery. Anglican bishops may deny some of the basic beliefs of Christianity but at least they live in palaces. They have sonorous titles. They are Divines; Prelates; two are even Primates. They sit in the Lords and dress in extraordinary clothes on occasions—more so than Catholics these days. They use pre-war expressions like "let us take counsel together," often delivered in pre-war accents. They do their business in some of the most beautiful buildings in the country, mounting fancy-dress ceremonials . . . which make good television.

S., JULY 14, 1990

CHURCH AND STATE

We must not imagine that the battle between Church and State took place only at the highest level. . . . Of course there had been tension between the clerical and secular elements in Christianity since very early times. The exaltation of the clerical caste had always been connected with the development of authority in Church discipline, and orthodoxy in dogma. Montanism, in the second century, had been a protest against all three, and Tertullian, in embracing it in the third, became the first articulate Christian anti-clerical.

H.C., P. 203

The birth of Protestant America was a deliberate and self-conscious act of Church-State perfectionism. . . . dissenting groups were fleeing an Anglican Jacobean England of whose "reformation" they had despaired. But they were not fleeing to religious liberty and diversity. On the contrary: like the Carolingians, they were seeking to create a total Christian society, where the divine instructions on every aspect of life would be obeyed to the letter, and a city of earth created as the antechamber or prelude to entry into God's city. The original vision of America was Augustinian, rather than Erasmian. There could be no question of religion being "private": civil and religious society were one, inseparable.

H.C., P. 421

THE CIVIL WAR

The Civil War can be described as the most characteristic religious episode in the whole of American history since its roots and causes were not economic or political but religious and moral. It was a case of a moral principle tested to destruction—not, indeed, of the principle, but of those who opposed it. But in the process Christianity itself was placed under almost intolerable strain. . . . But the answer to this was that the bulk of Christian opinion and teaching had been anti-slavery for more than a millennium, that Christianity was the one great religion which had always declared the diminution, if not the final elimination, of slavery to be meritorious; and that no real case for slavery could be constructed, in good faith, from Christian scripture. The fact that Southerners from a variety of Christian churches were prepared to do so, in the second half of the nineteenth century, was a shocking and flagrant stain on the faith.

H.C., PP. 436–37

CIVILIZATION

The essence of civilization is the orderly quest for truth, the rational perception of reality and all its facets, and the adaptation of man's behaviour to its laws. So long as we follow the path of reason we shall not move far from the lighted circle of civilization. Its enemies invariably lie among those who, for whatever motive, deny, distort, minimize, exaggerate or poison the truth, and who falsify the processes of reason. At all times civilization has its enemies, though they are constantly changing their guise and their weapons. The great defensive art is to detect and unmask them before the damage they inflict becomes fatal. "Hell," wrote Thomas Hobbes, "is truth seen too late." Survival is falsehood detected in time.

E.S., P. 85

Looking back, one is appalled to think of the number of occasions when the civilized world was in real danger of extinction. I am old enough to recall at least three: 1940, when the Nazi system, the most dynamic of all the ideological Frankenstein's monsters . . . had overrun continental Europe and seemed poised to take over Africa and Asia too; 1945–46, when America seemed about to pull all its forces home, leaving the rest of the world to Stalin; and the mid-1970s, when the aftermath of Watergate left the United States almost leaderless and encouraged Brezhnev and his surrogates to resume taking over the world.

N.R., DECEMBER 14, 1992

CIVILIZATION AND TRUTH

Civilization . . . is the rational pursuit of truth within a framework of order. The discovery of truth, of course, is part of this ordering process, the way by which man locates himself in the universe. This is a very long, complicated and cumulative process. Man needs to orientate himself in time, by discovering and perfecting chronology; in space, by acquiring geographical and astronomical knowledge; in nature, by discovering its laws and using them to master his environment. He is also engaged in a continuous effort of moral and social orientation, reflected in his attempts to improve his designs for civil government, for legal and ethical codes, and his image of what a just society should be. There is, likewise, a process of moral ordering, in which man seeks to discover his worth in relation to other men, and to the potentialities of his surroundings. Human beings need to know where they stand in all these matters, for such knowledge is an essential element in their security, and . . . their happiness . . .

E.S., P. 192

CLERIC

Behind the clericalist movement was, . . . in a more realistic way, a sense of superiority: clerics carried out the whole administrative side of government, running chanceries . . . and keeping accounts and records of every kind. The last point . . . is the most important of all: the Church had the literate manpower and the techniques to produce more sophisticated forms of government than any available to the secular world. In the Dark Ages these had been placed at the disposal of the barbarian tribal states: the Church, for instance, gave them written legal codes. But all the time the Church retained its old traditions of separate canonical legislation, dating back to the fourth century.

H.C., P. 204

COLD WAR

. . . Korea . . . provoked the permanent arms-race . . . [and] revolutionized the Congressional and national attitude to defence: defence allocations passed the $50 billion watershed [in 1953]. The increases made possible the development of tactical nuclear weapons . . . the rapid construction of overseas air-bases, a world-wide deployment of the Strategic Air Command, a nuclear carrier fleet and mobile conventional capability . . . If the Cold War began over Poland it reached maturity over Korea and embraced the whole world. In effect, Stalin had polarized the earth.

M.T., P. 452

COLERIDGE, SAMUEL TAYLOR

He always accepted the reality of evil, as distinct from mere error, and this acceptance rightly tempered any optimism he might feel about the future of mankind. He never fell into the crucial error, made so significantly by Shelley, by his mentor Godwin and by so many Continental idealists and utopians and their countless followers, of loving mankind in general but treating human beings in particular with heartless contempt or cruelty. Coleridge saw personal affections as the key to any true humanitarianism. They expand "like the circles of a Lake—the Love of our Friends, parents and neighbours leads us to the love of Country to the love of all Mankind."

B.M., PP. 825–26

. . . the teachings of Coleridge and those he influenced, following in the tradition of Burke, were one reason why Britain did not take the totalitarian path at any time in the future.

B.M., P. 828

COLLECTIVIZATION

Until 1914, agricultural modernization and the creation of large and relatively efficient peasant farms (and voluntary cooperatives) meant that Russia was one of the world's largest exporters of agricultural goods, sending up to 40 per cent of its produce abroad. Under Lenin it became a net importer of food, and the deficit widened as the years passed. Stalin's collectivization policy led to the murder or death by starvation of most of Russia's best peasant farmers. It branded a mark of Cain on the brow of the regime, which burned more deeply over the decades.

M.T., P. 725

The essence of statesmanship is the fine adjustment of rival forces by political contrivance. The essence of public philosophy is the identification and measurement of those forces. Naturally the balance of forces is constantly changing, not least as a result of adjustments which statesmen make. The overwhelming imbalance in our age has been caused by the huge increase in collectivism. The power of the state has increased, is increasing and ought to be diminished: there, in a sentence, is the great redressment problem of our times.

R.F., P. 5

Left and Right are now increasingly meaningless terms; the true dividing line runs between those who put their trust in the individual and those who insist on the moral righteousness of the collective. It is no accident that the collectivists, from whatever end of the spectrum they claim to come, always tend, in the end, to hate parliamentary institutions, because such free assemblies at their best exalt and ennoble individuals, and at the worst accord them some degree of protection.

R.F., P. 58

COLONIALISM

The biggest mistake made by the colonial powers—and it had political and moral as well as economic consequences—was to refuse to allow the market system to operate in land. Here they followed the procedures first worked out in the British colonies in America in the seventeenth century, elaborated to develop the American Midwest and West (to the destruction of the indigenous Indians) and refined, on a purely racial basis, in South Africa. It involved human engineering, and was therefore destructive of the individualistic principle which lies at the heart of the Judaeo-Christian ethic.

M.T., P. 159

Colonialism was important not for what it was but for what it was not. It bred grandiose illusions and unjustified grievances. The first had a major impact on events up to 1945; the second thereafter.

M.T., P. 161

Colonialism has been presented as a conspiracy of capitalist states; decolonization as a further conspiracy when it became economically more prudent to switch to "neo-colonialism." But if there was a conspiracy, why did the conspirators never meet or exchange plans and ideas? The truth is colonialism was born in intense rivalry and died in it. The colonial powers did not conspire against the natives. They conspired against each other. Each colonial power hated all the rest, despised their methods, rejoiced in their misfortunes and happily aggravated them when convenient. They would not cooperate even when imperative self-interest demanded.

M.T., P. 506

Comte, the most considerable of Saint-Simon's onetime disciples, . . . originally held violently hostile views on women, no doubt . . . because of his unfortunate first marriage to a Palais Royal prostitute, Caroline Massin. He told Mill that in the whole of the animal creation, the exceptions to the principle of male superiority were found only in the lowest reaches, among the invertebrates; that women were incapable of abstract thought; that they had done nothing in poetry, music, or painting; and that they should not only be denied power but forbidden to enter public offices.

B.M., P. 479

. . . the worst writer who ever lived . . . He said he wrote "scientifically." Later, however, he laid down rules of style: no sentence longer than five lines of print; each paragraph to have no more than seven sentences; all books to have seven chapters, each chapter to have three parts and each part seven sections; each section must have a lead paragraph of seven sentences, followed by three paragraphs of five sentences each.

B.M., P. 821

Comte was to become by far the most revered figure of the 1840s. John Stuart Mill, George Eliot and Professor Huxley thought the world of him. Comte's positivism was as attractive to the radical intelligentsia in the mid-19th century as Marxism was in the mid-20th century. Nor is this surprising: Positivism and Marxism have a good deal in common.

B.M., P. 822

COMMISSION

When Harold Wilson did not know what to do about a problem, or knew what to do but was afraid of the political consequences of doing it, he would set up a Royal Commission. If, as he rightly said, a week is a long time in politics, the lifespan of such a body is an eternity, and by the time it reports, the problem will have gone or changed and in all likelihood there will be a new government.

S., APRIL 29, 1989

COMMUNISM

It is a dismal fact that, during the 1970s and 1980s, the policies followed by Russia and its Cuban, Ethiopian and Indo-Chinese satellites added around 12–15 million to the world total of displaced persons: not unworthy of comparison with the horrific statistical achievements of Stalin or Hitler.

M.T., PP. 719–20

. . . if we look at the ravages which Communist politics . . . inflicted on those areas where they were allowed full play—the sheer destruction of resources . . . the obliteration of morality and truth-telling, the contempt for life, the ubiquitous corruption, the long-term poverty—we have to count as an immeasurable blessing that Marxism took over only one-fifth of the world. . . . Supposing it had triumphed and run the entire planet by its catastrophic system of wealth-destruction. The whole of humanity would have then entered a new dark age of savagery and want.

N.R., DECEMBER 14, 1992

COMMUNISM AND FACISM

. . . the Communist alternative was merely one form of state to-talitarianism. It had much more in common with the Nazi or Fascist solution to capitalist crisis than any of them had with free-enterprise capitalism. . . . all these state-power theories sprang from . . . Hegel. He taught that the state represents the principle of absolute reason and spiritual power, which bestows upon man whatever value he has. . . . in the collective whole, the individual is lifted to a higher sphere in which his real will is realized. As the state is the embodiment of absolute power, its actual policies must not be judged in terms of "subjective morality." Power is the basic fact of political life, and the political order must be judged and justified within its own terms—this is the central argument of Hegel's *Philosophy of Right* (1821).

E.S., PP. 77–78

COMMUNISM AND RACISM

I read recently an attempt by Robert Harris, a left-wing columnist in the *Sunday Times*, to differentiate morally between Nazism and communism, arguing that at least communist theory was free of the supreme sin of racism. Not true: Marxism sprang directly from anti-semitic conspiracy theory. Marx's essays on the way in which the "money-Jew" and his "hucksterism" had corrupted society, written in 1843–44 and published in the *Deutsch-Französische Jahrbücher*, were the immediate precursors to the emergence of his mature political philosophy in the years 1844–46. In effect Marx decided that the evil element in society, the agents of the money-power which revolted him, were not just the Jews but the bourgeois class as a whole: he simply extended his anti-semitic conspiracy theory to take in the entire capitalist class. But he remained strongly anti-semitic . . .

S., FEBRUARY 17, 1990

COMMUNIST RITUALS

Marxism-Communism in all its myriad varieties loves the splendour and language of ritual: the Red Square parades; the Peking displays of ritual gymnastics and its miracle- and mystery-plays; its hymns, like "The East Is Red," its catechism, the "Little Red Book," its ritual praises and abuse, so similar to [those of] the fourth-century Byzantine church. It even has its own ecumenical movement now, as can be seen from a photograph (1973) of students demonstrating for "proletarian unity," and carrying embroidered banners to Marx, Engels, Lenin, Stalin and Mao Tse-tung, for all the world like young

[65]

clerics in a Holy Week procession of expiation for sin, schism and heresy.

E.S., P. 127

CONGRESS

. . . the . . . Congressional committee-system . . . empowers investigations. For the legislature to conduct quasi-judicial inquiries is legitimate. It . . . proved invaluable in Britain's establishing constitutional liberties in the seventeenth and eighteenth centuries. It was grievously abused, particularly in the conduct of political and religious witch-hunts. Two aspects were particularly objectionable: the use of inquisitorial procedure, so alien to the Common Law, and the power to punish for contempt anyone who obstructs this procedure. Congress inherited both the virtues and vices of the system, which were inseparable. . . . On the whole the advantages outweigh the defects, and therefore the system is kept.

M.T., P. 459

CONRAD, JOSEPH

From the perspective of sixty years later it must be said that Conrad is the only substantial writer of the time whose vision remains clear and true in every particular. He dismissed Marxism as malevolent nonsense, certain to generate monstrous tyranny; Freud's ideas were nothing more than "a kind of magic show." The war had demonstrated human frailty but otherwise would resolve nothing, generate nothing. Giant plans of reform, panaceas, all "solutions," were illusory.

M.T., P. 12

CONSERVATIVE PARTY (ENGLAND)

The Conservative Party is now the great—the only—repository of freedom in this country. It is the democratic party; the party of individual freedom, the party of the rule of law. It is the last line of defence we possess.

R.F., P. 124

CONSERVATIVE PARTY PRINCIPLES

It is sometimes said that the country can no longer afford to elect a Conservative government, for fear of a devastating conflict with the unions. It is likewise said, as a consequence of this fear, that the Conservatives must trim their sails accordingly, modify and tone down their programme and beliefs, and so cobble together a series of attitudes and proposals which will satisfy the union oligarchs and receive their contemptuous stamp of approval. But this is arrant and indefensible cowardice. It is appeasement in its most naked and shameful form. It is total and unconditional surrender to the very forces which are bent on destroying our democracy and removing freedom from our land.

R.F., P. 123

CONSTITUTION

Constitution-making is a thankless task. Constitutional analysis is a tedious aspect of history. But constitutions matter. Weimar failed because its constitution was clumsy. The Federal Republic succeeded because Adenauer gave it a skilfully balanced foundation. The constitution turned the Fourth Republic into a mere arena for what de Gaulle contemptuously called "the ballet of the parties." Thanks to its proportional representation system, no party could form a homogeneous government.

M.T., P. 590

COOLIDGE, CALVIN

Coolidge was the most internally consistent and single-minded of modern American presidents. If Harding loved America as Arcadia,

[67]

Coolidge was the best-equipped to preserve it as such. He came from the austere hills of Vermont, of the original Puritan New England stock, and was born over his father's store. No public man carried into modern times more comprehensively the founding principles of Americanism: hard work, frugality, freedom of conscience, freedom from government, respect for serious culture . . . and was exceptionally well-read in classical and foreign literature and in history . . .

M.T., P. 219

CORRUPTION

. . . the only way to reduce corruption in government is to reduce the size of government.

C., DECEMBER 1991

CORRUPTION (AMERICAN)

As a historian, I never fail to be astonished by the relative incorruptibility of American public life. It is a theory of mine that no political system, however well-thought-out and invigilated, and however permeated by strong religious sanctions, can remain entirely honest if the sums of money at stake are large enough.

C., DECEMBER 1991

CREDIT CARD

There was a time . . . when credit cards were entirely optional and some old-fashioned folk swore they would never have them. Today they are in practice compulsory for people who travel or lead complicated lives. Not to have one causes suspicion.

S., APRIL 15, 1989

CREED, POLITICAL

A political creed which respects [individual conscience]—whatever evil it may otherwise do or stand for—is inherently healthy, for it contains within it a self-correcting mechanism. But in a system of belief where conscience is collectivised, there is no dependable barrier along the highway which ultimately may lead to Auschwitz and Gulag. I do not intend to travel even one miserable inch along that fearful road.

R.F., P. 76

CRIMINOLOGY

Criminology . . . has tended to rest in the domain of the social sciences, or the immature physical sciences. Its predominant form, known as Radical Positivism, operates from a number of "common-sense assumptions," such as that there is such a person as a criminal, that a moral consensus does exist, and that a crime occurs when a criminal infringes the consensus. But it is highly critical of the way this situation is dealt with. Thus, it rejects the assumption that crime is an overwhelmingly youthful, masculine and working-class activity; it accuses police and judiciary of using non-scientific criteria in operating the system, and urges reform to ensure that social control operates more effectively and scientifically in accordance with the objective interests of all concerned.

E.S., P. 199

CRITICISM

What the Greeks in fact did was to develop the principle of criticism. . . . [This was] the most important event since the creation of language itself, since it allowed man to put to use whole new areas of his intellect and personality, hitherto dormant. To question received opinion had not, hitherto, been something that human beings did. But the taste, once acquired, became habitual . . . the cultivation of this technique not only enlarged human horizons but almost produced a new human being: alongside the Dogmatic Man of the archaic societies it placed a new creature—*Critical Man.*

E.S., PP. 7–8

CROSS (STONE)

Perhaps most spectacular of all was the development of the entirely new Celtic-Christian idiom of the stone cross. The stone-art of Ireland went right back to the La Tène period of the first century A.D. The Christian device of the cross gave pagan technology the opportunity to develop a unique art-world of its own, with a multitude of periods and schools, and an increasing elaboration of the message conveyed. Eventually what we have in these high stone crosses is a theology in stone, imparting a number of elaborate Mediterranean religious concepts in a purely Celtic artistic vernacular. The crosses stood at the wayside, throughout the western parts of the British Isles, wherever tracks converged and men gathered— lifted fingers both admonitory and benign, mute witnesses to Christianity which spoke powerfully to the eyes.

H.C., P. 158

CUBA

Cuba illustrated the gap between words and reality which was to become the most striking characteristic of the Third World. Everyone in politics talked revolution and practised graft.

M.T., PP. 619–620

In all essentials, the battle for Cuba was a public relations campaign, fought in New York and Washington. Castro's principal advocate was Herbert Matthews of the *New York Times*, who presented him as the T. E. Lawrence of the Caribbean. Just as the Hearst press helped to make the Cuban revolution in 1898, so the *Times* sponsored Castro. This swung round the State Department.

M.T., P. 621

CULTURAL REVOLUTION

There was later some misunderstanding of the Cultural Revolution in the West. It was represented as a revolt of intellectuals. In fact, it was quite the reverse. It was a revolution of illiterates and semi-literates against intellectuals, the "spectacle-wearers" as they were called. It was xenophobic, aimed at those who "think the moon is rounder abroad." The Red Guards had a great deal in common with Roehm's Brownshirts, and the entire movement with Hitler's campaign against "cosmopolitan civilization." It was the greatest witchhunt in history.

M.T., P. 556

CULTURE AND ART

The visual image, whether in paint or stone or marble, thus goes close to the sources of a culture, and the way it makes itself understood. It is a remarkably sensitive index. The dynamic of Greek culture was the desire to know about man and explore his potentialities; it was humanist, and because it was humanist it devoted enormous trouble to portraying the human form in its exact likeness, and to placing it by structures of natural optic array in its true setting. The freedom of man in society, as an economic and political being, was paralleled by the freedom with which the artist could accurately depict him in his optical environment. Only when this freedom was secured, by a process of trial, error and improvement, was the information about man complete.

E.S., PP. 43–44

CULTURE (JEWISH)

The Jews subsidized their culture many hundreds of years before the practice became a function of the Western welfare state. . . . The system whereby sages and merchants ran the community in tandem thus redistributed rather than reinforced wealth. It also ensured the production of large numbers of highly intelligent people who were given every opportunity to pursue ideas. Quite suddenly, around the year 1800, this ancient and highly efficient social machine for the production of intellectuals began to shift its output. Instead of pouring all its products into the closed circuit of rabbinical studies, where they remained completely isolated from general society, it unleashed a significant and ever-growing proportion of them into secular life. This was an event of shattering importance in world history.

H.J., P. 341

CULTURE (POP)

. . . if Einstein created the cosmology of the twentieth century and Freud its characteristic mental assumptions, it was the cinema which provided its universal popular culture.

H.J., P. 463

. . . this apotheosis of inanity. For more than two decades now, more and more intellectuals have turned their backs on their trade and begun to worship at the shrine of "pop culture." Nowadays, if you confess that you don't know the difference between Dizzy Gillespie and Fats Waller (and, what is more, don't care) you are liable to be accused of being a fascist.

S.N., P. 46

CULTURE WARS

As a historian I have become increasingly fascinated by the perennial culture conflict, at its sharpest in advanced societies, between radicals and conservatives: between, that is, those who believe the world can be reshaped by their own unaided intelligence and those who distrust reason in isolation and think it should be anchored in prescriptive wisdom, natural law and other restraints. This conflict is conducted mainly in books but powerful echoes are to be found on the stage, in music, in art and architecture and not least in public life itself. What is absorbing is to follow the generational swings in national (and also international) culture, in which first radicals, then conservatives, get the upper hand, and especially the way in which the balance is tipped by the shift of a great writer from one camp to the other—Coleridge and Victor Hugo are excellent examples, in different directions. The richness and variety, and indeed the advance, of our culture depend upon the continuation of this conflict, which is deeply rooted in human nature. If you believe in the Hegelian dialectic, this is an example of its powerful spirit in action.

s., OCTOBER 6, 1990

CUOMO, MARIO

Operators like Cuomo have hitherto traded on their religious status to corral the Catholic vote while feeling free to ignore their Church in fishing for the suffrages of anyone else.

s., JUNE 23, 1990

The London *Times* describes him as a "devout" Catholic. I don't know why. This is the politician who refused to condemn the homosexual-abortionists' demo in St. Patrick's Cathedral in which a consecrated host was desecrated—he thought it might lose him votes—and supports the public funding of pregnancy-terminations.

s., JUNE 23, 1990

CURZON, LORD GEORGE NATHANIEL

Unlike the vast majority of politicians, he believed facts were paramount.

S.N., P. 172

D

DANCE (NINETEENTH CENTURY)

Vienna was a dancer's paradise. . . . As with clothes and hairstyles, the kind of dance you practiced indicated your politics. The minuet stood for the ancien régime. In Washington they favored the cotillion, which was French and republican, at any rate not monarchical. Imperial Vienna had dropped the minuet—too old hat—but had produced its own extravaganza, new, exhilarating, daring, erotic and intensely athletic—the waltz. . . . As [Byron] enviously noted, the intimate and close physical contact between the couple made it an entirely new kind of dance, a sexual break with the past.

B.M., P. 106

DARWINISM

Darwin's ideas seemed to many Englishmen to give a new lease to the concept of a chosen race. The race, their own, owed its appointment with destiny not to spurious historical documents, or the supposed activities of first-century apostles, but to the processes of natural selection which allowed only the fittest to survive and rule: the English had been chosen not by God but by nature herself . . . demonstrated by irrefutable scientific theory. Of course Darwin had said nothing of the kind; he had always been careful to insist that natural progression was morally neutral. But the "survival of the fittest" seemed to describe so accurately the facts of English history, and the dominant position of the English race, that English pundits naturally assumed that the laws of science endorsed England's global policy.

H.E., P. 319

DARWINISM (SOCIAL)

. . . the most influential misconception in history, since it produced the Marxism of *Capital*, the imperialism of Joe Chamberlain, and the racialism of Adolf Hitler.

E.S., P. 186

The adoption of uniform by political leaders became commonplace in the violent inter-war years, being pioneered by Trotsky, Stalin and Mussolini, and enthusiastically imitated by Hitler and, later, Mao Tse-tung. It indicated a habitual tendency to view the evolution of society not as a process of debate and compromise, arbitrated by votes and verbal argument, but as a Darwinian survival of the fittest, with physical force determining the critical stages.

P.P.J., P. 257

Darwin himself always stressed the limits of his discoveries. He discouraged those who sought to build ambitious projections on them. That was why he gave no licence to the theories of the "social Darwinists," which terminated in Hitler's Holocaust, and why he likewise brushed off Marx's attempts to appropriate Darwinism for his own theories of social determinism, which eventually produced the mass murders of Stalin, Mao Tse-tung and Pol Pot.

M.T., P. 778

DAVID (KING)

The story of King David and the accession of Solomon, written evidently by a man who was an eye-witness at court, is a sustained masterpiece of historical literature, . . . [with] innumerable subplots, and handling with dazzling skill a huge cast of sharply-differentiated characters. The portrait of David himself, a great man torn by

conflicting emotions and urges, rivals any biography of antiquity
. . . And there is a masterly theme, a presentation in microcosm
of the theme which runs through all the Bible, and indeed throughout Jewish history: sin redeemed through suffering.

C.H.L., P. 82

DE GASPERI, ALCIDE

De Gasperi, indeed, was almost immune to the two great diseases
of modern times: ethnic nationalism and the belief that states based
upon it can be transformed into Utopias.

M.T., P. 578

DE GAULLE, CHARLES

. . . de Gaulle was never exactly what he seemed. He was one of
the master-intelligences of modern times, infinite in subtlety, rich
in paradox, fathomless in his sardonic ironies. He was a pre-war
figure with a post-war mind, indeed a futurist mind. . . . He was
born to love the French Empire and provincial France, *la France des
villages*—in fact he ended both.

M.T., P. 593

The most important point to be grasped was that the essential de
Gaulle was not a soldier or even a statesman but an intellectual. He
was an intellectual of a special kind, whose entire life was a med-
itation of the theme of mind, power and action. He had, moreover,
the historian's capacity to see current events *sub specie aeternitatis.*
. . . He was always anxious to woo intellectuals . . .

M.T., P. 593

DEATH

Perhaps the greatest of all twentieth-century follies is the belief that
we can ignore death, sweep it under the carpet as it were. It is

almost a truism to say that the present age, so brazenly outspoken about the physical realities of sex, recoils in horror at the prospect of mortality and talks of it only in hushed whispers, in euphemisms and circumlocutions, or not at all.

P.P.J., P. 249

DECEMBRIST

The Decembrist Movement of 1825 is of great importance because it was the first time a group of middle-ranking officers conspired to overthrow a regime they judged incapable of reforming itself. It set the pattern for countless such coups from that day to this, in Europe and the Middle East, in Africa and Asia, and throughout the Spanish-speaking world.

B.M., P. 838

In the short term, the Decembrists must be ranked among the most unsuccessful plotters in history. In the long term, they played a decisive part in delegitimizing and destroying the regime they hated. One reason they were able to do so was that . . . unlike most intellectuals [they were willing to sacrifice] themselves for their ideas . . .

B.M., P. 846

DECOLONIZATION

When the ex-colonial peoples received independence, they thought they were being given justice: all they got was the right to elect politicians. Colonialism, of course, could not produce political equality; what it could, and at its best did, provide was equality before the law. But the process of transfer, by making the vote the yardstick of progress, left the law to take care of itself, so that in the long run the vast majority of Africans ended with nothing.

M.T., P. 510

DEFAMATION

. . . to sue for defamation merely draws attention to the charge.

I., P. 302

DEMOCRACY

Democracy is an important factor in the material success of a society, and especially in its economic success; it should, other things being equal, produce rising living-standards. But of course the essence of democracy is not one-man-one-vote, which does not necessarily have anything to do with individual freedom, or democratic control. The exaltation of "majority rule" on the basis of universal suffrage is the most strident political fallacy of the twentieth century. True democracy means the ability to remove a government without violence, to punish political failure or misjudgement by votes alone.

E.S., P. 256

A democracy is a utilitarian instrument of social control; it is valuable in so far as it works. Its object is to promote human content; but perhaps this is more likely to be secured if the aim is rephrased. As Karl Popper says, the art of politics is the minimization of unhappiness, or of avoidable suffering. The identification of the cause and scale of suffering draws attention to, and defines, problems in society; and, since man is a problem-solving creature, eventually gets something done about them. The process of avoiding suffering is greatly assisted by the existence of free institutions. The greater their number, variety and intrinsic strength, and the greater their individual independence, the more effective the democracy which harbours them will be. All such institutions should be treated like fortresses: that is, soundly constructed and continually manned.

E.S., P. 256

We must, in the twenty-first century, banish from our thinking not only the utopian ideologies that did so much harm in the twentieth, but the illusions that made their careers of destruction so easy. We cling to our belief that all peoples are ready for and can practice democracy, and maybe we shall authenticate it. But a related belief, that all people are ready for independence, has been proved illusory, at incalculable cost in human misery.

N.R., DECEMBER 14, 1992

We live not so much in a parliamentary democracy as in a media democracy.

S., MARCH 18, 1989

DEMOCRACY, AGE OF

Toward the end of the 1820s, the world moved a decisive stage nearer the democratic age. This advance came about not through one dramatic incident, such as the storming of the Bastille, whose results were bound to be ephemeral, but by a combination of many factors and forces—the growth of literacy, the huge increase in the number and circulation of newspapers, the rise in population and incomes, the spread of technology and industry, the diffusion of competing ideas—and, not least, by the actions of great men.

B.M., P. 89

DEMOCRACY, SOCIAL

For, as an incurable social democrat, I state with absolute conviction that anything to the Left of social democracy, as a political theory, must to a greater or lesser extent be totalitarian, and therefore traffic in violence. And the victims of violence must almost invariably be innocent.

S.N., PP. 125–26

THE DEPRESSION

The 1929 crash exposed in addition the naivety and ignorance of bankers, businessmen, Wall Street experts and academic economists high and low; it showed they did not understand the system they had been so confidently manipulating. They had tried to substitute their own well-meaning policies for what Adam Smith called "the invisible hand" of the market and they had wrought disaster. Far from demonstrating, as Keynes and his school later argued—at the time Keynes failed to predict either the crash or the extent and duration of the Depression—the dangers of a self-regulating economy, the *dégringolade* indicated the opposite: the risks of ill-informed meddling.

M.T., P. 240

DETERMINIST

The trouble with [Enlightenment] determinist philosophers was that they were constantly changing their minds about what history was certain to do.

B.M., P. 820

DICTATORS

All mountebank dictators, from Napoleon III to Mussolini and Hitler, liked to be able to claim, with some plausibility, that they had been put in power by a "free vote," and that the people had, as it were, walked willingly into the dungeon before the portcullis slammed down for the last time.

R.F., P. 64

DIETS

I find something deeply corrupt and decadent in eating very expensive food especially designed to keep you slim. After all, the idea of the retributory coronary striking dead the self-indulgent patrician helps to persuade the poor that there is some justice in this world. A culinary system which mitigates this sanction is therefore antisocial.

P.P.J., P. 248

DIMINUTIVES AND AMERICA

It is an ineradicable human propensity to contract long words into short ones and we are not going to stop it. But that does not mean to say that the subs [sub-editors], a powerful tribe, should always get their way. I seethe with rage whenever I think of the manner in which they have foisted the term "gay" on us, thus destroying the original meaning of that delightful word. . . . Racial contractions, however useful to subs, are nearly always risky. Spiro Agnew (himself, it must be said, the object of much ethnic abuse) got himself into fearful trouble by referring to somebody as "the fat Jap." I suppose "the thin Jap" might just have passed, but you never know: America is a minefield of unacceptable diminutives.

s., NOVEMBER 26, 1988

DISARMAMENT

Scratch the surface of our modern world, and we find that it is as disorderly and vicious as ever, a world where rights which cannot be defended are worthless and where, in the last resort, the laws of force prevail. The fundamental objection to the process of unilateral disarmament is that it involves abandoning the arbitration of your own system of morality and accepting that of your potential enemies.

P.P.J., P. 256

DISRAELI, BENJAMIN

Disraeli wrote novels purely to make money and win notoriety. But in the process he became a political thinker.

S.N., P. 83

During his early struggles, he repeatedly reassured himself that failure did not matter, provided time was still on his side: time was the working capital of fortune. His tragedy is that when success finally arrived, time had run out.

S.N., P. 165

DOCUMENTARY

. . . the only really dishonest advertisements which now appear on television are the Party Political Broadcasts. Viewers are far more likely to be deliberately misled by a supposedly high-minded television documentary than by a soap commercial.

s., MAY 24, 1986

DOG

I do not know whether dogs have a soul, that is, a moral relationship with their creator. But they surely have a moral relationship with man, and we with them. We enter into a contract of honour with our dog and break or abide by it like any other bond. The dog feels a contract too, and usually sticks to it much more faithfully . . . owning a dog certainly can be a moral education.

P.P.J., P. 219

DREYFUS AFFAIR

The Dreyfus affair convulsed France for an entire decade. It became an important event not just in Jewish history but in French, indeed in European, history. It saw the emergence, for the first time, of a distinct class of intellectuals—the word intelligentsia was now coined—as a major power in European society and among whom emancipated Jews were an important, sometimes a dominant, element. A new issue was raised, not just for France: who controls our culture?

H.J., P. 387

The Dreyfus affair was a classic example of a fundamentally simple case of injustice being taken over by extremists on both sides. Drumont and the Assumptionists flourished Dreyfus' conviction and used it to launch a campaign against the Jews. The young Jewish intellectuals, and their growing band of radical allies, began by asking for justice and ended by seeking total victory and revenge.

H.J., P. 388

DUELING

In the early 19th century gentlemen ceased to wear swords and took to carrying umbrellas instead. Thereby hangs a tale. One of the infallible signs of modernity was the decline of dueling. Yet it did not vanish as quickly as sensible men expected. . . . Christian societies had always, officially at least, condemned dueling. All the churches opposed it vehemently, in practice as well as in theory; it was one of the few sins that clergymen did not commit (except, occasionally in Ireland).

B.M., PP. 462–63

. . . in Jena alone there were 147 duels during the summer, among a student population of 350. But the duels were fought with sabers, as a rule, and were rarely fatal, the object being to inflict and receive honorable scars.

B.M., P. 466

It was an Irish characteristic . . . that duelists often killed not merely their enemies but their friends and relations. Richard Martin of Connemara, member of Parliament for Galway . . . and often known as "the King of Connemara," killed his cousin in a duel and fought so often he was known as "Hairtrigger Rick." Oddly enough, he was also strongly opposed to capital punishment, deplored any kind of ill-treatment of dumb beasts, and helped to found the Society for the Prevention of Cruelty to Animals, ending his life with a new nickname, "Humanity Martin."

B.M., P. 468

DURANTY, WALTER

Duranty was a passionate apologist for the dictator. His favourite expression was: "I put my money on Stalin" . . . Indeed we have documentary evidence that he privately put the numbers of Stalin's famine victims at between seven and ten million. Yet not a word of this guilty knowledge appeared in his reports to his paper, which continued to paint the régime in glowing colours. Malcolm Muggeridge, who reported from Moscow for the *Guardian* during the Thirties and knew Duranty, described him as "the greatest liar of any journalist I have met in 50 years of journalism." Yet Duranty was given the Pulitzer Prize in 1932—at the height of the famine—for "dispassionate, interpretive reporting of the news from Russia."

S., JULY 20, 1991

DUTCH ECONOMICS

It can be argued that the Netherlands were the first country on earth to escape the Malthusian Trap. During the seventeenth century, they generated a substantial and sustained increase in per capital income, while supporting a much larger population. The relative freedom with which trade operated there allowed for the rapid development of paper techniques . . . and banking facilities. A genuine European capital market, centred in Amsterdam, developed. As security grew, rates of interest fell. . . . The development of commerce was accompanied by (and this is important) a sustained rise in agricultural productivity, as a result of capital investment and specialization, and a free labour force. In many agricultural methods, the Dutch were pioneers, and, though they had to import some food, they increased domestic supplies by land recovery and the more effective use of labour. The Dutch were the first people in history to achieve a measure of self-sustaining economic growth.

E.S., P. 59

E

ECOLOGICAL ALARMISM

Ecological alarmism . . . incorporates many aspects of Marxist mythology, especially the idea that capitalist society creates, then satisfies, artificial and wasteful appetites, and is ultimately self-destructive. But it is even more characterized by an irrational fear of science. Its visions are infested by Gothic devils in the shape of mad scientists and their lunatic benefactors, engaged in horrific experiments which must end in the destruction of the human race. . . . this form of millenarianism saw the H-bomb as the death agent; the popular nightmare of the 1950s was of an incinerated planet . . . and the level of argument—and the misunderstanding of how science and sciences actually work—was illustrated by an Anglican bishop, who wrote to *The Times* asking all nations to agree to destroy "the formula for the thermonuclear bomb." The level of argument has not improved but . . . there has been a change of location. The dangers of radiation remain as a carry-over from the thermonuclear eschatology, but they are now seen as part of a permanent peace-time threat posed by the demands of capitalist economies . . .

E.S., P. 88

ECOLOGISTS

The eco-lobby, . . . a middle-class movement, usually living in pleasant rural suburbia, brought down vengeance for the sin of growth on the innocent heads of the urban poor of the West's great cities. But the vengeance inflicted was even more painful for the poor countries of the world. Most of them have no indigenous sources of energy, except water-power, and are heavily dependent on imported oil for their development programmes. Tripling the price made nonsense of their planning forecasts, and everywhere brought wholesale cuts in targets. The effects were particularly serious in agriculture, where oil-fueled tractors and irrigation-plants were just becoming familiar features of the African and Asian scene. The drain on precious resources was compounded by the inevitable decisions in the West to cut overseas aid schemes . . . The precise economic effects, in terms of human misery and death, of the eco-lobby's *coup* will never be known. But in spring 1976, the United Kingdom House of Commons sub-committee on Overseas Aid published a document which calculated that more than 500 million people were then near the starvation level in the Third World.

E.S., PP. 100–1

Ecologists who worry about raw material shortages on the basis of reserve figures are rather like the nervous Daughters of the American Revolution, who insist, from time to time, the gold in Fort Knox be publicly counted, to make sure it is still there. The world does not count its real reserves of metal because counting is costly and it does not need to know the answer.

E.S., P. 97

ECOLOGY

Once ecology became a fashionable good cause, as it did in the late 1960s, reason, logic and proportion flew out of the window. It became a campaign not against pollution, but against growth itself, and especially against free enterprise growth—totalitarian communist growth was somehow less morally offensive.

R.F., P. 162

[86]

ECONOMIC FREEDOM

The storage economies of remote antiquity were often hideously unpopular. So was the slave-based economy, combined with corporatism, of the classical world. Agricultural feudalism was certainly unpopular; and mercantilism had to be enforced, in practice, by authoritarian states. But industrial capitalism from the very start received the demonstrable approbation of the masses. They could not vote in the ballot box, but they voted in a far more positive and impressive manner, with their feet. And this for a simple reason. The poorest member of society values political freedom as much as the richest and the well educated—that is my belief. But the freedom he values most of all, the freedom which means most to him, is the freedom to sell his labour and skills in the open market. It was precisely this that industrial capitalism gave to men for the first time in history.

R.F., P. 158

ECONOMICS AND EMIGRATION

. . . tens of millions of European peasants, decade after decade, moved relentlessly across the Atlantic in pursuit of that same freedom, from semi-feudal estates and smallholdings in Russia, Poland, Germany, Austria-Hungary, Italy, Ireland, Scandinavia, to the mines and factories and workshops of New York, Chicago, Pittsburgh, Cleveland and Detroit. It was the first time in history that really large numbers of ordinary people were given the chance to exercise a choice about their livelihood and destiny, and to move, not as a member of a tribe or a conscript soldier, but as free individuals, selling their labour in the open market.

R.F., P. 159

ECONOMIST

The rapid expansion of the world economy in the early 1820s marked the upswing of the first modern trade cycle. It had innumerable consequences. One was to make the new species of expert, the economist, appear—at least for a time—to be the guide and philosopher of mankind. Ricardo, whose great work, *The Principles of Political Economy and Taxation*, had first appeared in 1817, was not the only practitioner to catch the ear of the powerful, indeed the reading public as a whole. Thomas Carlyle had not yet denounced economics as "the dismal science." On the contrary, it was held in almost reverential respect.

B.M., P. 862

EDEN, SIR ANTHONY

. . . he was an honourable man. He made a half-hearted Machiavelli. As a proxy-aggressor he was wholly incompetent.

M.T., P. 492

EDITOR

All successful journals revolve around the principle of editor's prerogative, which is neither democratic nor constitutional but authoritarian, and a good editor reigns through a combination of fear and respect.

S., NOVEMBER 28, 1987

[Editors] feel they can never go to bed at night without, as it were, shutting their eyes to an unknown time-bomb which will explode the next day. Being human, they are less worried about non-libellous errors which merely offend against truth and taste.

S., OCTOBER 1, 1988

EDITORIAL

When I wrote my first leading article, I felt like a young priest who had just celebrated his inaugural Mass, having accomplished an act of transubstantiation, by turning mere cerebration into Editorial Policy.

S., JUNE 11, 1988

Professional politicians, a few diplomats, civil servants and academics—and of course journalists—take leading articles seriously; hardly anyone else.

S., JUNE 11, 1988

I always prefer news to views in a newspaper.

S., MARCH 15, 1986

The Queen no longer uses the royal we, except in formal documents; the editorial we is likewise obsolescent. But editors should not regard its decline with indifference as with royalty. It suggests power is slipping elsewhere.

S., JUNE 11, 1988

EDUCATION

No other society in human history has placed such a strong and consistent emphasis on education at all levels as the United States has from its very inception. But there has been a failure somewhere. . . . There is a universal complaint in Europe and North America that the young emerge from high school (and often from university) with only tolerable literacy, unable to write their own language well, ignorant of other languages, knowing little of their country's history, literature, and culture—fitter candidates for a mob than for a citizenry.

N.R., DECEMBER 14, 1993

For half a century [the educational system] has been in the hands of the educational experts: the ministry, the inspectorate, the NUT [National Union of Teachers], the colleges of education and local authority officers. Between them they have produced a multi-cultural, multi-ethnic gallimaufry, English without grammar or spelling, history without dates or facts, and sex instruction without morals. They have not yet completely killed the habit among children of reading worthwhile books but they have certainly had a go.

S., SEPTEMBER 26, 1987

EDUCATION (BRITISH)

The English education system was not designed to produce a happy and prosperous coal industry: it scarcely taught the miners how to read and write, and to the owners it gave, at best, a modest fluency in dead languages.

H.E., P. 341

EDUCATION (BRITISH ELITE)

The elite education system was geared to produce, above all, politicians, lawyers and churchmen. It inculcated habits of thought peculiarly well adapted to these professions. It deliberately and systematically encouraged the ablest young men to aspire to be prime ministers, lord chancellors, archbishops. And, within the limitations of its terms of reference, it was conspicuously successful. It is no accident that England was able to move from oligarchy to democracy, and then to social democracy, without revolutionary violence—the only country in the world to do so. It is no accident that England had, and has, the most stable political system of any major country.

H.E., PP. 339–40

EDUCATION (MEDICAL)

. . . medical education has always done violence to natural human feelings. The student is taken directly to the dissecting room where, probably for the first time in his life, he is confronted with a corpse—not just a corpse, but a roomful of corpses, starkly laid out naked and without dignity on white tables, the atmosphere heavy with the fumes of preserving fluid. . . . But no one dares show his repugnance, lest he be deemed unfit for a medical career. Before

[90]

long, a mood of forced levity is generated (dare I call it an *esprit de corpse?*), and the dissection-hardened students christen their specimen with a facetious nickname, and play practical jokes with severed parts of the human anatomy.

S., JANUARY 19, 1985

EINSTEIN, ALBERT

Einstein was not a practising Jew, but he acknowledged a God. He believed passionately in absolute standards of right and wrong. His professional life was devoted to the quest not only for truth but for certitude. He insisted the world could be divided into subjective and objective spheres. . . . In the 1920s he found the indeterminacy principle of quantum mechanics not only unacceptable but abhorrent. For the rest of his life until his death in 1955 he sought to refute it by trying to anchor physics in a unified field theory.

M.T., P. 4

He lived to see moral relativism, to him a disease, become a social pandemic, just as he lived to see his fatal equation bring into existence nuclear warfare. There were times, he said at the end of his life, when he wished he had been a simple watchmaker.

M.T., P. 4

EISENHOWER, DWIGHT DAVID

Eisenhower was the most successful of America's twentieth-century presidents, and the decade when he ruled [was] the most prosperous in American, and indeed world, history. His presidency was surrounded by mythology, much of which he deliberately contrived himself. He sought to give the impression that he was a mere constitutional monarch, who delegated decisions to his colleagues and indeed to Congress, and who was anxious to spend the maximum amount of time playing golf. His strategem worked. . . . He was

[91]

seen as well-meaning, intellectually limited, ignorant, inarticulate, often weak and always lazy.

M.T., P. 461

[Eisenhower] had three quite clear principles. The first was to avoid . . . occasions of unnecessary war. . . . Eisenhower's second and related principle was the necessity for constitutional control over military endeavour. . . . [The] third principle, reflected in his diaries and other personal documents, was that the security of freedom throughout the world rested ultimately in the health of the American economy. . . . But [he knew] the U.S. economy could itself be destroyed by intemperate spending.

M.T., PP. 463–64

Churchill was one of the few men who appreciated [Eisenhower] at his correct worth. It could be said that they were the two greatest statesmen of the mid-century.

M.T., P. 463

[What] Eisenhower strove mightily to avoid was a huge, permanent increase in federal commitments. He put holding down inflation before social security because he thought it was ultimately the only reliable form of social security. He loathed the idea of America becoming a welfare state. . . . His real nightmare was a combination of excessive defence spending combined with a runaway welfare machine—a destructive conjunction that became reality in the late 1960s. While he was in charge, federal spending as a percentage of GNP, and with it inflation, was held to a manageable figure, despite all the pressures. It was a notable achievement and explains why the Eisenhower decade was the most prosperous of modern times.

M.T., P. 464

ELECTION OF 1828, UNITED STATES

. . . the first successful smear campaign in American history.

B.M., P. 943

ELITISM

Elitism and its associated notions—the pursuit of excellence and of knowledge—form the very bedrock principle of a progressive civilisation; the history of human progress is essentially the history of elitism. The politics of pity, based on the notion of strengthening the weak by weakening the strong, must produce impoverishment; but the assault on elitism is still more socially destructive, for it overthrows the principle of leadership itself and reduces human societies to herds of Gadarene swine.

R.F., P. 220

ELIZABETH I

The difference between Elizabeth, and James I and Charles I, was that she could smell political danger, and knew when to draw back before her prestige and dignity were irrevocably committed. It was this capacity which made her such a remarkable, and durable, sovereign, so well equipped to run a political system based on ambiguity and dependent on a consensus.

E., P. 298

No woman in history, before or since, has been invested with such a degree of personal authority over so long a period, and has remained so acutely aware of its limitations and dangers. In this sense she was incorruptible, and so kept her balance and judgment to the end. Behind a meretricious façade of vanity, she imposed upon herself an internal discipline, fortified indeed by a fine and flexible intellect, but whose roots were essentially moral. All monarchs of her day believed themselves to be trustees of the deity; Elizabeth accepted the practical implications of her position and treated her public as well as her private actions as morally accountable.

E., P. 443

In her last years, many people throughout Christendom regarded Elizabeth as the most remarkable living phenomenon in the world. Her virginity, her wit and intelligence, her political and military

[93]

triumphs, her sheer endurance, her renowned skill as a states-woman—all these made her unique. She had reigned longer than any other European monarch of her time. She had outlived all her enemies: popes, kings, rivals, generals, conspirators. . . . It was already apparent that she had changed the course of history, broken the thrust of the Counter-Reformation, and established England as a great power in Europe and on the oceans. Yet here she still was, a living memorial to momentous changes and events, absolute mistress of a thrusting and dynamic people . . . and in a country which had ceased to be a backwater and was now regarded as a centre of the world's motions. She was, as the ballad singers called her, "the great lioness."

E., P. 424

Elizabeth's political genius consisted in . . . [not attempting] to disguise her sex; on the contrary she emphasised it. In her great speeches, she always reminded her hearers that she was a woman . . . *sui generis*. They could turn her out in her petticoats, she said, and she would make a living anywhere in Europe. She had a woman's body but "the heart and stomach of a king." She was careful not to say "of a man" . . . she did not believe in woman's liberation. She did not seek to play a masculine role, and so injure the men she had to control in their pride. The English had burnt Joan of Arc for precisely that mistake. Elizabeth vaunted her sex. Her weapons were an astonishing wardrobe, a collection of jewels which even the popes envied, false hair, paint and powder, and the universal knowledge that behind these trappings lay a resolute and imperious spirit which it was perilous to challenge.

H.E., P. 130

We owe a great deal to this remarkable woman. To be sure, she presided over a dazzling galaxy of talent: political, commercial, military, naval and artistic. But she herself took all the really important decisions—and non-decisions—of her reign, often against the advice of her ablest counsellors. It is impossible to read the letters and documents of this period to examine the domestic and foreign political strategy, culminating in the defeat of the Armada, to analyse the solutions to the problem of the succession, or the religious settlement, without concluding that her head and brain were firmly in charge of the national destiny. She was a political genius of a very rare kind, for her inspiration was a sense of tolerance, springing from a warm heart and a cool intellect. She inherited all her father's will-power, but none of his murderous instincts.

H.E., P. 165

When she said she loved the people of England—and they are not a people whom anyone can easily love—she meant it. The real measure of her achievement is that she was able to express this love in concrete terms, and impart to her people a taste for the new and unfashionable virtues she possessed.

H.E., P. 167

ELIZABETHAN PEACE

Although we tend to see Elizabeth's reign as dominated by the great struggle with Spain, to contemporaries its most marked character-istic . . . was the long continuance of internal peace. It was, in fact, unprecedented. Never before had the English ruling class con-trived to resolve its disagreements for so many years without re-sorting to the arbitration of force. . . . [But] it produced strains of its own, as politics grew more sophisticated, and men sought power increasingly through institutions—and the ideas that shaped them—rather than through an ancient hierarchy whose origins were military. Then, too, the spread of education, and the rapid diffusion of novel and complex secular notions, led to a willingness to chal-lenge received opinions over the whole spectrum of conduct. . . . Arguments hitherto accepted as circular were seen to be open-ended.

E., P. 364

EMPIRE

European empires began in paternalism and a denial of the spirit of politics. They ended at the opposite extreme, in over-democra-tization and political elephantiasis. The silver age of empire was completely dominated by endless conferences and constitution-making.

M.T., P. 508

One reason empires fail is that they are too big to run; they are easier to create than to administer, consolidate and defend.

S., MARCH 28, 1987

ENERGY CRISIS

"Energy Crisis" was a crisis of policy, not of nature. To handle it, all that was required was a progressive, and non-disruptive change in pricing policy. Instead, the panic generated by the eco-lobby . . . led the oil-exporting states abruptly to triple the prices of oil. The occasion was the Arab-Israeli war of 1973, but that this was merely a pretext is shown by the fact that the Iranians, who have no quarrel with Israel or the West, took the lead in insisting on massive increases. They were impressed by the argument that the greedy requirements of western growth for low-price oil were robbing them of their greatest, almost their only, national asset, and they jumped at the chance afforded by the war to get the Arab states into line.

E.S., P. 100

ENGELS, FREDERICK

. . . Engels, who specifically repudiated political anti-Semitism in 1879, saw Marxism as a sufficient warrant for genocide as well as class warfare.

C., APRIL 1984

ENGLAND VERSUS ROME

The English eventually approached the business of changing their religion . . . in the middle decades of the sixteenth century in a

[96]

characteristically haphazard and confused manner, and were later to congratulate themselves on the constitutional propriety with which it was done . . . Yet the breach with Rome . . . had comparatively little to do with religion as such; its principal dynamic was anticlericalism, which was itself a form of English xenophobia. The papal aggression of the twelfth century had ended the old easy relationship between Church and State which had been such a striking and constructive feature of Anglo-Saxon society.

H.E., P. 145

THE ENGLISH

The English are a huge force for good and evil: producing, with relentless energy and fertility, new ideas and concepts, and men of dauntless courage to thrust them on society; rich, also, in instincts of decency, imperious in asserting the moral law, remorseless enemies of injustice, avid for philanthropy, profoundly anxious to refashion the globe on lines of purity and reason; but also, and simultaneously, blind and prejudiced, clinging desperately and often violently to the past, worshipping unreason in a thousand ways, uniquely vulnerable to the corruptions of class and snobbery and xenophobia, cruel by indifference and conservative by tradition.

H.E., PP. 239–40

ENGLISH ELITE

Englishmen born to wealth or privileges have a special duty to society, to supply the defects of a mass-democracy which arise from the political consequences of inequalities which no human wisdom can finally eliminate. The English people will, from time to time, be deceived, and be their own worst enemies, for they will fail to exploit the potentialities of the power given to them. An elite is needed, not to govern, but to enable the people to govern themselves.

H.E., P. 314

[97]

ENGLISH IN IRELAND

The English presence in Ireland arose from the failure of Irish society to develop the institution of monarchy. The Irish, of course, had kingship; too much of it . . . The chief kings were those who held Meath and Leinster, Munster, Connaught and Ulster; but between the fifth and twelfth centuries, with a population which never exceeded 500,000, Ireland had about 150 kings at any given date, each ruling over a *tuath* or tribal kingdom.

H.E., P. 1

ENGLISH (MEDIEVAL)

The medieval English were exceptionally violent, aggressive, xenophobic and racialist; they were also greedy, parsimonious, business-minded and pharisaical. They applauded aggression; they were much less anxious to finance it. They thought war was a business, which should turn in a profit.

H.E., P. 115

ENGLISH POLITICAL SOCIETY

The development of English political society in the long shadow cast by Magna Carta is rich in irony and paradox. It cannot successfully be analysed in terms of conflict between the classes. Men believed that such conflicts were, or ought to be, unnecessary, for each section of the community had its ancient and predestined role to play, and conflict was a sign of malfunctioning, to be corrected by a return to the past. What everyone wanted was continuity; all men were, or believed themselves to be, conservatives; political progress was thus in fact achieved only by what might be termed constructive self-delusion, by the use of conservative instruments to achieve radical reform.

H.E., P. 123

The English love to inflict violence on foreigners; happily, they love money more. This is the hammer and anvil which forged the structure of English political society.

H.E., P. 116

THE ENGLISH AND RELIGION

The truth is that the English are not, and never have been, a religious people. That is why toleration first took root in our country. There were, to be sure, plenty of religious zealots in England; not just Protestants and Catholics, but Anabaptists and Huttites, Mennonites, Waterlanders, Socinians and men of Rakow. But all together they never made up more than a minority. It is a matter for argument whether England has even been a Christian country. The English like to be baptised, to get married in church, to be buried in consecrated ground; they pray in times of peril; they take a mild interest in religious controversy, and like to clothe the State in religious forms. But they are not truly interested in the spiritual life.

H.E., P. 164

THE ENGLISH AND VIOLENCE

No race on earth has such a consistent and rooted hatred of unauthorised violence. Extremely violent by nature and instinct, their political capacity for self-knowledge has always placed the highest premium on the control and subjugation of these terrible forces within them. From Anglo-Saxon times to the present, English history is the long record of the struggle for self-mastery, the remorseless, often unsuccessful, attempt to release themselves from the drug of violence. It has been, on the whole, a remarkably successful struggle; but for this drug there is no such thing as a wholly complete cure, and constant vigilance will be needed so long as the English race lasts.

H.E., P. 91

[99]

The Enlightenment

. . . by the 1790s, reason was no longer the guiding principle of the European intelligentsia. It was having to compete not only with the romantic movement, infused by Kantian spirituality, but a swelling variety of fashionable superstitions. The situation was not unlike that of the first century, with paganism, gnosticism and scepticism, as well as Christianity, all jostling each other.

H.C., PP. 358–59

To intellectuals in Christian society, the question posed by the enlightenment was really: how large a part, if any, should God play in an increasingly secular culture? To Jews, the question was rather: what part, if any, should secular knowledge play in the culture of God?

H.J., P. 299

For the first time in human history, and with growing confidence and audacity, men arose to assert that they could diagnose the ills of society and cure them with their own unaided intellects: more, that they could devise formulae whereby not merely the structure of society but the fundamental habits of human beings could be transformed for the better. Unlike their sacerdotal predecessors, they were not servants and interpreters of the gods but substitutes.

I., PP. I–2

The Enlightenment and Rationalism

. . . the guillotine, which served as it were to terminate awkward arguments in a thoroughly rationalistic manner.

H.C., P. 360

Enthusiasm, Religious

The central problem of the institutional church was always how to control the manifestations of religious enthusiasm, and divert them into orthodox and constructive channels. The problem was enormously intensified when large numbers of people were involved. At what point did mass-piety become unmanageable, and therefore heresy? . . . a dilemma as old as the Montanists. A crusade was in essence nothing more than a mob of armed and fanatical Christians. Once its numbers rose to over about 10,000 it could no longer be controlled, only guided. It might be used to attack the Moslems, or unleashed against Jews, or heretics; or it might become heretical and antinomian itself, and smash the structures of established society. This fear was always at the back of the minds of the clerical and secular authorities.

H.C., P. 249

ENTREPRENEUR

At his best the capitalist is a creator in the same sense as an artist. He is an innovator whose chief urge is to do something completely different and new, to astonish, even shock, to become *stupor mundi*. He is impelled by the excitement of his idea, and his reward is its realization in terms of factories, jobs, products; the riches it brings are almost incidental. The quest for novelty is the essence of capitalist endeavour, as it is of all human progress, and the appetite for adventure is a sharper spur than cupidity. Those who pillory capitalism for "creating artificial needs" strike me as timid and dismal souls. You might just as well denounce Monet for creating an "artificial need" for Impressionism.

P.P.J., P. 247

ENVIRONMENTAL APOCALYPTICS

It is characteristic of these wild philosophers, as indeed it was of medieval apocalyptics, that they attribute the approaching end of the world to quite different causes, and that they cannot agree on when it is likely to happen. At bottom, they seem to be no more rational than those old men one used to see in the streets of New

York or London carrying placards that read, "Repent: the end is nigh."

N.R., JUNE 29, 1984

ENVIRONMENTALIST LOBBY

One should never underestimate the ruthlessness of the men and women possessed with the transcendental notion that only their acts can save the human race from imminent destruction. Even in industry, scientists who get involved in controversies that invite unfavorable media attention—and the lobby is probably more influential in the media than anywhere else—make themselves unpopular with the corporation managers who are obsessed by public relations and the company image. So it is always better to play safe, just as scientists who privately agreed with Galileo thought it better to keep their mouths shut.

N.R., JUNE 29, 1984

[Scientists] quite literally believe that their livelihood will be affected if they take a stand against the [environmental] lobby. It is quite powerful in government, on which many scientists are wholly or partly dependent for research funds or employment. It is equally powerful in academia, where scientists who oppose the conventional wisdom may have their classes wrecked, lectures mobbed, funds removed, or entire research programs banned by frightened university authorities. This is not just speculation; it has actually happened, in such august institutions as Harvard.

N.R., JUNE 29, 1984

EQUALITY

In our times, liberty's chief conflict has been with equality. But absolute equality is not a good at all; it is a chimera . . . the unregarding and indiscriminate pursuit of relative equality, itself desirable, has led to many unwarrantable restrictions on human freedom without attaining its object. . . . for many years the bias has been in the wrong direction, and it is now necessary to strike a new balance of moral good by redressing it. Where there is genuine doubt between the legitimate claims of liberty and equality, the decision taken should be the one most easily reversed if it proves mistaken.

E.S. PP. 258–59

EQUALITY AND DIVERSITY

In fact diversity and equality are mutually destructive: if diversity is promoted, equality must be sacrificed.

H.E., PP. 402–3

ESSAY

. . . the essay is a piece of conjuring; it aims to convey sharp and often uncomfortable propositions, the result of much deep thinking, in a relaxed and seemingly effortless manner. To do this well takes hard work and a lot of experience; and you must have a gift for it —many great writers cannot do it at all. It requires, as it were, a certain looseness of the writing joints. Stiffness, formality, brute power are all amiss.

S., SEPTEMBER 1, 1984

ETHNIC EPITHET

The difficulty lies in the subtle distinctions these epithets convey, especially to those so described. In general people from actual or former top nations don't mind what they are called. New Englanders, in my experience, never resent the term Yank . . . I don't in the least mind being called a Pom by Australians, or a Limey by Americans (actually they always call me "Professor," which does irritate me). But I find the word "Brit," a recent and I suspect Irish

[103]

coinage, objectionable, as it lumps us with the Scots and Welsh, with a suggestion of football hooliganism thrown in.

S., NOVEMBER 26, 1988

EUPHEMISM

. . . a human device to conceal the horrors of reality.

N.Y.T.B.R., JUNE 27, 1986

EUROPE

Europe, as an entity, was the offspring of the marriage between the culture of ancient Greece and Rome and the morality of Judeo-Christianity. It has, therefore—or so visionaries and imperialists have long argued—a natural disposition toward a common system of law and government. . . . From early modern times onward, this centralizing aspiration was resumed by whichever nation-state was perceived to be most powerful and thus in a position to impose its own version of unity by armies, bureaucrats, and the extension of its legal system.

C., AUGUST 1992

[The] attempts to dragoon Europe into unity, or impose a centralizing hegemony upon it, ended in wars, the most destructive of which left the Continent in 1945 prostrate and impotent, its destinies for the first time in the hands of non-European powers, the U.S. and the U.S.S.R. From this nadir in its fortunes, the idea of a new Europe sprang; a Europe which would abolish its civil wars, and end its repeated suicide attempts, by moving toward a negotiated, voluntary, democratic union.

C., AUGUST 1992

In west, north-west and central Europe, the clearance of forest and the draining of swamp were the prime economic facts of the entire Dark Ages. In a sense they determined the whole future history of Europe: they were the foundation of its world primacy. The operation was so huge, and took place over so long a period—nearly a millennium—that no one element in society can claim exclusive credit: it was a collective effort. But it was the monasteries which led the movement and for long sustained it.

H.C., P. 149

In a sense Hitler had been the last truly European leader, able to initiate world events from a Eurocentric vision. He lost that power at the end of 1941. The vacuum opened by his colossal fall could not be filled by European rivals. At the end of the war, the two non-European superpowers stood, as it were, on the rim of a spent volcano, peering contemptuously into its still smouldering depths, uninvolved in its collapse but glad it no longer had the daemonic energy to terrify humanity.

M.T., P. 575

Once we begin to perceive Europe as a creation of its writers, and its painters and composers and architects too, we begin to see how impossible it is to set geographical limits and to say, "Thus far and no further." . . . It means that the future of Europe, and its relationships with the superpowers, in the 1990s and beyond, will be an expansive rather than a contracting one, that it will be a wider future rather than a narrow one. Any notion of a Europe consolidating itself behind a high tariff wall, of becoming a protectionist superstate, must be rejected. Europe must keep all its windows to the world flung wide open, letting in all the breezes and competition, ideas and innovation. It must be a fresh-air Europe.

S., NOVEMBER 11, 1989

[Today's] Europe is callous to culture, blind to beauty, without a whisper of romance or a spark of spirituality. It is a Europe of bureaucratic grocers.

S., DECEMBER 14, 1991

In 1952, the great French novelist André Malraux went so far as to declare: "America is now part of Europe." That remains true. Europe is essentially a cultural concept born of the union of two historical forces, the most powerful cultural current in human history: the

[105]

cultural legacy of the classical world and the moral legacy of medieval Christendom. The flow of European colonists all over the world was a human and cultural expansion that no amount of decolonization can ever efface.

W.P.R., MARCH 1990

EUROPE AND THE UNITED STATES

We have learned one lesson in the last half-century: the well-being of the world depends, above all, on the sensible pursuit of common aims by the United States and the free European peoples. That the Japanese are rapidly transforming this relationship into a triangular one goes without saying. But the U.S.-European axis remains the fulcrum of stability, and the Europeans know it: it is the one fixed point in their geopolitics. For this reason they are remarkably dependent on the workings of the American system, and the character of the man it places in the White House.

F.A., JANUARY 1989

EUROPE AND RONALD REAGAN

He thought Russia was winning the arms race. So he rearmed with all deliberate speed and on a considerable scale. He thought Russia and its surrogates had made unacceptable territorial gains during the 1970s. So he set about reversing these gains where possible and made it plain beyond any possibility of misunderstanding that any further attempts to advance would be resisted from the start. He thought the nuclear balance in Europe had been upset by recent Soviet deployments. So he set about restoring it with the deployment of American cruise and Pershing missiles in Europe. These actions won broad support in Europe, not least because of the self-confidence with which they were taken. It is remarkable, looking back on it, how quickly Reagan contrived to reestablish the concept of American leadership of the West as inevitable and right, part of the natural order of things.

F.A., JANUARY 1989

EUROPEAN COMMUNITY

We have hitherto seen the European Community as the institution whereby the old Franco-German hatred has been buried, for ever. But the truth is that it is a practical mutual-security system with a much wider scope, for by persistently enlarging the area of shared law and the authority of common institutions, it makes the frontiers of all its members, and their ethnicity too, seem less and less important.

s., NOVEMBER 11, 1989

The world is already drifting into three huge trading systems—the Americas, East Asia, and Europe. There is no doubt that the French, and the bulk of the Brussels machine, see the EC as an internal free-trading area, surrounded by a high protective wall—Fortress Europe. If the French determine the European pattern, then the Big Three will emerge as fiercely antagonistic, repelling one another's trade and fostering their own. The scene would be set for the greatest trade wars the world has ever known—and history teaches that trade wars lead to real ones. We could well face the nightmare of that tripartite world, engaged in perpetual warfare, foreseen in George Orwell's *Nineteen Eighty-Four*.

c., AUGUST 1992

There was here a confusion of ideas, which has become more impenetrable as the years have passed but which might have been avoided if the architects had studied the American precedent and laid down a clear separation of powers among legislature, judiciary, and executive. In the absence of these distinctions, in the absence indeed of an overriding constitutional document, the parliament has totally failed, so far, to become the equivalent of the American Congress—the fountainhead of law and finance—and has remained primarily a talking-shop. Nor has the Court of Justice taken on the role of validating the constitutionality of Community legislation: it has simply attempted to impose that legislation on the judicial systems of member-states. Finally, the Council of Ministers has failed to emerge as a true executive, instead remaining merely the conduit through which member-governments transmit their agreements or disagreements.

C., AUGUST 1992

EUROPEAN MIGRATION

Historians who study [the] sweeping European incursions into the last . . . pastures . . . of the primitive peoples tend to concentrate on . . . violent episodes and . . . the cruelty and folly of governors and generals. But the truth is that the principal damage inflicted on native stocks was not the result of deliberation or even unthinking savagery by the whites. As the Europeans spread into the wilderness, they brought with them their own cattle and crops, their animals and vermin, their insects and diseases. It was not just the human invader but their accompanying pathogens and microorganisms, animals, and weeds that, in deadly combination, destroyed the indigenous peoples. As Darwin put it, "Wherever the European has trod, death seems to pursue the aboriginal."

B.M., PP. 275–76

EVIL

The beginning of evil is the assault on truth. The first sin, of Adam, was preceded by the first lie, Satan's, and its unthinking repetition by Eve. The metaphor of Genesis teaches that anti-truth is the cause of active evil. Lying is the prolegomenon, the foreword, to the encyclopaedia of evil.

P.J., PP. 150–5

F

Fact

. . . in my experience, the great majority of people, including celebrated philosophy professors, are quite incapable of distinguishing the difference between matters of fact and opinion . . .

s., MAY 27, 1989

Factory System

The factory system, however harsh it may have been, was the road to freedom for millions of agricultural workers. Not only did it offer them an escape from rural poverty, which was deeper and more degrading than anything experienced in the cities, but it allowed them to move from status to contract, from a stationary place in a static society, with tied cottages and semi-conscript labour, to a mobile place in a dynamic one. That was why the common man voted for industrial capitalism with his feet, by tramping from the countryside to the towns, in enormous numbers, first in Britain, then throughout Europe.

R.F., P. 158

FAITH, FAILURE OF

Failure of faith almost always arises from lack of humility. Pride destroys faith, and pride is the *déformation professionnelle* of the theologian.

P.J., P. 153

FAMILY

. . . the family is essentially a protective force, and not least against the claims of the state. It is an area of private custom, as opposed to public law. It is an alternative to the state as a focus of loyalty, and thus a humanizing force in society. Unlike the state, it upholds non-material values—makes them paramount, indeed. It repudiates the exclusive claims of *realpolitik*. It scorns the exclusive economics of profit-and-loss. It rejects political ideology as a sole guide in life. The family, in fact, is a gentle ideology in itself, because it is inconceivable without a system of morality based on altruism. The family embraces tradition, rather than fashionable dogma. It upholds a balance of right and responsibilities, and not merely within generations: it insists on respect for the past, and concern for the future. We are to farm, not to plunder, the earth. We are to honour the memory and heed the wishes of our forebears. And we are to plan not just for ourselves but for our posterity—all this is family doctrine.

P.P.J., P. 137

. . . the threat to the family posed by modern radical collectivism is in the long run no less grave, and far more stealthy and difficult to fight. Nor is it a theoretical or distant threat. It is real and imminent, especially in the America of the 1980s. I can sum it up in one sentence: the United States is in the process of establishing a social and legal system in which marriage has no legitimate status and the family no natural role.

P.P.J., P. 138

The traditional legal concept of the family is one of the great jurisprudential pillars of Western society. As I have argued, our marriage and family law—which it took us over 1,000 years to define and clarify—has been an essential element in the structure of possessive individualism which underlies our democratic, free-enterprise system. Its destruction will have economic consequences which are quite unforeseeable but which are certain to be profound. No less important, the disappearance of the legally-constituted family will remove a formidable defensive barrier which, at the moment, still stands between the vulnerable individual and the burgeoning state. The family is still an emblem of freedom. But to keep it bright and aloft in a collectivist age, we must ensure that it retains its legal personality and its constitutional status.

P.P.J., P. 145

. . . family functions are being communalized and bureaucratized at precisely the moment the courts are demolishing the legal basis of marriage. And it is notable that, when the state moves into the parental role, it no longer makes much, if any, distinction between legal and *de facto* families.

P.P.J., P. 143

FAMILY, "ONE-PARENT"

In the West, the spread of contraception, in a variety of forms, and the growing availability of abortion on demand, made fortunes for pharmaceutical firms and clinics, but, in a hedonistic and heedless society, did not appreciably diminish the number of unwanted children. One striking and unwelcome phenomenon of the 1970s and still more of the 1980s was the growth of what were euphemistically termed "one-parent families," in most cases mothers, usually dependent on welfare payments, looking after children on their own. These deprived children were the products of promiscuity and divorce-by-consent. . . . There was no point in trying to pretend that one-parent families and illegitimacy were anything other than grave social evils, devastating for the individuals concerned and harmful for society, leading, as they inevitably did in many cases, to extreme poverty and crime.

M.T., PP. 781–82

FAMINES

Most 20th-century large-scale famines have been man-made. Like the Great Hunger Stalin created in the Russia of the early 1930s, repeated with variations in parts of Africa by Marxist régimes, modern famines spring from brutal attempts to impose collectivist agriculture on traditional societies and from the civil wars such brutality engenders.

S., MAY 18, 1991

FASCISM

From a historical viewpoint, fascism belongs with communism at the far Left end. It is a Marxist heresy, invented by Mussolini when he broke away from the communists during the first world war. With its cult of violence, its worship of the state and its totalitarian urge to control every aspect of life, it has more in common with communist practice than with any other political system.

S., DECEMBER 7, 1989

FASHION

The art of female fashion depends basically on only two variables: hemlines and necklines. By juggling artfully with them from season to season, the designer can persuade women to buy many more clothes than they need or want because these two lines date the dress infallibly. It is the original and classic illustration of the theory of planned obsolescence. But if the neckline disappears altogether, the designer's basic resources are automatically halved. From his point of view, the awful thing about the topless dress is that it does not date.

S.N., P. 50

FAX

Imagine what Jane Austen would have done with one. The last postal strike, which detonated the fax explosion here, must have suggested to many ordinary people, as well as businessmen, that there is now an easy, reliable alternative to sending letters by Her Majesty's mails. Once the cost comes down significantly, we will all be corresponding by fax, leaving the Post Office for junk mail. The danger, of course, is junk-fax, a phenomenon already appearing in the United States.

S., MAY 6, 1989

FEMINISM

Where . . . the ideas propagated by the Women's Movement have done great harm to the sex is in increasing the physical burden on women. The vast majority of women now feel, as a result of the propaganda, under a moral obligation to pursue a full-blown career, or at the least to take a full-time job. . . . But women . . . have found that their domestic obligations, to husbands, children, elderly parents and the home, have in no way lessened. Housework is much easier, but for technical reasons which have nothing to do with social ideology and which would have produced their effects had the banner of Women's Lib never been hoisted. I find it ironic that, at the very moment in history when women's traditional chores have been dramatically reduced by commercial technology, they have lost all the benefit by being hustled by their bossy leaders into factories and offices. As a result, they work as hard as they ever did; perhaps harder.

P.P.J., P. 232

[113]

FILM

There is still an innocent public belief that what you see on film must be true, that the camera—as opposed to the pen—cannot lie. That is one of the grand illusions of the 20th century.

S., APRIL 9, 1988

FISHING

Occasionally we passed grim and taciturn men, huddled from the wind under wide green umbrellas, working the waters with every conceivable device of piscatorial ingenuity, in the pursuit of bream, tench, gudgeon and other inedible creatures. What pleasure did they derive from this dank and unrewarding pastime? Was it, perhaps, the negative comfort of escaping from wives, mothers, girlfriends, into one of the last bastions of unreformed masculinity?

P.P.J., P. 239

FOOTBALL

The idea that football and similar team sports might be a form of education, particularly a way of producing healthy Christian gentlemen, would have struck most people before the year 1800 as absurd. Football was an ancient pastime, but it was almost invariably associated with hooliganism among the lower orders. All over Europe, governments had repeatedly banned it by proclamation and statute as being calculated to produce riot and injuries, sometimes deaths.

B.M., P. 705

FORD, GERALD

Gerald Ford had only two years in office, lacking the mandate of election. He spent the first desperately disentangling the Administration from Watergate, the second in a bid to put together a coalition to get himself elected. Behind the orderly façade of the

Ford White House there were inconclusive battles for power among rival subordinates, which Ford lacked the authority and the savagery to end. As a colleague put it, "Good old Gerry was too damned good for his own good." . . . he lacked *gravitas* . . . [and in] public, he developed an unfortunate tendency to fall over.

M.T., P. 672

FOURIER, CHARLES

Like Comte he had a passion for numbers and categories. He predicted the ideal world he was creating would last 80,000 years, 8,000 of them an era of Perfect Harmony. . . . the sea, no longer salt, would turn into lemonade, and the world would contain 37 million poets equal to Homer, 37 million mathematicians equal to Newton, and 37 million dramatists equal to Molière, though he modestly added, "These are approximate estimates." Every woman would have four lovers or husbands simultaneously. . . . Fourier himself was acknowledged later as one of the founding fathers of International Socialism, his ideas contributing, in due course, to Hitler's notions of town-and-country planning . . . and Stalin's grim agricultural communes.

B.M., PP. 822–23

FRANCO, GENERAL FRANCISCO

He hated politics in any shape. The Conservatives were reactionary and selfish landowners. The Liberals were corrupt and selfish businessmen. The Socialists were deluded, or worse. . . . Franco was never a fascist or had the smallest belief in any kind of Utopia or system. At his headquarters only one politician had influence; his brother-in-law, Ramón Serrano Suñer, and he was a functionary. . . . Franco said: "Spaniards are tired of politics and politicians." . . . "Only those who live off politics should fear our movement." He spent his entire political career seeking to exterminate politics.

M.T., P. 331

FREEDOM

It is not true, as Lenin contemptuously asserted, that "freedom is a *bourgeois* prejudice." Freedom is a good which any rational man knows how to value, whatever his social origins, occupation or economic prospects. Throughout history, the attachment of even the humblest people to their freedom, above all their freedom to earn their livings how and where they please, has come as an unpleasant shock to condescending ideologues. We need not suppose that the exercise of freedom is bought at the expense of any deserving class or interest—only of those with the itch to tyrannize.

E.S., P. 258

No student of history can have any doubt that, in the long run, the direction of mankind is towards greater freedom. We have moved progressively from the collectivist and tribal communities of antiquity to societies in which the uniqueness of the individual is conceded, theoretically at least, and the universality of human rights is given formal recognition. No one now denies, explicitly and publicly, the rights of man; all agree, as self-evident truth, that freedom is a public good. Just as hypocrisy is the tribute vice pays to virtue, so constitutions, endorsing human rights, are the homage which the most obdurate and enduring tyranny feels obliged to lay at freedom's feet. Even the most depraved African despot, who belabours his helpless subjects with every refinement of cruelty and savagery, sports some Utopian certificate to give his regime a spurious legitimacy.

R.F., P. 1

FREEDOM (ANCIENT)

Freedom, to the Greeks, was something indissolubly associated with city life; they could not conceive of it being created, let alone flourishing, in any other context. They thought, in fact, that all good things came from cities, and this belief, endorsed and fortified in Roman times, was the chief reason . . . why the ancient civilization

[116]

could not accommodate those they called barbarians because they
rejected urbanization.

E.S., P. 29

THE FRENCH

. . . the French have always been outstandingly gifted [at] taking
a German idea and making it fashionable with superb timing.

I., P. 231

FREUD, SIGMUND

Like other melancholic irrationalists, Freud wrote in terms of a
collective nervous breakdown—itself a relic of social Darwinism,
which compares societies to individuals. Of course, to speak of
civilization having a nervous breakdown has no meaning; one might
just as well say it has a hernia, or piles. But this misuse of figures
of speech is characteristic of secular eschatology, and helps to explain
the horror its faithful feel towards scientists, forever portrayed in
cataclysmic or violent activities, such as the "conquest" of space,
age, etc.—expressions, needless to say, coined by journalists, not
by men of science.

E.S., P. 89

. . . like Marx's followers, when evidence did turn up which appeared
to refute them, he modified the theories to accommodate it. Thus
the Freudian corpus of belief was subject to continual expansion and
osmosis, like a religious system in its formative period. As one
would expect, internal critics, like Jung, were treated as heretics;
external ones, like Havelock Ellis, as infidels, Freud betrayed signs,
in fact, of the twentieth-century messianic ideologue at his worst
—namely, a persistent tendency to regard those who diverged from
him as themselves unstable and in need of treatment. . . . Two
decades later, the notion of regarding dissent as a form of mental

[117]

sickness, suitable for compulsory hospitalization, was to blossom in the Soviet Union into a new form of political repression.

M.T., P. 6

After eighty years' experience, his methods of therapy have proved, on the whole, costly failures, more suited to cosset the unhappy than cure the sick.

M.T., P. 6

FREUDIANISM

Freudianism was many things, but if it had an essence it was the description of guilt. . . . Freud said he intended to show that guilt-feelings, unjustified by any human frailty, were "the most important problem in the development of civilization." It might be, as sociologists were already suggesting, that society could be collectively guilty, in creating conditions which made crime and vice inevitable. But personal guilt-feelings were an illusion to be dispelled. None of us was individually guilty; we were all guilty.

M.T., P. 11

FÜHRER

All the disciples of Nietzsche agreed a *Führer* would be necessary and would emerge, like a messiah. He was envisaged as the Knight from Dürer's famous print *Night, Death and the Devil*. Wilhelm Stapel in *The Christian Statesman* presented him as ruler, warrior and priest in one, endowed with charismatic qualities. The reality was rather different. Hitler was totally irreligious and had no interest in honour or ethics. He believed in biological determinism, just as Lenin believed in historical determinism. He thought race, not class, was the true revolutionary principle of the twentieth century, just as nationalism had been in the nineteenth.

M.T., P. 129

G

GANDHI, MAHATMA

Gandhi's eccentricities appealed to a nation which venerates sacral oddity. But his teachings had no relevance to India's problems or aspirations. Hand-weaving made no sense in a country whose chief industry was the mass-production of textiles. His food policy would have led to mass starvation. In fact Gandhi's own *ashram*, with his own very expensive "simple" tastes and innumerable "secretaries" and handmaidens, had to be heavily subsidized by three merchant princes. As one of his circle observed: "It costs a great deal of money to keep Gandhiji living in poverty." About the Gandhi phenomenon there was always a strong aroma of twentieth-century humbug. His methods could only work in an ultra-liberal empire.

M.T., P. 471

Gandhi was expensive in human life as well as money. The events of 1920–21 indicated that though he could bring a mass-movement into existence, he could not control it. Yet he continued to play the sorcerer's apprentice, while the casualty bill mounted into hundreds, then thousands, then tens of thousands, and the risks of a gigantic sectarian and racial explosion accumulated. This blindness to the law of probability in a bitterly divided sub-continent made nonsense of Gandhi's professions that he would not take life in any circumstances.

M.T., P. 472

[119]

GARAGE

Indeed one reason why garages tend to cheat customers today over repairs is that they had their origin in horse-mongering, thus preserving an unbroken tradition of fraud.

B.M., P. 172

"GAY"

. . . must we . . . be stuck with "gay" for male homosexuals? The homosexual lobby on both sides of the Atlantic has successfully sold the term . . . to . . . the sub-editorial establishment, and it is now in the process of being imposed on the rest of us, thus wrecking for ever some of the finest lines in English poetry. Nothing has done more to turn enlightened people against homosexuals than this impudent hijack, and in their own long-term interests they ought to switch. . . . My solution, which ought to appeal to the sub-editorial mind, is simply to reverse the terms and call them "yags."

S., JULY 3, 1986

GAY PAREE

The English notion of "gay Paree" dates from . . . 1802–03, when English visitors flocked to the French capital and brought back shocked-intrigued tales of how little the Parisian ladies wore. From that moment, French fashions dominated the lives of middle- and upper-class Englishwomen, who pored over Parisian magazines smuggled in at some danger, along with the brandy and scent. . . . They also adopted another French innovation, the corset, originally known as a divorce, because it was the first undergarment to separate the breasts, pushing them up to form a fleshy shelf.

B.M., P. 458

GENESIS

. . . the Hebrew presentation in Genesis shows a definite concern for moral values and presents history as the working out of a providential design. It is the difference between secular and religious literature and it is also the difference between the writing of mere folklore and determinist history.

C.H.L., P. 34

GENETICS

The speed with which the DNA discovery was developed and applied to practical problems raised questions about the macroscopic end of the biological spectrum: the process of explaining the evolution of social behaviour in terms of the growth and age-structure of whole animal populations, humanity included, and in terms of their genetic constitution. Granted the unitary nature of biological laws, if a scientific revolution could occur at one end of the range, was it not to be expected (or feared) at the other? It was in this area that the social sciences had most conspicuously failed, not least because they had been penetrated by Marxist superstition. The academic imperialism of some social scientists prevented much serious work being done on the lines Darwin's discoveries had suggested: that minds and mental attitudes evolved like bodies, and that behaviour could be studied like other organic properties, by means of comparative genealogies and evolutionary analysis.

M.T., P. 779

GENOCIDE

Once Lenin had abolished the idea of personal guilt, and had started to "exterminate" (a word he frequently employed) whole classes, merely on account of occupation or parentage, there was no limit to which this deadly principle might be carried. Might not entire categories of people be classified as "enemies" and condemned to imprisonment or slaughter merely on account of the colour of their skin, or their racial origins or, indeed, their nationality? There is no essential moral difference between class-warfare and race-warfare, between destroying a class and destroying a race. Thus the modern practice of genocide was born.

M.T., P. 71

GEOPOLITICS

It is of the essence of geopolitics to be able to distinguish between different degrees of evil.

M.T., P. 351

GERMAN WAR GUILT

I can understand why many Germans were deceived by Hitler in the 1930s. But I don't think they had the will to war, as they certainly had in 1914. They were the big losers in the conflict: their country partitioned, perhaps for a century or more, a long occupation, a humiliating struggle to be again recognised as a civilised people. On the whole, during the last 40 years, they have made reasonable efforts to pay their debt to international society and to perform a constructive role in Europe. Perhaps it is time for us to recognise the fact.

S., APRIL 27, 1985

GERMANY

Lenin once said that only a country like Russia could have been captured so easily as he took it. Germany was a different proposition. It could not be raped. It had to be seduced.

M.T., P. 132

GERMANY (POST-WORLD WAR I)

Germany emerged from the first world war . . . a stricken and demoralised country, swarming with penniless and often violent ex-servicemen. The number of political murders, many of them wholly unpunished, was terrifying. A violent spasm of inflation wiped out the savings of the middle class but left the rich industrialists and landowners richer because they were able to pay off all their debts in worthless paper. Germany enjoyed a few years of modern prosperity in the second half of the Twenties . . . [and what was] left of national morale [was] drowned in an ocean of unemployment. At the same time, the Weimar system of government . . . broke down. These desperate circumstances just enabled Hitler, the guttersnipe version of Bismarck, to slip into power, and once he had his hands on the levers he never relaxed his grip until his suicide 12 years later.

s., APRIL 27, 1985

GERMANY AND RACISM

There was a huge overlap between the slave system and German industry. It might be recalled that the Germans had used slave-labour and working-to-exhaustion in 1916–18; it was a national response to war, a salient part of the "war socialism" Lenin so much admired. Race paranoia was deeply rooted in German culture and had been fostered by generations of intellectuals. It antedated Hitler; dwarfed him. Forty years later it is difficult to conceive of the power and ubiquity of inter-white racism, especially anti-Semitism (and not in Germany alone). In a sense, then, it was the German people who willed the end; Hitler who willed the means.

M.T., PP. 419–20

GORBACHEV, MIKHAIL

Perhaps Gorbachev's most fundamental mistake was not to abolish the caste and its privileges right from the beginning: then all those

[123]

in positions of authority, brought up against the reality of shortages, would have accepted the inevitability of abolishing Leninism itself. But he left the privileges intact, and the U.S.S.R. remained two nations: the ruling class and the *hoi polloi*, just like a society in antiquity.

M.T., P. 766

GOSSIP COLUMNS

In some ways, gossip columns are a little like pornography: people turn to them despite their better judgment, knowing that they are yielding to a sleazy impulse. . . . What is even more curious is that readers don't mind whether the gossip is actually true or not . . . Among the most enthusiastic readers of the tabloid gossip columns are the people who feature in them—society riff-raff, people famous for being famous, showbiz "personalities" and the like—although they are aware from their own knowledge that many items which appear have only a remote connection with the truth. Why then do they read these farragoes? I suspect it is because they want to discover they really exist outside their own imaginations; the same motive sometimes prompts people to write diaries.

S., APRIL 13, 1985

. . .if I had to choose between bingo and gossip as devices for selling newspapers, I would pick bingo every time. It may appeal mildly to the cupidity in all of us, but I think its main attraction is simply that it gives a little tinge of excitement to life, and I can't see much harm in that. Gossip, on the other hand, trades in half-truth, exaggeration and downright falsehood, and it arouses some of our worst instincts: lack of charity and malice, *Schadenfreude*, a sneaking desire that calamity should strike those who are richer and more famous than us, and not least a propensity to pry into other people's private lives.

S., APRIL 13, 1985

GOVERNMENT

. . . if you wish to form a government you cannot afford to behave like one . . .

S.N., P. 179

GOVERNMENT ART SUBSIDIES

I suppose we have to reconcile ourselves to the fact that our subsidised theatres, especially the Royal Shakespeare and the National, exist mainly to give second-rate playwrights expensive opportunities to peddle left-wing propaganda—one good reason for starving such places of money.

S., MAY 11, 1985

GOVERNMENT POLICIES

Policies have a disconcerting habit of reminding people of things best forgotten.

S., JUNE 2, 1990

GOVERNMENT VERSUS THE PRIVATE SECTOR

The societies of antiquity were frequently destroyed by the growth of the state and its parasites. The process continues to our own day, changing only its outward form. It is one of the central themes of Smith's *The Wealth of Nations* that private individuals create wealth, and governments consume it. The more the government consumes, the less the private sector has to invest; so wealth accumulates more slowly, or not at all, or even declines.

R.F., P. 7

GOYA, FRANCISCO DE

He came from Saragossa, the son of a master gilder, and progressed through the royal tapestry factory, as a designer, to painting royal and society portraits. He was enormously successful, though he painted girths, warts, wrinkles, and all; he used to quote Cervantes: "Where truth is, God is, truth being an aspect of divinity."

B.M., P. 68

GRAMSCI, ANTONIO

Antonio Gramsci . . . came from exactly the same intellectual tradition as Mussolini: Marxism, Sorel, syndicalism, a repudiation of historical determinism, a stress on voluntarism, the need to force history forward by an emphasis on struggle, violence and myth; plus Machiavellian pragmatism. But Gramsci, though much more original than Mussolini, lacked his aplomb and self-confidence. . . . Unable to see himself in a leadership role, he drew from Machiavelli not a personal prince, like Mussolini, but a collective one. "The modern Prince, the myth-prince, cannot be a real person, a concrete individual: it can only be an organization."

M.T., P. 97

"GREAT LEAP FORWARD"

. . . the Great Leap produced a man-made famine on the scale of Stalin's catastrophe in the early 1930s, which lasted till 1962. To this day outsiders do not know exactly what happened to Chinese agriculture during these terrible years. The steel industry was wrecked and had to be rebuilt virtually from its foundations. Agriculture was yet again reorganized by a return to co-operatives and a fall in the size of commune units to 2,000 households. But the crops and livestock lost were lost for good. People just starved. How many millions died from the Leap is a matter of conjecture: figures are not available.

M.T., P. 551

GREEK SOCIETY

The Greeks, by the very act of creating a free man, found themselves producing a servile class. There were a very large number of Greek words for slave, and servile status, and infinite gradations of servitude. But it is notable that the two concepts of freedom and slavery advanced hand in hand as Greek civilization developed, and that those cities where chattel slavery flourished were also those where freedom was most fully developed. Thus Greek society was, not accidentally but essentially, a slave society, and, since war and conquest were the most fertile providers of slaves, the triumph of the Greek culture meant the spread and intensification of slavery.

E.S., P. 13

GUILT

. . . that corrosive vice of the civilized during the twentieth century . . . we shall meet in many forms: guilt.

M.T., P. 41

GULF WAR AND THE MEDIA

Television reporters (and ignorant anchormen at home) appeared to be much more interested in guessing at the propaganda effects of Khafji than in actually telling viewers the news. This is a prime example of the way in which television tends to be a disinformation rather than an information service. The first casualty in war is the objectivity and news-values of broadcasting. If the studio has pictures of a weeping U.S. marine widow, then that is the story: the fact that an entire Iraqi armoured force has been destroyed and all its equipment burned or captured is dismissed as a non-event if film is not available. Television is bear-led by its visuals, not to speak of the neuroses of the people who work for this irrational and self-corrupting medium. . . . in wartime, truth is hard to come by but you are more likely to find it in newspapers than in the flickering images and babble of the box.

S., FEBRUARY 9, 1991

H

HABSBURGS

. . . the Habsburgs had made their way in the world less by winning battles than by judicious marriages.

B.M., P. 72

HAIR, RED

. . . usually regarded as a bad sign in the 19th century . . .

B.M., P. 299

HAMMARSKJÖLD, DAG

Dag Hammarskjöld . . . came from a highly successful family of public servants in a nation uneasily aware that it had grown immensely prosperous by staying out of two world wars. He was guilt personified and he was determined that the West should expiate it . . . he exuded a secular religiosity. . . . It was Hammarskjöld's manifest intention to cut the umbilical cord which linked the UN to the old wartime Western alliance, and to align the organization with what he regarded as the new emergent force of righteousness in the world: the "uncommitted" nations.

M.T., PP. 493–94

Hammarskjöld paid scant regard to the lives, black or white, he was risking. Cold, detached, consumed by an overwhelming ambition masquerading as an ideal, he thought in terms of a political abstraction, not human beings. He formulated what became a characteristic UN double-standard: that whereas the killing of Africans by whites (as at Sharpeville in South Africa on 21 March 1960) was of international concern and a threat to peace, the killing of Africans by Africans (or of whites by Africans, or of Asians by Africans or all three races by Africans) was a purely internal matter outside the purview of the UN. Thus the UN became identified with a form of inverted racism, which was to cost an incalculable number of African lives over the next two decades.

M.T., P. 516

HANDSHAKE

Less politically committed visitors from Britain viewed the egalitarianism they found in America with mixed feelings. What they all noticed was the universal practice of shaking hands. In Britain handshaking was a sign of close friendship or kindly condescension. . . . But in America, the alternative, a mere bow, was regarded as anti-republican and pro-King.

B.M., P. 53

HARDING, WARREN

Harding won the election [and] . . . he celebrated by playing a round of golf. He did not believe that politics were very important or that people should get excited about them or allow them to penetrate too far into their everyday lives.

M.T., P. 214

Harding inherited an absentee presidency and one of the sharpest recessions in American history. By July 1921 it was all over and the economy was booming again. Harding had done nothing except cut government expenditure, the last time a major industrial power treated a recession by classic *laissez-faire* methods, allowing wages to fall to their natural level. . . . But the cuts were important. . . .

Harding can be described as the only president in American history who actually brought about massive cuts in government spending, producing nearly a 40 per cent saving over Wilsonian peacetime expenditure. Nor was this a wild assault. It was part of a considered plan which included the creation of the Bureau of the Budget, under the Budget and Accounting Act of 1921, to bring authorizations under systematic central scrutiny and control.

M.T., P. 216

HEBRAIC MORAL ORDER

It says something for the lasting impact of this Hebraic moral order on mankind that, in 1531, over 2,000 years after it had first reached written form, the tranquillity and concord of Renaissance Europe was broken by an argument between Henry VIII, based on Leviticus 19:16–21, and Pope Clement VI, who defended Catherine of Aragon's marriage on the basis of Deuteronomy 15:5, in Henry's eyes a much inferior text. Heads rolled, stake-fires burned in consequence.

R.F., P. 80–81

HEBREW PHILOSOPHY

Hebrew philosophy supposed there was a secret to the universe but of an altogether different order to the secrets of, say, mining technology. The secret was personified as Wisdom, as in some of the Hebrew proverbs, and wisdom came to man only through obedience, the true foundation of the moral order: "And he said to man: 'Behold, the fear of the Lord, That is wisdom: and to depart from evil is understanding.' "

C.H.L., P. 85

HEGEL, GEORG WILHELM FRIEDRICH

G. W. F. Hegel, from Stuttgart, ran a pro-French newspaper, the *Bamberger Zeitung*, mostly copied from the official French government organ, the Paris *Moniteur*; he thought Bonaparte, whom he had seen ride through Jena in 1806, was the *Weltseele*, the personification of reason, and he applauded Bonaparte's troops even though they stole all his money.

B.M., PP. 70–71

It is astonishing that Hegel's reputation survived his absurd declaration that history had ended with Bonaparte's victory over Prussia at Jena in 1806. Yet Hegel went on to hold what was then the most enviable academic post in Germany, the chair of philosophy in Berlin, and to write much more clever and influential nonsense. In due course his thoughts were transmuted by Marx not merely into a set of absolute answers about where history was heading but into a program for accelerating the process. Until recently this moonshine was believed by millions of comparatively well-educated people, and indeed there remain corners of university campuses where it is still upheld and taught.

C., MARCH 1992

HEINE, HEINRICH

Heine himself was both the prototype and the archetype of a new figure in European literature: the Jewish radical man of letters, using his skill, reputation and popularity to undermine the intellectual self-confidence of established order.

H.J., P. 345

HELL

Pastoral writers were much more specific about Hell than about Heaven; they wrote of it as though they had been there. . . . Jerome said that Hell was like a huge winepress. Augustine said it was peopled by ferocious flesh-eating animals, which tore humans to bits slowly and painfully, and were themselves undamaged by the fires. Another expert thought the damned would be nourished with green bread, washed down with a mere eggcupful of stinking water. German writers (and painters) were the most energetic in depicting the physical torments. They argued that a hundred million damned souls would be squeezed into every square mile of Hell, and would thus be treated "like grapes in a press, bricks in a furnace, salt sediment in a barrel of pickled fish, and sheep in a slaughterhouse." The French favoured more subtle psychological pains. Bridaine said that when the guilty asked, "What is the time?" a voice answered, "Eternity." There were "no clocks in Hell, but an eternal ticking."

H.C., P. 341

. . . with the eighteenth century . . . Scientific knowledge made much of the mechanism of Hell-fire seem wildly implausible, and cast doubt on any effort to visualize God's punishments. "Reasonable Christianity" needed Hell as the great deterrent, but it found the idea of a ferociously vindictive God unreasonable; Hell remained, but it had to be, as it were, cooled down a little. . . . The authorities considered Hell to be the most effective deterrent against crime; as fear of it declined, therefore, judges and Parliament agreed that the statutory penalties must be increased. During the eighteenth century and well into the nineteenth, a series of Acts, extending capital punishment to cover over 300 offences, tried to repair the yawning gaps in Locke's system of ethical enforcement.

H.C., PP. 342–43

HEMINGWAY, ERNEST

What Hemingway did is what all really original great writers do —he created his own market, he infected readers with his own taste.

I., P. 150

No writer in history ever gave more interviews and photo-calls.

I., P. 153

Despite the central importance of truth in his fictional ethic he had the characteristic intellectual's belief that, in his own case, truth must be the willing servant of his ego.

I., P. 154

Hemingway's awareness of his inability to recapture his genius, let alone develop it, accelerated the spinning circle of depression and drink. He was a man killed by his art, and his life holds a lesson all intellectuals need to learn: that art is not enough.

I., P. 172

HELLMAN, LILLIAN

Will Lillian Hellman, like her hero Stalin, ever be finally buried in decent obscurity, or will she—fables and all—remain a fighting symbol of progressive thought? We shall see. But the experience of the last two hundred years suggests that there is plenty of life, and lies, in the old girl yet.

I., P. 305

Far from being dedicated to the principles of freedom, Lillian Hellman was a notorious Stalinist who frequently went on sponsored trips to Russia and hotly defended the party line throughout Stalin's heyday in the Thirties. For her, the Moscow purge trials were models of justice, and the evil Vishinsky, who prosecuted at them, a jurisprudential hero. Not only did she defend the show trials: she fiercely attacked those Americans and European writers who dared to question their fairness. Later—much later—she renounced Stalinism, but her repentance was never more than perfunctory.

S., JULY 14, 1984

HENRY VIII

Henry VIII was idle, irresponsible, ignorant, lacking in judgment and totally oblivious to any sense of duty to the community. But he knew how to beat the big drum of monarchy, and the nation trooped in his wake. Through all the vicissitudes and miscalculated adventures into which he led the realm—disastrous foreign wars, state bankruptcy, the debauching of the currency, change of religion, government by confiscation and judicial murder—the great mass of the people obediently followed. The English have always responded to strong central government, invested with majesty and colour, and operated by a self-confident will.

H.E., P. 129

HERESY

. . . Jewish Christians in the fifties . . . had first introduced the idea of heresy in the portrayal of Paul as antichrist and the first heretic. It was in fact the Jewish Christians in the fifties who had first introduced the idea of heresy in the campaign against Paul and Hellenization. . . . Hence, following the collapse of Jewish Christianity, the orthodox Judaic authorities did not wait long to anathematize Christianity as such. Around [A.D.] 85, the judgment was incorporated in the synagogue liturgy: "May the Nazarenes and the heretics be suddenly destroyed and removed from the book of life." Heresy was another Judaic gift to the Christian Church, where it soon began to flourish mightily.

H.C., P. 43

. . . belief in celibacy necessarily proves fatal to a heretical movement.

H.C., P. 47

HERETICS (MODERN)

Their object is to destroy certitudes, to infect the corpus of received civilized knowledge with doubt, and so to dislocate western man, take him away from his natural, familiar defences, and set him up again, naked, on an empty and bewildering plain. This process of disorientation can be halted, as we have seen, by a careful and rational defence of truth. Unfortunately, the obfuscators have received the assistance of unconscious and unwilling allies in the realms of creative imagination—and this because of an inherent defect in the civilizing process itself.

E.S., P. 212

HERO

No man is a hero to his dustman.

P.P.J., P. 221

HEROD

Herod was, by any standards, a great man. The New Testament and Christian tradition present him as a monster and the Massacre of the Innocents, though we have no secular authority for it, has a plausible ring . . . Orthodox Jewish tradition also presents him as a tyrant. The pseudepigraphic *Assumption of Moses* says: "He shall slay the old and the young, and shall not spare. . . . And he shall execute judgments on them as the Egyptians executed upon them, during thirty and four years, and he shall punish them." Herod was a kind of Peter the Great, dragging a conservative and obstinate people into the modern world. He realized that the suppression of piracy and banditry which Rome's power and new-found unity made possible was bringing in an economic golden age in which he wanted his country to participate. This meant knocking heads together, and in particular destroying the selfish oligarchy of families which controlled Jewish religion. He did this single-handed. But he also wanted to show the world that Jews were civilized and gifted people, capable of entering fully into the new expansive spirit of Mediterranean civilization.

C.H.L., P. 112

HERZL, THEODOR

Herzl is one of the most complex characters in Jewish history. Like Disraeli's, his flashy theatrical manner concealed tragic depths.

H.J., P. 391

Herzl began by assuming that a Jewish state would be created in the way things had always been done throughout the Exile: by wealthy Jews at the top deciding what was the best solution for the rest of Jewry, and imposing it. But he found this impossible. Everywhere in civilized Europe the Jewish establishments were against his idea. Orthodox rabbis denounced or ignored him. To Reform Jews, his abandonment of assimilation as hopeless represented the denial of everything they stood for. The rich were dismissive or actively hostile. Lord Rothschild, the most important man in world Jewry, refused to see him at all and, worse, made his refusal public. . . . the intellectuals dismissed Herzl too, especially in the prophet's home town, Vienna. The joke was: "We Jews have waited 2,000 years for the Jewish state, and it had to happen to me?" . . . Nevertheless, what Herzl quickly discovered was that the dynamic of Judaism would come not from the westernized elites but from the poor, huddled masses of the *Ostjuden*, a people of whom he knew nothing when he began his campaign.

H.J., PP. 397–98

HIROSHIMA AND NAGASAKI

The use of nuclear weapons . . . saved Japanese, as well as Allied, lives. Those who died in Hiroshima and Nagasaki were the victims not so much of Anglo-American technology as of a paralysed system of government made possible by an evil ideology which had expelled not only absolute moral values but reason itself.

M.T., P. 427

HISTORY

The more I study history, the more convinced I am that what happens is influenced as much by the willpower of key individuals as by the underlying pressure of collective forces. If we look at the interwar period, for instance, the history of Europe was settled to a great extent by the overwhelming personalities of two extraordinary men, Hitler and Stalin. Without them, events would have taken a totally different course, just as the history of Europe in the twenty years 1795–1815 would have been almost unimaginably transformed without Napoleon.

A.S., JULY 1988

Educated people have an extraordinary appetite for absolute answers to historical questions, answers which wise historians know cannot be forthcoming. It is astonishing that Hegel's reputation survived his absurd declaration that history had ended with Bonaparte's victory over Prussia in Jena in 1806. . . . The latest intellectual entrepreneur to supply the appetite is Francis Fukuyama, whose 1989 article "The End of History" . . . so got the 1990's off to a muddled start. . . . History does not end; it simply becomes more complicated . . . more fascinating, as well as more difficult to predict. *Pace* Fukuyama, we face new nightmares in the 21st century as well as realized dreams, and the really disturbing prospect is that they will be nightmares of a kind we have never before experienced.

C., MARCH 1992

History is concerned not merely with moments, and decades, of time but with the long-term consequences of actions which change their significance and value continuously as the years unfold.

P.J., P. 234

There are no inevitabilities in history.

M.T., P. 43

. . . there is no logic or justice in history. It is all a matter of chronology.

M.T., P. 249

[137]

There is no such person as History. It is human beings who decree.

M.T., P. 484

. . . reality cannot for long be banished from history. Facts have a way of making their presence felt.

M.T., P. 696

. . . the historian of the modern world is sometimes tempted to reach the depressing conclusion that progress is destructive of certitude. In the eighteenth and the nineteenth centuries the Western élites were confident that men and progress were governed by reason. A prime discovery of modern times is that reason plays little part in our affairs.

M.T., P. 699

What is important in history is not only the events that occur but the events that obstinately do not occur. The outstanding event of modern times was the failure of religious belief to disappear. . . . By the end of our period, even the term "secularization" was in dispute.

M.T., P. 700

The study of history is a powerful antidote to contemporary arrogance. It is humbling to discover how many of our glib assumptions, which seem to us novel and plausible, have been tested before, not once but many times and in innumerable guises; and discovered to be, at great human cost, wholly false. It is sobering, too, to find huge and frightening errors constantly repeated; lessons painfully learnt forgotten in the space of a generation; and the accumulated wisdom of the past heedlessly ignored in every society, and at all times.

R.F., P. 3

HISTORIAN

. . . in 1815 a poet, a scientist and a painter spoke the same language . . . but by 1830 it was increasingly difficult for them to understand each other; the sad bifurcation into two cultures was beginning. One impression the historian must always convey is this sense of the turning of the years, sometimes slow, sometimes fast, always relentless in its motion.

B.M., P. XIX

HISTORIAN (CHRISTIAN)

For Christianity, by identifying truth with faith, must teach—and, properly understood, does teach—that any interference with the truth is immoral. A Christian with faith has nothing to fear from the facts; a Christian historian who draws the line limiting the field of enquiry at any point whatsoever is admitting the limits of his faith. And of course he is also destroying the nature of his religion, which is a progressive revelation of truth. So the Christian, according to my understanding, should not be inhibited in the smallest degree from following the line of truth; indeed, he is positively bound to follow it. He should be, in fact, freer than the non-Christian, who is pre-committed by his own rejection.

H.C., P. VIII

HITLER, ADOLF

[The Jews'] history told them that all persecutions, however cruel, came to an end; that all oppressors, however exigent, had demands that were ultimately limited and could be met. Their strategy was always geared to saving "the remnant." In 4,000 years the Jews had never faced, and had never imagined, an opponent who demanded not some, or most, of their property, but everything; not just a few lives, or even many, but all, down to the last infant. Who could conceive of such a monster? The Jews, unlike the Christians, did not believe the devil took human shape.

H.J., P. 506

Hitler appears always to have approached politics in terms of visual images. Like Lenin and still more like Stalin, he was an outstanding practitioner of the century's most radical vice: social engineering—the notion that human beings can be shovelled around like concrete. But in Hitler's case there was always an artistic dimension to these Satanic schemes. Planning a world empire radiating from Berlin, it was the colossal state structures of the capital which sprang first to mind and were then modelled down to the smallest detail. When . . . Hitler gave directives for the political, demographic and economic transformation of tens of millions of square miles of Europe, right up to the Urals, he spoke in elaborate terms of the Babylonian gardens which were to adorn the cities of the master-race. It was highly characteristic of him that he put an architect in charge of war production. Indeed he should have been an architect himself.

M.T., P. 130

Hitler's artistic approach was absolutely central to his success. Lenin's religious-type fanaticism would never have worked in Germany. The Germans were the best-educated nation in the world. To conquer their minds was very difficult. Their hearts, their sensibilities, were easier targets. Hitler's strength was that he shared with so many other Germans the devotion to national images new and old: misty forests breeding blond titans; smiling peasant villages under the shadow of ancestral castles; garden cities emerging from ghetto-like slums; riding Valkyries, burning Valhallas, new births and dawns in which shining, millennian structures would rise from the ashes of the past and stand for centuries. Hitler had in common with average German taste precisely those revered images which nearly a century of nationalist propaganda had implanted.

M.T., PP. 130–31

Hitler was the first to appreciate the power of amplification and the devilry of the searchlight: he seems to have invented *son et lumière* and used it with devastating effect at his mass night-meetings. He imported political costumery and insignia from Mussolini's Italy but improved upon them, so that Hitlerian uniforms remain the standard of excellence in totalitarian sumptuary. Both Stalinism and Maoism imitated Hitler's staging, exceeding it in scale but not in style.

M.T., P. 131

As Hitler's vision expanded, in the heady days of 1941, it came to embrace all Europe. . . . The Pope would be hanged in full pontificals in St. Peter's Square . . . New crops, such as perennial rye, would be invented. He would forbid smoking, make vegetarianism compulsory, "revive the Cimbrian art of knitting," appoint a "Special Commissioner for the Care of Dogs" and an "Assistant Secretary for Defence Against Gnats and Insects."

M.T., PP. 381–82

Hitler learnt from Lenin and Stalin how to set up a large-scale terror regime. But he had much to teach too. Like Lenin, he wished to concentrate all power in his single will. Like Lenin, he was a gnostic, and just as Lenin thought that he alone was the true interpreter of history as the embodiment of proletarian determinism, so Hitler had confidence only in himself as the exponent of the race-will of the German people.

M.T., P. 296

Being a race-socialist as opposed to a class-socialist, Hitler believed the dynamic of history was race. The dynamic was interrupted when race-poisoning took place. The poison came, above all, from the Jews. He admired Jews as "negative supermen." In his *Table-Talk* he said that if 5,000 Jews emigrated to Sweden, in no time at all they would occupy all the key positions . . . The Germans, on the other hand, had been "poisoned." That was why they lost the First World War. Even he was poisoned: that was why he occasionally made mistakes . . .

M.T., P. 342

. . . [Hitler] was always raising the stakes on the table and seeking to hasten the pace of history. He feared his revolution would lose its dynamism. He thought himself indispensable, and at least four of his phases must be accomplished while he was still not only alive but at the height of his powers. It was his impatience which made him so dangerous in the short term and so ineffectual in the long term (the very reverse of the Soviet strategists).

M.T., PP. 343–44

[141]

Despite the attempts of both Protestant and Catholic clergy to delude themselves, Hitler was not a Christian, and most of the members of his movement were avowedly anti-Christian. Of course Hitler was sometimes deceptive. He never officially left the Church; he sometimes referred to "providence" in his speeches, and he attended church several times in his first years of power. In the 1920s he told Ludendorff that he had to conceal his hatred of Catholicism, because he needed the Bavarian Catholic vote as much as he needed the Prussian Protestants—"the rest can come later."

H.C., P. 485

HITLER AND V. I. LENIN

Hitler, like Lenin, was the product of an age increasingly obsessed by politics. . . . and he was only really at home, like Lenin, in a world where the pursuit of power by conspiracy, agitation and force was the chief object . . . of existence. But in that barren and cheerless world he, like Lenin, was a master. He had the same intellectual egoism . . . ruthlessness in personal relations, preference for force as opposed to discussion and, most important, the ability to combine absolute fidelity to a long-term aim with skilful opportunism. The two men shared a certain puritanism: Hitler, like Lenin . . . had little personal vanity and was not corrupted by the more meretricious aspects of power. But in one essential respect they were quite different. Whereas Lenin was the religious type of revolutionary, Hitler was a romantic. Indeed he was an artist.

M.T., P. 129

HITLER TERROR

With the mature Soviet model to guide him, Hitler set up the apparatus of terror and the machinery of the police state even more quickly than Lenin—and soon on a scale almost as large as Stalin's. The initial agent in this endeavour was Goering, using the Prussian police and his newly created Gestapo of SA and SS men, operating from its Berlin HQ on Prinz Albrechtstrasse. It was Goering who destroyed the Communist Party in the space of a few weeks by a policy of murder—"A bullet fired from the barrel of a police-pistol is my bullet" was the assurance he gave his men—or internment in the concentration camps he began setting up . . .

M.T., P. 286

HITLER'S POPULARITY

. . . from 1933 until the beginning of 1939, Hitler was one of the most popular leaders in German history. Most Germans accepted his totalitarian cruelty because of the benefits he brought them. He was the only leader of a major country to bring back full employment in the 1930s, and he did it with astonishing speed. . . . Just as important, Hitler restored national morale. . . . Most Germans applauded Hitler when, at no cost in human life, he got back the Rhineland, absorbed Austria and "liberated" the Sudeten Germans. But they parted company from him when, in March 1939, he invaded the rest of Czechoslovakia. Then they knew he would undoubtedly get them into another war. The actual onset of war was received by most Germans in grim silence, and thereafter Hitler rarely addressed big public gatherings or appeared in the streets. His popularity was gone and only his apparatus of terror remained. Moreover, in the secrecy and darkness imposed by war he could stealthily begin his evil schemes of extermination.

S., APRIL 27, 1985

HOBBES, THOMAS

He was an agnostic, possibly an atheist, who presented the deification of the Commonwealth as a convenient substitute for conventional faith. The idea was broadened by Rousseau, whose concept of the General Will made it possible, eventually, to deify the Common Man, collectivized as the proletariat and endowed with dictatorial powers.

E.S., P. 126

HOLOCAUST

The Holocaust was planned; and Hitler planned it. That is the only conclusion which makes sense of the whole horrifying process.

H.J., P. 484

. . . bureaucratization . . . made possible its colossal scale and transformed a pogrom into genocide.

H.J., P. 486

The Jews had been for two millennia an oppressed minority who had never possessed the option of force. They had therefore been habitually obliged to negotiate, often for bare existence, and nearly always from a position of great weakness. Over the centuries they had developed not merely negotiating skills but a philosophy of negotiation. They would negotiate against impossible odds, and they had learned to accept a negotiated status, however lowly and underprivileged, knowing that it could later be improved by further negotiations and their own efforts. The paramountcy of settlement, as opposed to force, was built into their very bones. That was one reason they found it so difficult, even when the evidence became overwhelming, to take in the magnitude of Hitler's evil: it was hard for them to comprehend a man who wanted no settlement at all with them, just their lives.

H.J., P. 529

. . . just as the collective memory of pharaonic bondage dominated the early Israelite society, so the Holocaust shaped the new state. It was, inevitably, pervaded by a sense of loss. Hitler had wiped out a third of all Jews, especially the pious and the poor, from whom Judaism had drawn its peculiar strength. The loss could be seen in secular terms. In the nineteenth and early twentieth centuries the world had been immeasurably enriched by the liberated talent streaming out of the old ghettos, which had proved a principal creative force in modern European and North American civilization. The supply continued until Hitler destroyed the source for ever. No one will ever know what the world thereby sacrificed. For Israel the deprivation was devastating. It was felt at a personal level, for so many of its citizens had lost virtually all their families and childhood friends, and it was felt collectively: one in three of those who might have built the state was not there. It was felt spiritually perhaps most of all.

H.J., P. 559

HOLY ALLIANCE

The French invasion of Russia in 1812, and still more their expulsion, served to give Russia a unity it had never before possessed, and this in turn intensified the territorial drive once it was resumed in 1815. Russia, like Austria and Prussia, was the great gainer from Bonaparte's long wars—the Holy Alliance, as it were, was a grace after meat.

B.M., P. 272

HOWLEY, WILLIAM, ARCHBISHOP OF CANTERBURY

[A man guilty] ". . . of the most extraordinary indolence in history."
B.M., P. 378

HUGO, VICTOR

Having chosen his battlefield, Hugo had no intention of fighting fair. Where his artistic aims were at stake, he was totally unscrupulous, thus setting a pattern for the future: that art is more important than fusty notions of right and wrong. . . . More important, he did not hesitate to engage in cultural terrorism to ensure the play an enthusiastic reception, employing all the ruffianism of the claque system on an unprecedented scale.

B.M., P. 963

Human Conduct and Moral Absolutes

It is not true that all codes of human conduct are relative, and reflect cultural assumptions and economic arrangements which do not necessarily possess any authority. It is not true that there is no such thing as absolute right, and absolute wrong. It is not true that our behaviour is wholly determined by environment. Nor is it true that to seek to impose moral norms is an arrogant and unwarrantable assumption of infallibility; on the contrary, in the long run it is a necessary condition of human happiness, and even of human survival. What *is* true is that every rational human being is in a moral sense free, capable of reacting to moral absolutes, and of opting for good or evil.

E.S., P. 255

Hunting

. . . most of those who follow the hounds are now very ordinary people, and presumably ordinary newspaper readers too. . . . Anyone who has studied the history of law will know that, by one of the most ancient of paradoxes, those who hunt animals are the ones who love them most realistically, and therefore wisely, and are the most successful at defending their long-term interests.

S., OCTOBER 31, 1987

I have never hunted, and it is many decades since I shot any kind of animal. Indeed nowadays I am reluctant to kill even an annoying housefly—such a miracle of God and nature is its complex, super-efficient body, when studied closely—and I give it three public warnings, as in all-in wrestling. So blood sports as such do not interest me. But, as a historian, I can accept the paradox that carefully-controlled hunting, and the survival of species, go together. If we want foxes, to observe and delight in, we must have hunting.

S., SEPTEMBER 28, 1991

But supposing we all agree that hunting debases, does that automatically give us a right to stop it? Here we touch at the heart of the conflict between libertarianism and social morality in English life. At what point should the state intervene to prevent an activity which harms those who indulge in it and is, in a general sense, noxious to society? There are all kinds of things—smoking, drinking, driving private motor-cars—which bring death and misery on the widest scale, but are allowable. All of us would like to legislate against activities we deplore; all of us would like unlimited freedom to indulge in those we enjoy.

S.N., P. 43

HUSSEIN, SADDAM

Saddam was well-known to Western governments as a man of exceptional depravity, from a clan of professional brigands. He had acquired his first gun at the age of ten (and committed his first murder, it was claimed, two years later). As head of the secret police from 1968, and as president from 1979, his career had been punctuated both by the slaughter of his colleagues and rivals, often by his own hand, and by atrocities on the largest possible scale, not least mass public hangings of Jews.

M.T., PP. 714-15

He trained his own son in the science of cruelty by taking him, when a boy, to witness political prisoners being tortured in one of his Baghdad security prisons, and he himself has been reliably described as watching one of his political opponents being cast alive in a bath of acid to be slowly dissolved.

S., FEBRUARY 16, 1991

Saddam's murder of thousands of Kurds by chemical weapons, his slaughter of 7,000 Kuwaitis—including babies torn from life-support machines which were then stolen—and his systematic stripping of this small country of all its valuables, public and private, are well authenticated. That has not prevented clerics, actors and playwrights from publicly voicing views which would ensure his survival. Of course they go through the perfunctory motions of saying they condemn his atrocities—thereby adding what many would regard as a dimension of hypocrisy to their conduct. But the net effect of the policies they urge, to have an immediate cease-fire, to withdraw all Western forces from the area, and to rely entirely on "sanctions" and United Nations exhortation, would be to leave Saddam in possession of his war-making machine . . . and therefore of his capacity to savage his neighbours and brutalise his own people. Unless they are unusually stupid and ill-informed (which of course, some of them may well be), these "anti-war" agitators must know this to be true.

S., FEBRUARY 16, 1991

I

IBSEN, HENRIK

. . . the whole of Ibsen's life is a furtive Ibsenesque drama.

I., P. 92

On 20 March 1888 he sent a cable to the Christiania Workers Union: "Of all the classes in my country, it is the working class which is nearest to my heart." This was humbug. Nothing was near to his heart except his wallet.

I., P. 99

The difficulty with [Ibsen's elitist] view, which was typically Victorian in its way, was that it assumed that humanity, led by the enlightened minority, would always progress in a desirable direction. It did not occur to Ibsen that this minority . . . might lead mankind into the abyss. Ibsen would have been surprised and horrified by the excesses of the twentieth century, the century whose mind he did so much to shape.

I., P. 99

IDEAS

Most people are resistant to ideas, especially new ones. But they are fascinated by character. Extravagance of personality is one way in which the pill can be sugared and the public induced to look at works dealing with ideas.

I., P. 12

The cruelty of ideas lies in the assumption that human beings can be bent to fit them.

I., P. 268

Above all, we must at all times remember what intellectuals habitually forget: that people matter more than concepts and must come first. The worst of all despotisms is the heartless tyranny of ideas.

I., P. 342

IDEALIST

It is always dangerous to confront idealists with a situation which, to put it mildly, is far from ideal.

S.N., P. 226

IDEOLOGICAL SPECTRUM

I have long been uneasy at the way the media unthinkingly accept confusions in categorising the ideological spectrum. The truth is, the spectrum ought to go through totalitarian-radical at one end to traditional-archaic at the other. Thus you begin on the Left with communism and fascism, progress through various degrees of state socialism (including the Latin American varieties) to parliamentary socialism (democratic socialist being the left-wing variety, social democrat the more right-wing), then to old-style liberalism, parliamentary conservatism and church-and-king Tories. At this point the parliamentary-democratic element declines again and you get, on the extreme Right, autocratic monarchism based on the doctrine of Divine Right.

S., OCTOBER 7, 1989

IDEOLOGY (MODERN)

. . . the new creeds are all variations, sometimes exalted, sometimes debased, of political nostrums long since tried, and found wanting—or indeed wholly destructive. The only novelty lies in the permutations of falsehood and unreason which academic ingenuity has contrived to concoct. Some cults preach varieties of Marxism, some proletarianised refurbishings of Hitlerism, some a combination of both. Unknowingly, the ancient and dusty battles of nineteenth-century revolutionaries are re-fought in new and fashionable trappings. With each successful assault on the customary standards of deduction and logic, of proof and plausibility, the threshold of reason is lowered.

H.E., P. 417

IMAGINATION

Imagination is a powerful rewriter of history.

S., MAY 14, 1988

IMITATIONS

The trouble with imitations is that they make one appreciate the genuine article.

S., JANUARY 10, 1987

IMPERIALISM (BRITISH)

Imperialism concealed the truth of decadence, inhibited inquiry into its causes, and blocked the search for remedies. It led the English to forget that they are a small people, inhabiting a tiny island not rich in natural resources, and that in a hostile and competitive world they must always live on their wits and their realism. It persuaded them to overestimate their strength and ignore their weaknesses. In this sense it was a true opium of the people, a drug which bred ruinous fantasies and produced a dismal awakening when the dreams were over.

H.E., P. 346

. . . imperialism as a matter of practical necessity corrupted the master-race. It forced ordinary white men to behave like gods— false gods. A tiny *élite*, governing multitudes, had to acquire, or assume, a Jupiter-complex simply to get through the business of decision-making. The thunderbolts had to be rained on the heads of the wicked, the good rewarded with miracles. To many of the *élite* the illusion . . . became reality: they thought themselves gods. To others . . . [it] became a hollow and cynical routine. In either case, the imperialist made himself into a lesser man. The Empire did not so much shape "character," as deform it.

H.E., P. 349

THE INDIVIDUAL

Where individual and corporate rights conflict, the political balance should usually be weighted in favour of the individual; for civilizations are created, and maintained, not by corporations, however benign, but by multitudes of individuals operating independently.

E.S., P. 257

INDUSTRIAL REVOLUTION

The Industrial Revolution, which first developed its irresistible momentum in the 1780s . . . is often presented as a time of horror for working men. In fact it was the age, above all, in history of matchless opportunities for penniless men with powerful brains and imaginations, and it is astonishing how quickly they came to the fore.

B.M., P. 188

The common philosophical thread which runs through all aspects of the Industrial Revolution story is a libertarian one. The more perceptive men realized this at the time, and argued that, once property was effectively guaranteed, the fewer regulations the better. As early as 1702, parliament passed the motion "That trade ought to be free and not restrained." The view was growing, even in absolutist France, where it was voiced by Mirabeau, that laws which conformed to nature were unnecessary, and those which contradicted it were impracticable.

E.S., P. 66

INDUSTRIALIZATION

For 150 years, almost from the point when they grasped it had happened, political radicals have insisted that industrialization took place at the expense of the working classes: that the capital needed for the first phase of industrial capitalism was accumulated by "forced savings" extracted from the workers by lowering their living standards. . . . This thesis . . . is now quite untenable. Indeed the opposite is true. The latest and most thorough statistical examination . . . shows that even the first phases of the Industrial Revolution, 1781–1851, brought huge rises in living standards for all broad categories of British workers: an improvement of 140 per cent for the working population as a whole.

P.P.J., PP. 175–76

INFANTICIDE

There are, as it happens, inconsistencies in our attitudes to the moral issues raised by our growing knowledge of biological processes. The [British] state has only recently withdrawn its legal ban on abortion in any form, and now permits the embryo to be destroyed, or murdered, up to 28 weeks from conception. In this case the destruction is carried out with no direct social purpose at all, merely (in effect) on the desire of the mother, and in accordance with the moral principle that "a woman should decide what happens to her own body." Now, however, the Warnock Committee comes along and says that, once the embryo is 14 days old, you can destroy it

[153]

but you may not carry out experiments on it. . . . [if] the state declares that I become Me after two weeks, why does it allow "Me" to be annihilated for a further 26?

s., JULY 28, 1984

INFLATION

. . . hyperinflation sets up a voracious moral corruption eating out the heart of society. It is the very antithesis of the communal ideal. Where social morality teaches us to see ourselves as part of a whole, members of a human society based on comradeship, mutual help, friendliness, trust, magnanimity and hope in the future, wage inflation sets group against group and makes self-interest the guiding principle of life. It makes money seem the only social nexus and the only criterion of well-being. It forces on all of us the aggressive posture of comparative envy.

E.S., P. 192

It turns money and its ever-changing value into the chief preoccupation not only of the miser and the banker but of every human being, the dominant topic of conversation, the source of all anecdote, the ever-present, ever-nagging worry behind every plan and move. It makes the young predatory, the middle-aged mean and acquisitive, the old fearful. It penalizes not just the poor, the old, the sick and the weak, but the decent, the diffident, the unselfish, the reasonable, the temperate, the fair-minded, the loyal and the generous. It allows the social mood to be determined by the rapacious, the unscrupulous, the anti-social and the bully. Uncontrolled inflation creates a world of blind materialism, where ideals cannot be realized, where force, power and selfishness are the only dynamics, and where charity is dead.

E.S., P. 192

INSTITUTIONS

Civilisation is not merely created and advanced by individuals; it is promoted and above all upheld by institutions. Loyalty to institutions is therefore a vital cement which holds civilisation together. Institutions have lives of their own, longer than the human span, developing their own standards and disciplines, codes of ethics and—most important—their own creative energies. Whether they are schools or colleges, ballet companies or orchestras, magazines or newspapers, these corporate entities need the human nourishment of devoted service to give their best to society.

S., FEBRUARY 8, 1986

INTELLECT

It is a fact, and in some ways a melancholy fact, that massive works of the intellect do not spring from the abstract workings of the brain and the imagination; they are deeply rooted in the personality.

I., P. 69

INTELLECTUAL

The common assumption is that intellectuals and soldiers are natural enemies. Not so. Intellectuals tend to be fascinated by power, not least military power, and are only too anxious to harness the soldiers to the chariots of their ideas. Equally, the soldiers and the politicians who both direct and are carried along by them have no objection to attaching intellectual horsepower to their gun carriages. Hegel illustrated this tendency better than anyone. No intellectual has ever been a more dedicated servant of state power. In appearance, temperament, habits, virtues and vices, he was the archetypal academic.

B.M., P. 811

Nothing appeals to intellectuals more than the feeling that they represent "the people." Nothing, as a rule, is further from the truth.

B.M., P. 847

[155]

. . . for 1,500 years Jewish society had been designed to produce intellectuals. It is true they were sacerdotal intellectuals, in the service of the god Torah. But they had all the characteristics of the intellectual: a tendency to pursue ideas at the expense of people; endlessly sharpened critical faculties; great destructive as well as creative power.

H.J., PP. 340–41

. . . it is a habit of intellectuals, who write everything with an eye to future publication, to use their diaries as *pièces justificatives*, instruments of propaganda, defensive and offensive weapons against potential critics, not least their loved ones.

I., P. 134

. . . the private lives and the public postures of leading intellectuals cannot be separated: one helps to explain the other. Private vices and weaknesses are almost invariably reflected in conduct on the world stage.

I., P. 274

. . . the great crux of the intellectual life: the attitude to violence. It is the fence at which most secular intellectuals, be they pacifist or not, stumble and fall into inconsistency—or, indeed, into sheer incoherence. They may renounce it in theory, as indeed in logic they must since it is the antithesis of rational methods of solving problems. But in practice they find themselves from time to time endorsing it—what might be called the Necessary Murder Syndrome—or approving its use by those with whom they sympathize. Other intellectuals, confronted with the fact of violence practised by those they wish to defend, simply transfer the moral responsibility, by ingenious argument, to others whom they wish to attack.

I., P. 337

Now it is a characteristic of such intellectuals that they see no incongruity in moving from their own discipline, where they are acknowledged masters, to public affairs, where they might be supposed to have no more right to a hearing than anyone else.

I., P. 339

There seems to be, in the life of many millenarian intellectuals, a sinister climacteric, a cerebral menopause, which might be termed the Flight of Reason.

I., P. 341

One of the principal lessons of our tragic century, which has seen so many millions of innocent lives sacrificed in schemes to improve the lot of humanity, is—beware intellectuals. Not merely should they be kept well away from the levers of power, they should also be objects of particular suspicion when they seek to offer collective advice. . . . For intellectuals, far from being highly individualistic and non-conformist people, follow certain regular patterns of behaviour. Taken as a group, they are often ultra-conformist within the circles formed by those whose approval they seek and value. That is what makes them, *en masse*, so dangerous, for it enables them to create climates of opinion and prevailing orthodoxies, which themselves often generate irrational and destructive courses of action.

I., P. 342

The belief seems to be spreading that intellectuals are no wiser as mentors, or worthier as exemplars, than the witch doctors or priests of old. I share that scepticism. A dozen people picked at random on the street are at least as likely to offer sensible views on moral and political matters as a cross-section of the intelligentsia.

I., P. 342

In the outside world, the magnitude of the Stalin tyranny—or indeed its very existence—was scarcely grasped at all. Most of those who travelled to Russia were either businessmen, anxious to trade and with no desire to probe or criticize, . . . or intellectuals who came to admire and, still more, to believe. If the decline of Christianity created the modern political zealot—and his crimes—so the evaporation of religious faith among the educated left a vacuum in the minds of Western intellectuals easily filled by secular superstition. There is no other explanation for the credulity with which scientists, accustomed to evaluating evidence, and writers, whose whole function was to study and criticize society, accepted the crudest Stalinist propaganda at its face value. They needed to believe; they wanted to be duped.

M.T., P. 275

A visit to "our" Spain was essential to the self-respect of a progressive intellectual. Just as the Germans, Russians and Italians used Spain to test their new military equipment—exploitation by hardware— so writers went there to acquire material for their next novel or poem, what might be termed exploitation by software.

M.T., P. 337

The trouble with intellectuals is that, once they get a modicum of authority, . . . they tend to be arrogant in exercising it.

S., JANUARY 17, 1987

. . . the intellectuals who proclaim our freedoms are being eroded do not want balance. They want bias—their bias—and that is what, up until now, they have been getting from the duopoly. They demand tolerance and the widest possible exposure of their own views—but deny them to others.

S., FEBRUARY 4, 1989

The middle-class intellectual element, while overwhelmingly white, is simply trying . . . to have its cake and eat it; it supports mul- tiracial/culturalism *except* when it conflicts with the still more cher- ished doctrine of absolute freedom to publish (left-wing) views, especially the right to spit in the face of religious belief.

S., AUGUST 12, 1989

INTELLECTUALS (POLISH)

The coming of the Communist regime may, paradoxically, have strengthened Catholicism among the Polish intelligentsia, not only for the obvious reason that it gives religion the invaluable attraction, among intellectuals, of the opposition role, but also because about half of those officially classified as belonging to the intelligentsia are of lower-class (chiefly peasant) origins, where faith is stronger.

Poland is perhaps the only country on earth where religious fervour among intellectuals is higher than it was half a century ago.

P.J., P. 18

INTELLECTUAL (SECULAR)

. . . the rise of the secular intellectual has been a key factor in shaping the modern world. . . . intellectuals have laid claim to guide society from the very beginning. But as guardians of hieratic cultures . . . their moral and ideological innovations were limited by the canons of external authority, and by the inheritance of tradition. . . . With the decline of clerical power in the eighteenth century, a new kind of mentor emerged. . . . The secular intellectual . . . was just as ready as any pontiff or presbyter to tell mankind how to conduct its affairs. . . . the collective wisdom of the past, the legacy of tradition, the prescriptive codes of ancestral experience existed to be selectively followed or wholly rejected entirely as his own good sense might decide. . . . Unlike the sacerdotal predecessors, they were not servants and interpreters of the gods but substitutes.

I., PP. 1–2

INTELLIGENCE

The truth is, when we say, "That's not a very intelligent remark," what we usually mean is: "I don't agree with you."

S., MARCH 15, 1986

INTERVIEW

The ideal interview, like good prose, should be a sheet of perfect glass, through which the person under scrutiny is seen clear and whole.

S., OCTOBER 27, 1990

[159]

INTOLERANCE

The study of history suggests that the sum total of intolerance in society does not vary much. What changes is the object against which it is directed. Those who shape the conventional wisdom at the top are always anxious to censor unorthodoxy, thus demonstrating their power and consolidating their grip.

S., NOVEMBER 21, 1987

IRELAND

It is often argued that, except for short periods of crisis, Ireland has never stood in the forefront of British policy or attracted the services of her best statesmen and thinkers. . . . [But] for the British, Ireland has proved a well-stocked graveyard of reputations. It effectively destroyed Richard II and the Earl of Essex, it fatally damaged the cause of Charles I and James II, it wrecked the careers of a long procession of Lords Lieutenant and ministers, of whom we remember only a handful—Forster and Wyndham, Seely and Greenwood, for instance. A few used Ireland to add to their contemporary fame: Mountjoy and Cromwell, Castlereagh and Balfour. But today Mountjoy survives only as the name of a prison, and the other three have been condemned by posterity.

Id., P. 235

Ireland was the joker in the English pack. It always had been. It was a living, ocular refutation of the English claim to have the genius and temperament for an imperial mission. English statesmanship had been . . . exercised in Ireland for seven and a half centuries, and had invariably been found wanting. The English liked to think they were a tolerant people, easy-going, not inclined to press logic to unreasonable lengths, pacific unless provoked, adept at compromise, skilful in devising political solutions as an alternative to violence . . . unrivalled in fashioning institutional frameworks which canalised passion, . . . above all, just. This was the image the English sought to present to themselves and to the world: they had built it up from innumerable examples . . . But the moment

[160]

the history of Ireland was mentioned, the whole shaky structure collapsed in ruins.

H.E., P. 350

. . . the British Army has contrived to prove, by its conduct, . . . that Britain has no other object in Ulster but to secure a lasting peace and a just settlement. And that, perhaps, is a more important object gained than military victory. If there is one lesson the history of Ireland teaches, it is that military victory is not enough.

Id., P. 233

THE IRISH

Are the Irish, indeed, the children of wrath? Looking back over their history, we are tempted to think so, and to credit Edmund Spenser with a gift of prophecy when he wrote of Ireland that "Almighty God hath not yet appointed the time of her reformation," but "reserveth her in this unquiet state still for some secret scourge, which shall by her come into England." The outstanding fact of the British-Irish connection has been the fearful toll it has exacted of human life, and not merely of the anonymous multitude. How many holders of famous names in that long story have died by violence or on the scaffold! "Silken Thomas" Kildare and Thomas Wentworth, Archbishop Plunkett and Phelim O'Neill, Lord Edward Fitzgerald and Wolfe Tone, Robert Emmet and Lord Frederick Cavendish, Pearse and Connolly, Casement and MacBride, Collins and Henry Wilson, Childers and Rory O'Connor, Brugha and O'Higgins, Airey Neave and Mountbatten—and how many more to come?

Id., P. 234

IRISH CATHOLICISM

Religion, indeed, is not the root of the problem in Ireland; it is merely the colouration of an underlying racist division which is much more ancient. The identification of Irish nationalism with

[161]

Roman Catholicism was largely accidental. It was the fanatical Catholic sovereign Queen Mary who began the systematic plantation of English settlers in the confiscated lands of Irish rebels. Hence, when England turned to Protestantism under Elizabeth, the older Anglo-Irish landed class clung to the Church of Rome more as a protest against the newer English plantations than for doctrinal reasons. Catholicism and the Pope became an expression of Irish nationalism, and the Papacy, which had given Ireland to England, now exhorted the Irish to resist. . . . but the main impulse in Ireland's religious choice was political and racial. If England had remained Catholic, and France had turned Protestant, there is little doubt that Ireland would have turned Protestant too.

H.E., P. 105

THE IRISH ON THE ENGLISH

Seen from an Irish perspective, the English were ruthless, but also irresolute; tyrannical, but cowardly; inconsistent even in their violence, oscillating wildly between repression, indifference and appeasement. Whatever the English genius was, in Ireland it had conspicuously failed. There, the English had imposed neither justice nor stability; they had created no durable institutions; they had generated no wealth. A long gallery of English potentates had impinged on the Irish scene: Henry Plantagenet and Richard of Bordeaux, Elizabeth and Cromwell, William of Orange and Walpole, Pitt the Younger and Robert Peel. Ireland had baffled them all, left them, indeed, angered at their own impotence. Confronted with Ireland, the English usually in the end took refuge in the bitter consolation that the Irish were incorrigible and worthless: thus attributing the consequences of their own criminal incompetence to the inborn nature of a hapless people who had never, in all those centuries, sought an English connection.

H.E., PP. 350–51

Irish Famine

What stayed longest and deepest in the collective memory of the Irish peasants was not so much the hunger itself as the way in which the landlords exploited the famine to disencumber their estates, actually emerging better off from the disaster.

id., PP. 104–5

Irish Nationalism

By tamely accepting the [Irish] union, the Protestant Ascendancy effectively forfeited its right to lead the Irish nation. By reneging on its bargain, and by delaying Catholic emancipation for nearly thirty years, the British government turned Catholics away from union and made the Catholic Church the central depository of Irish nationalism.

id., P. 91

Irish Playwrights

Indeed, if we subtract from British theatrical history the works of Goldsmith, Sheridan, Oscar Wilde and George Bernard Shaw, we are left with precious little that is durable from the Restoration to the Edwardians.

id., P. 117

The Irish Problem

. . . the modern Irish problem, as it existed until the twentieth century: a landless Catholic peasantry governed by a legally exclusive Protestant ruling class, with a small predominantly Protestant middle class sandwiched in between, and a multi-class Protestant enclave in Ulster. The separate communities were divided not only by religion but by race and, not least, by culture: they learned different poetry, sang different songs, celebrated different victories, mourned different calamities and, above all, swore different oaths. Ireland became a country where privilege was upheld, and revenge planned, by the swearing of oaths. Catholic oaths were secret and furtive. Protestant oaths were public and assertive, indeed vainglorious and provocative, being turned into toasts.

Id., PP. 63–64

IRISH UNION ACT

This rapid reconciliation of the Protestant ruling class to the fact of union reminded the great mass of Irishmen that the "English garrison" had another country to go to and serve; in the last resort they could do without independence and still flourish. By accepting the union they necessarily relinquished the leadership of the nationalist movement to the Catholics and in a few years they found themselves transformed into a colonial ruling class. Thereafter, it was the Catholics who stood for an independent parliament, and the Protestants for union. The idea of a Protestant nation was dead.

Id., P. 90

IRONY

Irony is an exceedingly dangerous weapon in journalism. However clearly it is labelled, you can be absolutely certain that a lot of readers will not get the point.

S., MAY 19, 1984

IRVING, WASHINGTON

He was the first American to achieve celebrity through literature. That was an important step in the growth of America's cultural self-confidence. It was also a critical stage in Britain's recognition of the United States not only as a legitimate entity but as a civilized one.

B.M., P. 60

Isolationism

. . . the isolationist instinct remains . . . The strains are felt particularly in the Presidency itself. The conflict between America's national impulses and international duties destroyed that powerful and able man Lyndon Johnson. It lay at the heart of Richard Nixon's battle with the media, the real cause of Watergate and so his downfall. It made the decent, well-meaning Gerald Ford seem out of his depth, and turned Jimmy Carter, who took office with high hopes and ideals, into a near disaster. The great merit of Ronald Reagan is that he has ended this run of debilitated Presidents and speaks for America in confident . . . tones . . . because he is a man of few . . . and clear ideas, deeply and sincerely held, which happen to be shared with most Americans.

U.S.N., DECEMBER 30, 1985

Israel

There is, indeed, something biblical in the battles among Israel's founders and pioneers . . . and the way in which their enmities were eventually submerged by time and chance and the slow erosion of events. All of them in different ways were outsized characters, touched by messianic delusions . . . Together, they give the lie emphatically to the claims of determinists that history is made by impersonal forces rather than great individuals. Israel, like most other nations, was built by inspired egoism.

C., OCTOBER 1987

No nation in antiquity was so self-conscious, so well-informed about its origin and progress, so anxious to amass documentary evidence of its past. Indeed, the desire for a general explanation giving a gigantic answer to the big question of life, but capable also of supplying satisfactory answers to all the little ones, is central to Hebrew monotheism and the concept of a god with limitless power.

C.H.L., P. 82

The building of Israel was the twentieth-century equivalent of re-building the Temple. Like the Temple under Herod the Great, it had unsatisfactory aspects. But it was there. The very fact that it existed, and could be visited and shared, gave a completely new dimension to the diaspora. It was a constant source of concern, sometimes of anxiety, often of pride. Once Israel had been established and proved it could defend and justify itself, no member of the diaspora ever had to feel ashamed of being a Jew again.

H.J., P. 560

The Balfour Declaration and the idea of a Jewish National Home was one of the post-dated cheques Britain signed to win the Great War.

M.T., P. 481

American backing for Israel in 1947–48 was the last idealistic luxury the Americans permitted themselves before the Realpolitik of global confrontation descended. The same time-scale influenced Russia. It backed Zionism in order to break up Britain's position in the Middle East. . . . These considerations would not have prevailed a year later, when the rush for Cold War allies was on. Israel slipped into existence through a crack in the time continuum.

M.T., P. 485

Just as no non-Jew can grasp the centrality of the holocaust in Jewish experience, so non-Polish Jews find it hard to understand the totality of its destructiveness. In consequence, Israel as a City of Refuge has a unique symbolic importance in the eyes of the survivors of Polish Jewry. Whereas Weizmann and the Israeli Labour establishment always saw Israel as a "light to the gentiles," with a role to guide and assist the poor peoples of the Middle East, for Begin it was essentially a fortress to ensure that the murder of a defenceless people should never again occur.

S., MARCH 3, 1984

Israel's future is incomparably more secure than when [Begin] took over in 1977. In the process, Israel has forfeited some of the sympathy it once enjoyed with "world opinion," whatever that is. But such sympathy is no substitute for safety. It is the fundamental assumption of Begin's policy that the Israelis could enjoy all the sympathy in the world and still end up as dead as the millions of Polish Jews he remembers and laments. There is absolutely no answer to this argument.

S., MARCH 3, 1984

J

JAPAN

Japan is the most elusive and impenetrable nation on earth, which in some ways has more in common with the Middle Kingdom of ancient Egypt than anything in contemporary society.

C., MARCH 1992

Japan, so far, has clung to democracy because it is convenient, and safe, and has proved mighty profitable. If these conditions should change, will Japan, a country with a large and now-affluent population and few natural resources, look elsewhere for political salvation? Has democracy, let alone liberalism, struck deep, self-sustaining roots in Japanese civic habits and attitudes? How can we possibly say? The Japanese, or so many of them tell me, do not even know themselves; or if they do know, are not saying.

C., MARCH 1992

No western scholar who studies modern Japan can resist the feeling that it was a victim of the holistic principle whereby political events and moral tendencies have their consequences throughout the world. Japan became infected with the relativism of the West, which induced a sinister hypertrophy of its own behavioural weaknesses and so cast itself into the very pit of twentieth-century horror.

M.T., PP. 176–77

Long before the European war broke out, Japan was a tense, underfed, increasingly desperate totalitarian country which had alienated all its neighbours, abolished its constitutional and democratic

[168]

system, abandoned the rule of law, had no long-term strategy which made any sense, and had adopted the expedient of using force to smash its way out of its difficulties, which were increasingly self-created. Here, at the end of the 1930s, was one exemplar of relative morality in practice.

M.T., PP. 318–19

. . . [during the] Occupation, under which America had sole power, . . . General MacArthur proved a decisive blessing. He was able to play the role of enlightened despot, and impose on Japan a revolution from above, like the Meiji Restoration of the 1860s which launched the Japanese as a modern nation. The 1947 constitution, drawn up in MacArthur's headquarters, was not an inter-party compromise, representing the lowest common denominator of agreement, but a homogeneous concept, incorporating the best aspects of the British and U.S. constitutions . . .

M.T., P. 730

The American occupation of Japan was probably the greatest constructive achievement of American overseas policy in the whole postwar period, and it was carried through virtually single-handed. And, as with Britain's creation of a model trade union movement for West Germany, it raised up a mighty competitor.

M.T., PP. 730–31

JAPAN (POSTWAR)

There was nothing miraculous about this miracle. It was a straightforward case of Adam Smith economics, with no more than a touch of Keynesianism. A high percentage of fixed capital formation, very little of it in non-productive investment. Moderate taxation. Low defence and government spending. A very high rate of personal saving, efficiently channelled into industry through the banking system. Shrewd import of foreign technology under licence.

M.T., P. 733

[169]

THE JAPANESE

The Japanese are the most remote of all great peoples and the most xenophobic; they have, when they choose, an unrivalled capacity to absorb what is useful to them from other civilisations, while preserving their essential cultural values completely intact. They are becoming a major, soon perhaps will be a dominant, force in the modern world while remaining isolated from it. Our ignorance of them, and what little I know of their history, fills me with foreboding.

S., APRIL 11, 1987

JAZZ

To buttress their intellectual self-esteem, these treasonable [intellectuals] have evolved an elaborate cultural mythology about jazz, which purports to distinguish between various periods, tendencies and schools. The subject has been smeared with a respectable veneer of academic scholarship, so that now you can overhear grown men, who have been expensively educated, engage in heated argument on the respective techniques of Charlie Parker and Duke Ellington. . . . One might, I suppose, attribute such intellectual treachery to the fact that, in jazz circles, morals are easy, sex is cheap and there is a permissive attitude to the horrors of narcotics. Men are, alas, sometimes willing to debauch their intellects for such rewards.

S.N., P. 46

JEROME, ST.

Jerome was the first Christian, of whom we have intimate knowledge, whose interpretation of his faith was quite incompatible with the realization of his nature—the result being profound misery. As Ambrose is the prototype of the medieval prelate, Jerome is the precursor of the agonized Christian intellectual, whose flesh is in

[170]

irreconcilable conflict with the spirit, and whose enforced continence is bought at the cost of human charity.

H.C., P. 111

JESUS CHRIST

This meek Messiah was not a danger to any existing order, or any particular throne, or ruling class . . . at any rate in a direct or immediate sense. He was not a mob leader, a democrat, or a guerrilla. He was talking, it is true, of freedom. But it was not the freedom of Republican Rome, the freedom, within a firm framework of orderly government, to move, trade and worship where you will; nor was it the freedom of the Jewish priesthood to carry out the commands of the Torah . . . it was, rather, the internal freedom of the conscience at ease with itself . . . And this new freedom, which could not be measured in terms of frontiers and forms of government, and would be won by a degraded sacrifice of the Messiah himself, was offered not merely to Jews but to all mankind in accordance with the prophecy of Isaiah: "In thee shall all families of the earth be blessed."

C.H.L., P. 122

. . . if we reduce our knowledge of Jesus to points where there is unanimity, plausibility and an absence of objections, we are left with a phenomenon almost devoid of significance. This "residual" Jesus told stories, uttered various wise sayings, was executed in circumstances which are not clear, and was then commemorated in a ceremony by his followers. Such a version is incredible because it does not explain the rise of Christianity.

H.C., P. 27

How could the intentions of God be conveyed so as to be understood by all men, and for all time? Equally, how could any solution contain elements meaningful for all types and temperaments of men, as well as all races and generations: the activist, the militant, the doctrinaire, the ascetic, the obedient, the passive, the angular, the scholar, and the simple-hearted? How could it impart both a sense of urgency and immediacy, and at the same time be valid for all eternity? How could it bring about, in men's minds, a confrontation with God which was both public and collective, and individual and intimate? How could it combine a code of ethics within a framework of strict justice and a promise of unprecedented generosity? . . . But a great deal [of this variety] is essentially part of Jesus's universalist posture: the wonder is that the personality behind the mission is in no way fragmented but is always integrated and true to character. Jesus contrives to be all things to all men while remaining faithful to himself.

H.C., P. 28

. . . the revelation of his own position . . . was always to some extent ambiguous. He radiated authority—it was, from the very start, the most conspicuous thing about him. But of what kind? He was anxious to show that he was not a priest-general, performing a military role against a foreign oppressor. He was not the Messiah in *that* sense. On the other hand, he was not just the articulator of suffering and sacrifice: he had come to found a new kind of kingdom and to bring a message of joy and hope. How to convey that his triumph had to be achieved through his death? It was not an idea which appealed to the ancient world, or any world. Then, too, there was the central paradox that the mission had to be vindicated by its failure.

H.C., P. 29

JESUS CHRIST AND THE JEWS

He was, in effect, giving the Jews a completely new interpretation of God and, in delivering his message, claiming not merely divine authority, but divine status. . . . He was telling the Jews that their theory of how God made the universe work was wrong, and that he had a better. For the Sadducees to follow was out of the question. . . . they did not even believe in life after death . . . With the Pharisees he was in effect asking them to abandon their profession as canon lawyers, accept a theory which enabled men to justify themselves without the law, and a doctrine of grace and faith which made legalism impossible. In the end, then, his real appeal was to ordinary, uninstructed Jewish lay opinion, the *Am Ha-Aretz*, the "people of the land" or lost sheep, especially to the outcasts and the sinners for whom the law was too much. This was Jesus's constituency . . .

H.C., P. 31

JEWS

No people has ever insisted more firmly than the Jews that history has a purpose and humanity a destiny. At a very early stage in their collective existence they believed they had detected a divine scheme for the human race, of which their own society was to be a pilot. They worked out their role in immense detail. They clung to it with heroic persistence in the face of savage suffering. Many of them believe it still. Others transmuted it into Promethean endeavours to raise our condition by purely human means. The Jewish vision became the prototype for many similar grand designs for humanity, both divine and man-made. The Jews, therefore, stand right at the centre of the perennial attempt to give human life the dignity of a purpose.

H.J., P. 2

The Jews gave the world ethical monotheism, which might be described as the application of reason to divinity. In a more secular age, they applied the principles of rationality to the whole range of human activities, often in advance of the rest of mankind. The light they thus shed disturbed as well as illuminated, for it revealed painful truths about the human spirit as well as the means to uplift it.

H.J., P. 582

Over 4,000 years the Jews proved themselves not only great survivors but extraordinarily skilful in adapting to the societies among which fate thrust them, and in gathering whatever human comforts they had to offer. No people has been more fertile in enriching poverty or humanizing wealth, or in turning misfortune to creative account. This capacity springs from a moral philosophy both solid and subtle,

[173]

which has changed remarkably little over the millennia precisely because it has been seen to serve the purposes of those who share it. Countless Jews, in all ages, have groaned under the burden of Judaism. But they have continued to carry it because they have known, in their hearts, that it carried them. The Jews were survivors because they possessed the law of survival.

H.J., P. 582

The Jews have been great truth-tellers and that is one reason they have been so much hated. A prophet will be feared and sometimes honoured, but when has he been loved? Yet a prophet must prophesy and the Jews will persist in pursuing truth, as they see it, wherever it leads.

H.J., P. 583

To [the Jews] we owe the idea of equality before the law, both divine and human; of the sanctity of life and the dignity of the human person; of the individual conscience and so of personal redemption; of the collective conscience and so of social responsibility; of peace as an abstract ideal and love as the foundation of justice, and many other items which constitute the basic moral furniture of the human mind.

H.J., P. 585

JEWS (AMERICAN)

. . . during the second half of [this] century, [their] aristocracy of success became as ubiquitous and pervasive in its cultural influence as the earlier elite, the White Anglo-Saxon Protestant. Jews ceased to be a lobby in American society. They became part of the natural organism itself, a limb, and a powerful one. They began to operate not from without the American body inwards, but from within it outwards. With their historic traditions of democracy, tolerance and liberalism, they assumed to some extent the same role in America as the Whigs had once played in England: an elite seeking moral justification for its privileges by rendering enlightened service to those less fortunate. In short, they were no longer a minority seeking rights but part of the majority conferring them.

H.J., P. 567

JEWS AND RELIGIOUS IMAGES

Jewish hostility towards images is curious, since Yahweh himself was a personal deity who spoke and did things; there is plenty of anthropomorphism in the Old Testament. Moreover, it was not true, as the Hebrews supposed, that the devotees of the religions they condemned regarded images as gods; on the contrary, as Egyptian theology for instance makes abundantly clear, they recognized that gods were spiritual in essence and in no sense bound by the material of which images were made. In at any rate the more sophisticated cults of the ancient Near East, the image was a means by which the worshipper communicated with and drew nearer to God—as it still is in Roman Catholicism, for instance.

C.H.L., P. 62

JOB, BOOK OF

. . . the Book of Job illuminates all that central area of religious philosophy which contrasts the moral with the physical order; and it serves to remind us that the heritage of Hebrew civilization is not primarily in stones and artefacts but in the imperishable thoughts it has implanted in the minds of all succeeding ages.

C.H.L., P. 85

JOHN XXIII

His fascination as a public person lies in his efforts to apply strictly spiritual principles to the solution of temporal problems. But beyond this, though directly related to it, was his lifelong personal struggle to acquire goodness, and so to save his soul. He is thus of equal interest both to students of human wisdom and students of moral

[175]

philosophy; and his magnetism transcends intellectual categories. Pope John illustrates the continuing power of moral forces to influence events.

P.J., P. 5

In fact, he was exceptionally agile at establishing close personal relationships without conceding issues of principle—the essence of diplomatic method.

P.J., P. 48

When the task was finally presented to him—aged seventy-six, almost seventy-seven—he had no hesitations, no doubts. He simply did what, unconsciously, he had been training himself to do since he first became a priest: he spoke and acted as a wise pastor, but from the universal vantage point of the papal throne. This, indeed, is what Christianity is about; it is what the papacy should be about.

P.J., P. 118

Unlike so many of his predecessors, he appeared not as a divisive, but a unifying, force in the Christian community; and, more than that, he represented to many believers of divers faiths, and to millions of men and women of no faith, the pure and elementary virtues of the religious disposition. In the aftermath of the Cuban missile crisis, as humanity realized how close it had come to the brink, Pope John seemed, by the serenity and optimism of his words, a protective figure, a guarantee in his own calm and benignant person, that the world would not destroy itself, and that a mysterious Providence, as he said, was watching over the earth.

P.J., P. 229

He wanted the sincere Christian to redefine his religious life: to see it not as a cult, to be ritually observed, in isolation from the rest of his existence, but as an all-pervading attitude of mind which embraced every aspect of human consciousness, and which linked him to every section of humanity, regardless of race or belief. This universalism was a projection of his own personal spirituality, at the center of which was a profound belief in the intimate unity of God and the creatures he had brought into existence.

P.J., PP. 241–42

JOHN PAUL I

John Paul I's pontificate lasted only thirty-three days. He seems to have been stunned by his elevation, bewildered by the variety and complexity of the tasks facing him, shocked by the number of decisions required of him, each day, from rising to repose, and perhaps above all disheartened by being wrenched from familiar faces and surroundings and placed in the splendid and impersonal isolation of the Apostolic Palace. No doubt in time he would have achieved some sort of control over his court and surroundings— after all, he had been a more than adequate Patriarch of Venice, always regarded as a difficult and unmalleable see. As it was, his manifest disorientation seemed to confirm the complacent curialist view that, while pastoral experience might be desirable—was, indeed, very desirable—experience of central government was essential. . . . Was he praying for guidance or relief from his burdens?

P.J., P. 42

His life was Spartan: rising at five, retiring at nine; he ate, as the Romans say, "like a canary." On 5 September he had a shocking experience when the Orthodox Metropolitan Nikodim of Leningrad, paying him a courtesy call, collapsed and died in the papal study. A little over three weeks later, at 5:30 a.m. on Friday, 29 September, the Pope himself was found dead in his chamber, after he had failed to respond to his morning call. The lights were still on. He had evidently been reading Thomas à Kempis's *Imitation of Christ*. Medical examination suggested he had died at about eleven the previous night. The knowledge that the Pope had been dead for many hours before his condition was discovered added a chilling pathos to his distressing end.

P.J., PP. 42–43

JOHN PAUL II

As pope, he has repeatedly referred to Auschwitz as "the Golgotha of the modern world," the stage chosen by history for the representative enactment, in our age, of the Christian drama of suffering and redemption. There, the consequences of enormous sin were made manifest in this world; and there, the human heart was able, from time to time, to raise itself above that scene of unprecedented wickedness, and turn unspeakable horror into spiritual beauty. The analogy of Golgotha applies with equal force and on a larger scale to Poland as a whole, a sacrificial nation whose dolours have been unrivalled in our time.

P.J., P. 4

. . . looking at the life of Karol Wojtyla, Pope John Paul II, it is difficult to dismiss entirely the notion of a providential destiny. . . . [His] childhood and adolescence coincided with the brief, doomed moment of Polish independence: his early manhood with its savage martyrdom under the Nazis; his maturity with the long struggle to breathe under the suppressive tyranny of Soviet-imposed Communism. Nurtured in the very hothouse of suffering, acquainted with grief and forearmed against misfortune, this man born in the eye of the world's storm seemed peculiarly equipped by experience to be summoned to the chair of Peter at a moment of crisis in Roman Catholicism.

P.J., P. 34

John Paul is a priest's pope. Wherever he goes, it is on the serried ranks of the priests who come to greet him that he casts the fondest and most watchful eye. In Paris in 1980 he told young French people in the Parc des Princes: "I've been pope for nearly two years, a bishop for over twenty years, but for me the most important thing is still the fact that I am a priest."

P.J., P. 128

To John Paul a prelate who becomes separated from the duties of the priesthood is a man doomed to progressive spiritual starvation, for the priest is the prime agent of evangelization, and the chief

[178]

minister of the sacraments. John Paul has striven, as pope, to cling to his pastorate, to administer the sacraments as often as possible. That is why he takes so close an interest in his own diocese and its central parishes, in his ancient cathedral of St. John Lateran, and in the inner workings of his pontifical basilica, St. Peter's. From time to time he hears confessions there. Thus, on Good Friday 1981 he replaced, for an hour or two, one of the regular multilingual confessors in St. Peter's, and heard confessions in German, Hungarian, Italian and Spanish.

P.J., P. 130

The new Pope personified the paradoxical vigour of this ebullient Polish religious spirit springing from within the framework of an atheist state. He was a paradox in himself: an intellectual, a poet, a playwright, a professional philosopher trained in the Phenomenologist tradition which sought to Christianize Existentialism; yet also a passionate devotee of the culture of populist Catholicism: shrines, miracles, pilgrimages, saints, the rosary and the Virgin.

M.T., P. 702

The Pope, with all his virtues, . . . has an anti-American streak. He is much concerned in the religious politics of the Near East and listens to prelates from the Arab world who are strongly anti-Israeli. Most important of all, I believe John Paul felt that the Gulf was a needless distraction from events in Eastern Europe, and made it easier for the hard-liners to win back power in Moscow and so make trouble for his beloved Poland and the Catholics of Lithuania. All this is old-style papal *Realpolitik*, strongly reminiscent of Pius XII, who was as ambiguous about Hitler's Germany as John Paul appears to be about Saddam's Iraq.

S., MARCH 16, 1991

I call John Paul's view of man Promethean because he appears to see man as a creature of almost limitless gifts and unimaginable destiny. Now here is the poignancy of the threat which totalitarian atheism poses: for it, too, takes a Promethean view of man but, by depriving man of his true origins and destiny, threatens to turn him into a collective Frankenstein's monster.

P.J., P. 66

JOHN PAUL II (ELECTION OF)

Despite his comparative youth (fifty-eight), he was a very experienced diocesan bishop. No one who had any knowledge of his record could dispute his strength of character, his toughness as a negotiator or his loyalty to Catholicism. . . . In one important respect, however, he had exactly the same appeal as Luciani [John Paul I]: he was known to be a reformer within the Catholic *ethos*.

P.J., P. 45

His orthodoxy on all essentials was established beyond possibility of doubt. To the cardinals, many of them elderly men who had become increasingly alarmed by the drift to anarchy within the church, Wojtyla must have seemed—as the balloting proceeded and they contemplated the possibility of his election—a young and virile champion of the church's true interests, not afraid to welcome and use change, but wedded to that changelessness of the spirit which is the very heart and essence of Catholic traditionalism, and can be summed up in four words: the acceptance of authority. Here was a paladin from the church's far-flung and embattled frontiers, steeled in action, fervent in duty, born to obey but willing to command.

P.J., P. 46

JOHN PAUL II AND FREEDOM

John Paul not only rejects but positively hates determinism. Like all those who have been influenced by existentialism, he is concerned to affirm the reality of human freedom and responsibility against every scientific or philosophical or indeed religious theory (such as Calvinism) which denies them. Yet he agrees with Pascal that human freedom cannot be absolute—it is limited by desire—and therefore there is no necessary conflict between human freedom and divine grace. To Pascal, an "autonomy" which means remoteness from God is not freedom but a form of bondage; and that is a thought constantly in John Paul's sayings.

P.J., PP. 187–88

JOHNSON, LYNDON BAINES

Nor was Johnson a victim of lost illusions alone. He was also . . . a victim of the media, and especially of the East Coast liberals who controlled the most influential newspapers and the big three TV networks. The two points were connected, for one of the deepest illusions of the Sixties was that many forms of traditional authority could be diluted: the authority of America in the world, and of the president within America. Lyndon Johnson, as a powerful and in many ways effective president, stood for the authority principle. That was, for many, a sufficient reason for emasculating him. Another was that he did not share East Coast liberal assumptions, in the way that Roosevelt and Kennedy had done.

M.T., P. 646

JOHNSON, PAUL

. . . I have striven hard not to fall into the trap which sometimes swallows social historians—that is, to leave out chronology and show a world which appears static. I hold strongly that chronology forms the bones of history on which all else is built.

B.M., P. XVIII

I like to think of myself as a fanatic for factual accuracy, but a legion of errors are in print to reproach me. Moreover, despite all my efforts, I remain a poor speller, a characteristic I inherit from my father. My mother, by contrast, never made a spelling mistake in her life, and happily I am married to someone similarly gifted, who goes through everything I write and saves me from much shame.

S., OCTOBER 1, 1981

What worries me most [about spelling mistakes] are proper names. I suffered nightmares when writing my *History of the Jews*, not least because so many modern Jews have surnames of Polish origin, notoriously the most difficult of all to spell. Despite endless checking by many experts, some mistakes survived and I continue to receive reproachful letters from far-flung shores.

S., OCTOBER 1, 1988

I try to cover myself by writing for the long-term: that is, imagining a book which will be still selling in ten years (Cyril Connolly's definition of the crucial span), and with luck in 20. It is also vital nowadays to write for the world market . . . The United States is the biggest of all, for Americans do buy a great many books, and this is the one which most merits careful study and cultivation by authors. But there are important English language markets in such places as Australia, South Africa, Canada, Hong Kong and west and south Asia. The Japanese, German, French and Italian markets are now huge, and there are immense opportunities for Spanish and Portuguese translations. Scandinavia and the Netherlands constitute worthwhile markets too, and unknown opportunities are opening up in Eastern Europe. Such potential armies of readers throughout the world are unlikely to be much interested in books written simply to suit the chattering classes here.

S., DECEMBER 23, 1990

[*Birth of the Modern*] is my 27th (or possibly 28th) book, and a rather sad landmark in my writing life since it will be the last produced by traditional technology. It was written directly onto two Olympia Electronic Compact typewriters, placed side by side or in L-formation. I use one for the text and one for the source-notes, moving between them on a secretary's chair with wheels, so that text and sources are typed at the same time. It always amazes me when experienced writers tell me they compile the source-notes after they have finished the book—an infinite and quite unnecessary added labour, and one certain to produce avoidable errors. Yet I don't remember anyone having advised me to adopt my simultaneous technique. I must have discovered it for myself . . . I suspect most of the secrets of book-writing are thus learned by trial and error.

[182]

Those who claim to teach the craft are, almost by definition, failed writers, with not much of value to impart. Most successful writers cannot talk about their books coherently or are unwilling to divulge what they have acquired the hard way.

s., DECEMBER 23, 1990

I went on to write [A *History of Christianity*] and emerged from that experience with my faith strengthened. I discovered that the calamities of mankind during the Christian centuries occurred not because men and women practiced Christianity but because they failed to do so. Bad as it was *with* religion, mankind would be infinitely worse off without it.

R.D., JUNE 1985

JOKES

. . . what the world really needs is not more equality or social justice or even a good five-cent cigar but new jokes.

s., SEPTEMBER 1, 1984

From the beginning, it has been men who have defined what a joke is and what constitutes a sense of humour. They have always set the agenda and decided which areas are suitable for comedy and which are sacred. It is the commonest of all masculine prejudices that women "have no sense of humour" (i.e., they do not always laugh at jokes tailored for male minds).

s., AUGUST 6, 1988

JOURNALISM

It must never be forgotten that journalism is primarily a commercial activity. It may have an altruistic side, but the chief aim of editors is to raise circulation, the chief aim of managements is to make profits, and the chief aim of individual journalists is to enhance their own professional reputations and so their earning-power. At the same time, a journalist is a citizen first and a professional man second. His primary loyalty must be to the country and the society of which he is part, and so his first duty must be to obey the law and help to enforce it.

s., DECEMBER 19–26, 1987

Good writing and an obsession with politics are, in my view, nearly always mutually exclusive.

s., AUGUST 23, 1986

. . . the Age of Sleaze, which dominated . . . the 1970s and the 1980s, is now on the wane.

s., JANUARY 23, 1988

A serious quality newspaper, which aims to make a contribution to the good government of our country, as opposed merely to selling copies and making money, ought at all times, but particularly during periods of crisis, to try and see government from the inside. In a parliamentary democracy like ours, all governments, whether left or right, are trying to serve the public interest according to their lights, often in the face of difficulties which it is not really in their power to control. Equally, prime ministers are usually doing no more than seeking, sometimes a bit desperately, to keep the coach on the road. They should be judged in that spirit. Words like "lying" and expressions like "saving her own skin," are crude, inaccurate, and childish.

s., NOVEMBER 18, 1989

JOURNALISM AND WORLD WAR II

Fleet Street is particularly fond of articles on the second world war, nearly all of which have an explicit or implicit anti-German flavour. Curiously enough, these papers rarely make any reference to the holocaust of the Jews, the one gigantic episode in Hitler's wicked career which ought to be kept fresh in our minds because of its unique barbarity and because of the lesson it teaches about the irrationality of human beings. But there is no newspaper glamour in that grim record of murder factories.

S., APRIL 27, 1985

JOURNALIST

. . . a journalist cannot divorce himself from history even if he wishes. He cannot prevent the past from intruding. The more he tries to understand the present, the further he is driven to probe into the past, in the search for explanations.

H.E., P. 3

I have no time for workers' control on a newspaper. I cannot imagine any body less competent to select a good editor than its assembled editorial staff. Journalists who as individuals working on their own may be absolutely brilliant seem to take leave of their senses when they come together in collective conclave.

S., DECEMBER 15, 1984

. . . there is one fundamental and insuperable objection to this kind of feature, which marks the real distinction between a reporter and a gossip-columnist. A reporter deals in news; if it is not genuine news, it does not get in the paper. Space in the news pages is always limited, and unless a news story is valid, its chances of reaching print are slim. A gossip column, on the other hand, is a fixed space; it has to be filled every day.

S., APRIL 13, 1985

The trouble with our national newspapers . . . lies in the journalists: in their false values, their lack of education, their appalling disregard for accuracy and their sheep-like propensity to move in flocks instead of thinking for themselves.

S., MAY 11, 1985

Journalists should understand that, in law, they have exactly the same duties and responsibilities as any other citizens. There is no analogy whatever between a journalist and a priest or a doctor or even a lawyer. They cannot plead a relationship of confidentiality, as with a penitent or patient or client. If they know a serious offence has been committed, and they can help in apprehending its perpetrator, they are bound to do so.

s., OCTOBER 19, 1985

. . . a man or a woman, by becoming a journalist, does not . . . cease to be a citizen. He has all the legal and moral responsibilities to obey the law and serve his country which citizenship implies. His calling gives him no exemption from any of them. On the contrary: in so far as his duties cover important aspects of state security and the safety of his fellow-citizens, his citizenship obligations are enhanced, not diminished. The penalties for breaking the law, or evading his responsibilities, ought to be greater, not less, than for any other citizen.

s., MAY 17, 1986

The rest of society must be protected from any abuse of their power; the inequalities of nature and art must be redressed against them.

s., JUNE 28, 1986

Having worked with journalists all my adult life I would hate to live in a country where they were accorded, *de jure* or even *de facto*, privileged status. The doctrine of media triumphalism is, in my view, a much greater practical threat to the liberties of ordinary folk in this country than anything a parliamentary government is likely to cook up.

s., FEBRUARY 14, 1987

. . . journalists are now even more hated than social workers.

s., FEBRUARY 2, 1988

. . . journalists are fundamentally writers. They are bemused by the magic and majesty of words. However dusty and cynical they may be, inside them, struggling to get out, is the deeply chaotic, anarchic, autarchic spirit of the writer, with his passionate individualism, his belief in his own God-given uniqueness. No writer worth tuppence wants to be part of a field-grey army of word-tradesmen, on hourly rates and overtime, however munificent. His ego screams out for individual recognition.

s., JULY 1, 1989

In journalism, above all professions, he who can does; he who cannot teaches. Good political journalists rarely have . . . the skill, to tell others how to do it. . . . A journalist, like an actor, learns chiefly by watching others perform, and from his own mistakes.

s.n., p. 8

He should try to develop a sense of history, and constantly widen his knowledge of the past, particularly of the 19th and early 20th centuries. He should acquire a library of historical works: not the instant books published today, which tell us a great deal about the sex-lives of people, . . . but the solid, multi-volume biographies, which give copious extracts from letters, speeches, debates, and articles: Moneypenny and Buckle on Disraeli, Morley on Gladstone, Gwendolyn Cecil on Salisbury, Churchill on his father, Lord Randolph; there are scores of others . . . the two volumes of Cabinet diaries written by Tom Jones [are] perhaps the most precious glimpse into the mysteries of British government we are ever likely to get. The recent past is a rich repository of truth for the modern political writer.

s.n., p. 14

The trouble is that journalists are often flattered out of their senses by contact with the great. They should develop a proper pride in the profession they represent, and deal with politicians on a basis of friendly and civilized equality. They must seek information, but never cringe for it; if they know their job, the politicians will always be prepared to meet them on fair terms. They should not have favourites or develop personal animosities; in either case the informed public will quickly spot the bias and discount their judgements accordingly.

s.n., p. 15

He must establish himself on easy terms with men and women of all parties. . . . But he must never allow friendship to develop to

[187]

the point at which his views are warped by prejudice or inhibited by the fear of causing offence. Nor should he ever purchase information at the cost of silence.

S.N., P. 15

Above all, they must not fall into the trap of regarding politics as a cynical game, played by people with unworthy motives.

S.N., P. 15

JOURNALIST AND HISTORIAN

They are both in the same business: to communicate an understanding of events to the reader. Both are involved in the discovery and elucidation of truth—that is, the search for the facts which matter, and their arrangement in significant form. No one can possibly say where the historian's work ceases, and the journalist's begins. The present is continuously in process of becoming the past: the frontier of history ends only with yesterday's newspaper. A good journalist casts anxious and inquiring glances over his shoulder, and a good historian lifts his eyes from the page to look at the world around him.

H.E., P. 3

JOURNALIST (POLITICAL)

There are nearly always two points of view, and remember that a good many readers will take the view opposite to ours. The object of a leader is to reinforce the convictions of your friends and, if possible, undermine the convictions of your enemies. Admit to your friends that there is a case to answer; then demolish it. Permit your enemies the luxury of an argument; then show it's unsound.

S.N., P. 10

Political journalism is a splendid career: to describe great events, even to influence them; to inform the millions of the mass-electorate of what is being done in their name, and why; to seek to guide those who have charge of our affairs—what more can a young writer who cares about his fellow-humans ask?

S.N., P. 16

JOURNALIST (WARTIME)

They occupy about the same moral position as arms salesmen and suppliers. That is, they are there for the money. Whatever they may say, newspapers and television networks welcome wars and exploit them. Wars raise circulations and ratings, provided they are covered in an exciting manner. So great sums are spent to provide coverage, and the journalists involved are highly rewarded. . . . If they get good stories (in print or film), that is stories stressing the horror and slaughter and pathos of war, . . . they are praised and promoted and their reputations are enhanced. More journalists have made their name from war coverage than from any other form of professional activity.

S., MARCH 30, 1985

It is a fantasy, entertained by many journalists, that in the event of war they have an automatic God-given right to cover it . . . both in compiling that material and getting it home; to be given military protection and to have their safety guaranteed; and then to pronounce moral judgment on the proceedings. Some journalists seem to think they now have a special extra-territorial (almost extra-terrestrial, you might say) status, akin to diplomats, UN officials or Red Cross representatives, so that they may sit above the battle, like Jove, divinely immune, while hurling editorial thunderbolts where they choose.

S., MARCH 30, 1985

JOURNALISTIC AWARDS

Journalistic awards do more harm than good. In the first place there are far too many of them and the selection often has the unmistakable whiff of Buggins's Turn. Then again these are the kind of accolades the Left is extremely adept at manipulating, taking over the selection committees, infiltrating the secretarial staff. Key prizes often go not to good journalists but to political propagandists.

s., july 20, 1991

Judaism

Judaism is a perfectionist religion. It contains the strength of its weaknesses. It assumes that those who practise it are an elite since it seeks to create a model society. That made it in many ways an ideal religion for a new state like Israel, despite the fact that its law was in process of being formed about 3,200 years before the state was founded.

h.j., p. 553

K

KENNEDY, JOHN F.

His career shows that one of the most dangerous kinds of politician is a man who is good at public relations and nothing else. In the end, all the Kennedy presidency consisted of was the myth of Camelot, and that was essentially Jackie's—not Jack's—creation. She even gave it the name.

A.S., SEPTEMBER 1991

Immediately after the 1960 presidential election, a victorious John F. Kennedy contemptuously summed up . . . : Nixon, he said, "went out like he came in—no class." To a European, this comment, coming from the son of a man who was little better than a financial gangster, is full of ironies. Visiting Washington as British Prime Minister shortly after Kennedy was elected, Harold Macmillan commented: "It's rather like watching the Borgia brothers take over a respectable North Italian town." As times goes by, and the sins of the Kennedys multiply with the generations, the comparison seems ever more apt.

C., OCTOBER 1988

To some extent, Jack's sexual antics and his Mafia links made him the prisoner of J. Edgar Hoover. It is impossible not to conclude from [Thomas C.] Reeves's account [in *A Question of Character*] that Jack's presidency might well have ended in a grave public scandal rather than assassination, and that his deteriorating health and growing drug dependence could have ruled out a second term.

A.S., SEPTEMBER 1991

KENNEDY, JOSEPH P.

He set up trust funds of $10 million apiece for his children and squirreled away vast sums for a variety of other purposes, chiefly for buying people, whether politicians, newspaper publishers, or cardinals. His range of contacts and collaborators was enormous, and included the mob leader Frank Costello and Meyer Lansky's lieutenant Doc Stacher. One can't help feeling that old Joe was actually a more interesting personality than his son—certainly a more powerful one—and one would welcome a full exploration of his business career and a detailed account of exactly what happened to his money, during his lifetime and since.

A.S., SEPTEMBER 1991

KENNEDY ONASSIS, JACQUELINE

. . . [Jack] had gone through the motions at Choate, Princeton, and Harvard, but was basically uneducated and a thorough philistine; she was a culture snob with, on the whole, excellent taste. While he was rich, she was penniless, and, once married, she went on regular spending orgies, which of course continued after she became Mrs. Onassis. In acquiring clothes and shoes she was almost in the Imelda Marcos league.

A.S., SEPTEMBER 1991

KEYNES, JOHN MAYNARD

It is important to get clear that Keynes was never a socialist. . . . At heart he believed in liberal capitalism not only because he thought it more likely to produce the goods than any other imaginable system, but for moral reasons: he thought the destruction of economic freedom must, in practice, lead to a progressive diminution of political freedom.

E.S., PP. 79–80

Keynes was an empiricist and an original who had no attachment
to theory—hated theory in fact. His method was to look at new
facts squarely, and then seek to explain them, and devise methods
to cope with them. The only trouble with Keynesianism in the later
1970s was that Keynes was dead, and so unable to bring his uniquely
creative mind to bear on its problems.

E.S., P. 86

KHOMEINI REGIME

The Khomeini regime could . . . inspire fear but it could not make
friends in any quarter. The only merit of its isolation was that it
ended the Shah's social engineering. . . . [Nevertheless, it] brought
the modern sector of the Iranian economy to a juddering halt . . .
The inevitable consequences followed: unemployment, breakdown
of health and other basic services, mass epidemics, malnutrition and
even starvation. Iran's horrifying experiences illustrated yet again
the law of unintended effect. The Shah's state road to Utopia led
only to Golgotha.

M.T., P. 717

"KITCHEN CABINET"

When the Americans set up their own government, they adopted
the cabinet from Britain, though in strict constitutional terms they
gave the Institution little status. . . . Jackson, however, was the
first president to be elected by an overwhelming popular vote and
this fact, in a sense, gave him an unprecedented mandate to exercise
the truly awesome powers which the U.S. Constitution confers on
its chief executive. From the outset of his tenure, an informal group
of cronies had begun to confer with him in the White House.

B.M., P. 946

KITCHENER, FIELD MARSHAL HERBERT

He was a trophy-hunter, with the instincts of a looter; even imperialist Britain could not always approve of his treatment of prisoners. But he was efficient, an imperial engineer. His campaigns were exercises not in strategy, or valour, but in logistics, skilfully and systematically, and above all remorselessly, employing the railway and the steam-boat and the electric telegraph to effect the concentration of fire-power which ensured automatic success against barbarous armies. Moreover, Kitchener was cheap. His wars were based on principles of (to use a later term) cost-effectiveness. He "costed" them in advance, and conducted operations within the strict framework of Treasury control.

H.E., P. 348

L

LABOUR PARTY

Labour has lost its secure anchorage in the wealth-creating sector of the nation and is drifting to sea in a swell of sterility.

R.F., P. 72

Labour today is so deeply anti-creative, so organically and instinctually lacking in any positive impulses, that it actually likes banning things or people, for its own sake. Its motto is: accentuate the negative. To ban, to boycott, to embargo, to exclude, blacklist, close down, shut up, silence, censure—these are the things which now come naturally to it, perhaps the only things it really knows how to do.

S., NOVEMBER 14, 1986

In the old days, the wiseacres of the Communist Party used to claim that, within three months of their putting forward a new policy, it was sure to be taken up at the Labour Party conference. The CP having been subsumed, it is now only a month or two between Labour adopting a line and top clerics parroting it.

S., NOVEMBER 23, 1991

LANGUAGE

It is both a consequence, and a guarantee, of the innate freedom conferred on man by mind. So long as we have language, we cannot be wholly enslaved, or wholly uncivilized. Equally, one of the factors

[195]

which nourishes our freedom and our civilization is the degree to which we cherish our linguistic skills, and relate them to truth and imagination. For language is the framework of reason; unless it is ordered and related to truth, reason cannot express itself.

E.S., P. 116

A man who deliberately inflicts violence on the language will almost certainly inflict violence on human beings if he acquires the power. Those who treasure the meaning of words will treasure truth, and those who bend words to their purposes are very likely in pursuit of anti-social ones.

E.S., P. 259

LATIN

By the eighth century, nobody learned Latin as his vernacular language; but no learned, devotional or liturgical work was written in any other. Latin became the clerical language. Thus proof of ability to speak or write it became the usual test of a claim to clerical status (and privilege). It became the mark of civilization, and so the badge of arrogance.

H.C., P. 203

THE LATIN CHURCH

. . . the Church acted as a "carrier" of civilization rather as, in its formative period, the Hellenistic religious-culture machine had "carried" Christian Judaism into a Roman, universalist context. The great merit of the Latin Church—the chief reason for its success— was that it was not anchored in any particular racial, geographical, social or political context. It bore the marks of its development but it was still genuinely universalist, the church of St. Paul: "all things to all men."

H.C., P. 127

[196]

LAW, ENGLISH COMMON

The only form of progression is to move backwards into the past—
but a past so imaginatively reconstructed that, in reality, it contains
the necessary elements of novelty. This is the essential principle
behind the development of English law, indeed of English constitutional history as a whole. The present is reformed by rewriting
the past in such a way that it becomes the future.

H.E., P. 84

LAW AND GOD

The phrase "a society under God and law" is appropriate because
Parliament is not the primeval legislature. It does not, and cannot,
create law from nothing. Rather it inherits, and interprets, a system
of moralistic law, much of which is enshrined in the organic corpus
of Common Law. Hence we might define the function of Parliament
as making the necessary adjustments between the system of fundamental law and the changing needs of society. Its primary function
is therefore as a revising body: it is a law-making body only in a
secondary sense. It cannot make fundamental law. It cannot make
marriage a crime, murder a duty, or falsehood meritorious.

R.F., P. 179

LAW VERSUS MORALS

The disintegration of doctrine has, inevitably, been followed by a
clouding of the moral vision. In the early sixties, it was argued, by
those who wished to disembarrass the criminal law of its less tenable
moral assumptions, that it was possible to make an absolutely clear
distinction between what was "legally wrong" and "morally wrong."
Thus, homosexual behaviour between consenting adults, to cite a
typical example, was considered inappropriate for legal prohibition.
But we were told that reforming the law would in no way legitimise
the sin.

R.F., P. 149

[197]

Law, Rule of

One thing we have learnt in this terrible century of ours is that the rule of law, with its notion of inalienable right, is a far more valuable safeguard to the individual than the delusory "one-man-one-vote."

R.F., PP. 183–84

Free institutions will only survive where there is the rule of law. This is an absolute on which there can be no compromise: the subjection of everyone and everything to the final arbitration of the law is more fundamental to human freedom and happiness than democracy itself. Most of the post-war democratic creations have foundered because the rule of law was broken and governments placed themselves above the courts. Once the law is humbled, all else that is valuable in a civilized society will vanish, usually with terrifying speed. On the other hand, provided the rule of law is maintained intact, the evil forces in society, however powerful, will be brought to book in the end—as witness the downfall of the Nixon administration.

E.S., PP. 256–57

. . . the rule of law is essential, not merely to preserve liberty, but to increase wealth. A law which is supreme, impartial and accessible to all is the only guarantee that property, corporate or personal, will be safe; and therefore a necessary incentive to saving and investment.

E.S., P. 257

League of Nations

The League, indeed, was the way out of the dilemma which the war posed for Christians. Christianity had been powerless to stop the war, or to shorten it, or to mitigate the "frightfulness," or to prevent both sides—with scarcely a dissenting clerical voice—from invoking the aid of the same God. But at least Christianity could be identified with the peace-solution. . . . The righteous Wilson wanted the League; and official religious opinion in America was overwhelmingly in favour of American participation. It greeted the Senate rejection with dismay, but was unable to reverse it. Thus Christian impotence in war was confirmed by Christian impotence in peace.

H.C., P. 479

The handling of the Abyssinian crisis, in which Britain was effectively in charge, is a striking example of how to get the worst of all possible worlds. Abyssinia was a primitive African monarchy which practised slavery; not a modern state at all. It should not have been in the League. The notion that the League had to guarantee its frontiers was an excellent illustration of the absurdity of the convenant which led Senator Lodge and his friends to reject it. The League should have been scrapped after the 1931 Manchurian fiasco.

M.T., P. 320

THE LEFT

What should distinguish the Left is an all-embracing humanism, which places the highest possible value on life and identifies itself with those societies striving to preserve and enrich it. The Left abandoned its principles in the 1930s by deliberately ignoring or discounting the Stalinist terror, and by defending the debased form of government which made it possible. Now it is committing a new form of the same treason by endorsing indiscriminate violence as the prime weapon of political action. Let us not mince our words about this. There is now a growing number of people on the Left, in this and other advanced countries, who deliberately associate themselves with international terrorist groups, with conferences held to promote the aims of terrorism, with the supply and manufacture of explosives, and, above all, with the ideology of violence. These people claim the name of socialist, though it is characteristic of them that they regard with peculiar detestation the world's most advanced social democracy, Israel. And among their heroes is Gaddafi of Libya, whose passion for violence is such that he favours the IRA and the UDA with almost equal approval.

R.F., P. 194

[199]

. . . there is a distinctive section of the educated middle class who seem to enjoy the contemplation of misery, and these people tend to write left-wing journals and dominate the thinking echelons of the Labour movement. There is a reason for their pessimism, which almost verges on the masochistic. Early socialists did not forbear to dwell on life's horrors or abuse villains. . . . But they were uplifted by tremendous hopes of ideal societies just round the corner. . . . All that has now vanished with the discrediting alike of Soviet and Chinese communism on the one hand and of social democratic nationalisation on the other. So all that remains is the discontent with existing society, which has filled the vacuum left by the collapse of idealistic solutions and now dominates the minds of the middle-class Left almost to the exclusion of anything else. They have developed a positive taste for misery-mongering and expect the rest of us to share it. We decline to do so, and that is why both their journals and their political campaigns fail.

s., JULY 4, 1987

. . . capitalism, pronounced dying in the Seventies, is in boisterous health. The British intellectual Left, in particular, have found the times almost unbearable, Thatcherism riding high, Labour unelectable, the workers devoting themselves to getting and spending. With nothing to believe in and no socialist utopia to look forward to, no wonder the cerebral Left or what little remains of it is engaged in myth-making.

s., FEBRUARY 4, 1989

THE LEFT AND NEWSPEAK

The Left is very clever at relabelling to produce an inversion of reality, as their categorisation of fascism shows (and look at what they did to "democratic"). In the West it is now recognised, even among the socialist intelligentsia, that Soviet Russia is a failure, and they want to distance themselves from it. What easier way to do it than by labelling those identified with the failure as "conservatives" and "the Right"? In the same way, Pol Pot, once hailed

[200]

by Leftists in the West as the ultimate Marxist social engineer, has been subtly reclassified as a fascist operated by the CIA.

S., OCTOBER 7, 1989

LENIN, VLADIMIR ILICH

[Lenin] systematically constructed, in all its essentials, the most carefully engineered apparatus of state tyranny the world has yet seen. In the old world, personal autocracies, except perhaps for brief periods, had been limited, or at least qualified, by other forces in society: a church, an aristocracy, an urban bourgeoisie, ancient charters and courts and assemblies. And there was, too, the notion of an external, restraining force, in the idea of a Deity, or Natural Law, or some absolute system of morality. Lenin's new despotic utopia had no such counterweights or inhibitions. . . . All rights whatsoever were vested in the state. And, within that state, enormous and ever-growing as it was, every single filament of power could be traced back to the hands of a minute group of men—ultimately to one man.

M.T., P. 48

Lenin hated the essence of democracy; and he regarded its forms merely as a means to legitimize violence and oppression.

M.T., P. 48

He saw the people with whom he dealt, his comrades, not as individuals but as receptacles for his ideas. On that basis, and on no other, they were judged. So he had no hierarchy of friendships; no friendships in fact, merely ideological alliances. He judged men not by their moral qualities but by their views, or rather the degree to which they accepted his. He bore no grudges. A man like Trotsky, whom he fought bitterly in the years before the Great War, and with whom he exchanged the vilest insults, was welcomed back with bland cordiality once he accepted Lenin's viewpoint. Equally, no colleague, however close, could bank the smallest capital in Lenin's heart.

M.T., P. 51

[201]

No man personifies better the replacement of the religious impulse by the will to power. In an earlier age he would surely have been a religious leader. With his extraordinary passion for force, he might have figured in Mohammed's legions. He was even closer perhaps to Jean Calvin, with his belief in organizational structure, his ability to create one and then dominate it utterly, his puritanism, his passionate self-righteousness, and above all his intolerance.

M.T., P. 51

Just as the warring theologians felt they were dealing with issues which, however trivial they might seem to the uninitiated, would in fact determine whether or not countless millions of souls burned in Hell for all eternity, so Lenin knew that the great watershed of civilization was near, in which the future fate of mankind would be decided by History, with himself as its prophet. It would be worth a bit of blood; indeed a lot of blood.

M.T., P. 54

. . . for all his proclaimed orthodoxy, Lenin was very far from being an orthodox Marxist. Indeed in essentials he was not a Marxist at all . . . he exploited the Dialectic to justify conclusions he had already reached by intuition. But he completely ignored the very core of Marx's ideology, the historical determinism of the revolution. Lenin was not at heart a determinist but a voluntarist: the decisive role was played by human will: his. Indeed, for a man who claimed a special "scientific" knowledge of how the laws of History worked, he seems to have been invariably surprised by the actual turn of events.

M.T., P. 54

What made Lenin a great actor on the stage of history was not his understanding of its processes but the quickness and energy with which he took the unexpected chances it offered. He was, in short, what he accused all his opponents of being: an opportunist.

M.T., P. 54

Lenin scorned the antithesis between the individual and the state as the heresy of the class society. In a classless society, the individual

[202]

was the state, so how could they be in conflict, unless of course the individual were a state enemy? Hence there was no such thing as equality of rights; or one man, one vote.

M.T., P. 78

In all his remarks on economic matters once he achieved power, the phrase which occurs most frequently is "strict accounting and control." To him, statistics were the evidence of success. So the new ministries, and the new state-owned factories, produced statistics in enormous quantities. The output of statistics became, and remains to this day, one of the most impressive characteristics of Soviet industry. But the output of goods was another matter.

M.T., P. 89

LENIN AND BENITO MUSSOLINI

As Marxist heretics and violent revolutionary activists, Lenin and Mussolini had six salient features in common. Both were totally opposed to bourgeois parliaments and any type of "reformism." Both saw the party as a highly centralized, strictly hierarchical and ferociously disciplined agency for furthering socialist objectives. Both wanted a leadership of professional revolutionaries. Neither had any confidence in the capacity of the proletariat to organize itself. Both thought revolutionary consciousness could be brought to the masses from without by a revolutionary, self-appointed élite. Finally, both believed that, in the coming struggle between the classes, organized violence would be the final arbiter.

M.T., P. 58

LENIN AND RELIGION

Lenin took religion much more seriously than Marx. It was a gigantic conspiracy. Religious motives were behind virtually every philosophical opinion. . . . In his view, the purer and more disinterested religious faith and observance are, the more dangerous they become. Since those who are saintly and selfless have more influence than the immoral and egotistical, clerics who make common cause with the proletariat against the capitalists are much more dangerous than those who defend exploitation.

P.J., P. 68

LENIN TERROR

. . . the most disturbing and, from the historical point of view, important characteristic of the Lenin terror was not the quantity of the victims but the principle on which they were selected. Within a few months of seizing power, Lenin had abandoned the notion of individual guilt, and with it the whole Judeo-Christian ethic of personal responsibility. He was ceasing to be interested in *what* a man did or had done—let alone *why* he had done it—and was first encouraging, then commanding, his repressive apparatus to hunt down people, and destroy them, not on the basis of crimes, real or imaginary, but on the basis of generalizations, hearsay, rumours.

M.T., P. 70

LENINISM AND FASCISM

Leninism was not only a heresy; it was exactly the same heresy which created fascism. . . . In 1903, the year after Lenin first used the term "vanguard fighters," Roberto Michaels, in his introduction to the Italian translation of Sorel's *Saggi di critica del Marxismo*, urged the creation of a "revolutionary élite" to push forward the proletarian socialist millennium. . . . These ideas were taken up by . . . Italian Marxist Benito Mussolini, [who] was much more broadly read than Lenin, . . . [and whose] political formation was fundamentally Marxist.

M.T., PP. 56–57

LIBEL

Words are very potent things. They can cause as much if not more pain than physical blows. Their effects can be more lasting than physical injury. Their destructive power, whether measured in financial, psychological or social tems, can be devastating. Abuse of the published word can be almost the precise equivalent of a physical assault or a financial fraud.

S., JUNE 28, 1986

Newspapers . . . are wrong to regard an apology as a defeat. . . . Unwise and even reckless remarks are allowed to slip into print occasionally. A paper's primary concern should be to publish the truth. A willingness to correct error, promptly, gracefully and in full ought to be part of this concern. The public is much more likely to trust a paper which voluntarily makes amends for its mistakes than one which tries to present a brazen front of infallibility.

S., JUNE 28, 1986

It is probably right that the libel law should err on the side of strictness. If outraged, inarticulate men feel they cannot get redress in the courts, they will be tempted to resort to force. It is better that editors and writers should be sued than assaulted, horsewhipped, challenged to duels or simply murdered.

S., JUNE 28, 1986

. . . there is a *lacuna* in our system of legal remedies against the outrageous use of words. Parliament has already shown that, in extreme cases, it is prepared to provide against those who use words to hurt racial sensibilities. It should now consider, as it is already considering in the case of the right of reply and privacy-invasion, whether the law should specifically deal with other kinds of verbal abuse, including the abuse of religious sentiment. This is tricky territory, since it is guarded by one of the great irrational dogmas of our times, the Divine Right of Writers, itself an aspect of Media Triumphalism.

S., MARCH 4, 1989

LIBERAL

The person who is in the weakest moral position to attack the state is he who has largely ignored its potential for evil while strongly backing its expansion on humanitarian grounds and is only stirred to protest when he falls foul of it through his own negligence.

I., P. 267

LIBERAL EMPIRICISM

For the English, and ultimately, I believe, for the world, there is no alternative to liberal empiricism. There is no cause for despair, and no case for desperate remedies. There is nothing that is wrong in English society, or in world society, that cannot be adjusted for the better, provided we keep our heads and exercise our reason. Everything worthwhile the English have achieved, for themselves and others, has been built upon the great tripod of the liberal ethic: the rejection of violence, the reaching of public decisions through free argument and voluntary compromise, and the slow evolution of moral principles tested by experience and stamped with the consensus. All English history teaches that these are the only methods which, in the end, produce constructive and permanent results.

H.E., PP. 421–22

LIBERAL FASCISM

It is constituted not so much by liberals themselves as by the well-organised and increasingly aggressive pressure groups liberal triumphalism has spawned. Its two most dangerous manifestations . . . are the race relations industry and the homosexual lobby, though there is a growing number of other objectionable groups, such as the animal rights campaigners [or the eco-lobby]. What worries me is not so much the demands of these liberal fascists as the willingness of the rich and powerful, both people and institutions, to bow to them. There is the stench of cowardice in the air, as in the original fascist heyday of the Thirties.

S., MAY 5, 1990

LIBERALISM

Whereas capitalism, judged by its historical performance over two centuries, is a self-correcting system, being a form of economic activity which tends to occur at a certain stage in human development unless you do something specific to stop it, liberalism is an intellectual concept which to some extent has to be imposed on societies by its better-educated elites: no large democracy, for instance, has ever abolished capital punishment by referendum. That, of course, is why liberalism tends to be self-defeating—because it often runs across the grain of popular sentiment, based on harsh experience.

C., MARCH 1992

The disenchantment with liberalism springs not so much from its premises as from its performance. The theoretical assault on its aims and methods is little more than an angry attempt to rationalise the disappointment, even disgust, which radicals rightly feel at its failure to maintain, let alone increase, the pace of reform. All societies are mobile, in the sense that they have an inherent tendency to produce inequalities and social injustice unless political correctives are constantly applied: thus action is required merely to counter the vicious thrust of uncontrolled human greed and ambition. Liberalism must move even to keep society from receding into the darkness.

H.E., P. 422

. . . liberalism has a streak of masochism, verging at times on self-destruction. The terrorists know it, and exploit it ruthlessly. . . . by a grim paradox, their most effective weapons are not their own bullets and explosives but our liberal virtues which they plan to destroy: our fair-mindedness, our willingness to see both sides of an argument, . . . our reluctance to take life or exert strong authority, especially force in any form, our pity for the underdog, real or imaginary, and, not least, our desire for a quiet life at almost any price, which at times verges on cowardice.

S., APRIL 26, 1986

LIBERATED

How has the human race contrived to create such hells at the end of the twentieth century? Nearly all of them are in areas formerly controlled by the European colonial powers, and hastily "liberated" in response to liberal opinion.

A.S., OCTOBER 1990

LIDDY, G. GORDON

. . . for a first offense, taking part in a burglary in which nothing was stolen, no one hurt, and no resistance offered to police, G. Gordon Liddy was sentenced to twenty years in jail, of which he served nearly five before President Carter took pity on him. His real crime was not burglary at all but his refusal to participate in the campaign of judicial terrorism then being waged by Judge John Sirica.

C., MARCH 1989

LIVERPOOL

. . . Liverpool is a pretty lawless city, yet it has been the object of more social and political activism, and subsidies and subventions and theorising and, above all, planning, than almost any other city in the kingdom. Like Glasgow—its chief rival for violence—it has been practically planned to death. Yet curiously enough, it is not dead. It is a living city, and in some respects a majestic and noble one; and what continue to make it majestic and noble are precisely those elements which fall outside the sphere of collectivised planning and political activism.

R.F., P. 97

LLOYD GEORGE, DAVID

It is impossible to analyze his political philosophy because any theory built up on his words and actions is invalidated by episodes in his life which cannot be reconciled to the theme. A Welsh democrat; a Liberal; a non-party radical; an anti-party man of the Centre; a natural progressive corrupted by power and money; a pure opportunist from start to finish; a simple patriot . . .

S.N., P. 209

No political talent in British history has been so prodigally squandered by a blind and unimaginative nation.

S.N., P. 215

LOUIS XIV

Louis XIV . . . was a man exercising power, in all its plenitude, from early manhood to decrepit age; and dispensing not merely the effective, closet-power of a Richelieu or a Mazarin, but in addition the public and ceremonial power of a demi-god, his days passed in stupefying and chiliastic ritual, most of it designed and ordered by himself. So Louis was engulfed by absolutism, which numbs the mind and deadens the moral sense, but also suffered, to an exquisite degree, from that occupational disease of monarchy, selfishness— even those he most respected or feared, such as Madame de Maintenon, testified to his habitual disregard to the sufferings of others.

P.P.J., P. 236

LUTHER, MARTIN

. . . "the just shall live by faith." To Luther this was the whole answer to the superstructure of sacramental and mechanical Christianity which the Church had erected. The scriptures said plainly that man was saved by faith, not by good works—the fact that he

[209]

performed good works was merely an outward confirmation of his consciousness of being saved.

H.C., P. 281

Luther, as a heresiarch, had begun by pleading for tolerance, for (this was a new expression) "freedom of conscience." This early moderation did not survive Luther's increasing dependence on the princes. Once his teaching became established as a state religion, all other forms of Christianity had to be eliminated, at least in their open expression. By 1525, he had forbidden the mass, "that this blasphemy may be suppressed by the proper authority," and this ban was soon extended to other forms of Protestantism . . . Two years later he agreed that anabaptists and other Protestant extremists "should be done to death by the civil authority."

H.C., PP. 288–89

LUXEMBURG, ROSA

Rosa Luxemburg's moral and emotional distortions were characteristic of an intellectual trying to force people into a structure of ideas, rather than allowing ideas to evolve from the way people actually behaved.

H.J., P. 449

M

MAN

Man owes his humanity to the notion of God, and if this notion disappears from his thoughts and his vocabulary, the humanity would disappear too.

P.J., P. 108

Man is the most insatiably active animal in creation. He is compelled not only to do things but to be constantly seeking to do new things. That means he is also freedom-loving, impatient of any restraint. None of this is to say that he favours anarchy: on the contrary, it is his nature to abhor chaos. He has a passion for order, an instinct for regularity and an inveterate habit of devising rules. His zeal for action and innovation is competitive; competition implies comparisons, and so judgments under authority. As Thomas Hobbes pointed out, life in society can be compared to a race, and a race must be regulated to retain its zest. But, he added, the race of humanity has no finish: the excitement and point of life is to be in it, and happiness consists in being in front: . . . "there can be no contentment but in proceeding." To proceed, we must be free; and since the race is unending, the whole of human history is the pursuit of freedom.

R.F., P. 1

Man, as history shows only too clearly, has that element of the divine in him, the element which causes him ceaselessly to strive for the ideal. It is his glory and his ruin. For in his Utopian quest he embraces the political process as the road to perfection. But this

[211]

political process itself is a delusion, more likely to lead to hell than
to heaven. If a society is unlucky, the political road, pursued relentlessly enough, will carry it straight into Auschwitz or the Gulag
. . . But even the most fortunate society will find nothing at the
end of that dusty track but the same man-made monster—the
state—as greedy and unfeeling as it was when man invented it in
the third millennium B.C. . . .

R.F., P. 3

Man is a creature of infinite variety who seeks and finds felicity—
in so far as he finds it at all—through a boundless plurality of forms.
Where the state is limited by law and custom, these forms flourish
and proliferate. Where the state is ubiquitous and unconfined it
presents an irresistible temptation to the monist simplifiers and their
fanatical adherents, a huge machine for the imposition of their
solutions, if necessary—and in the end, of course, they always judge
it necessary—through aeons of misery and oceans of blood.

R.F., P. 5

MAN (CRITICAL)

The great power of Critical Man is not that he can avoid error but
that he can turn it from disaster to advantage. He does not stand
or fall by his theories because in a sense he has none, merely working
hypotheses.

E.S., P. 8

MAN (WORKING)

Since the earliest times, he had rarely been fully free in an economic
sense. He had been classified and bound, not by his ability and his
willingness to work, but by his status. In the declining Roman
Empire, he had been herded into state-defined corporations, which
compelled him to exercise a certain trade, and no other, during his
lifetime; and later, the idea of the corporation was extended, to
cover his children and grandchildren, so that status and trade became

not merely compulsory, but hereditary. It was on this basis that the serfdom and rigid categories of the feudal society evolved; and when, after centuries, the feudal ties were loosened, they were replaced by the guild system, which again rigidly defined and controlled occupational status, prevented freedom of movement, especially upward progression, and was backed up by government legislation—known in England as the Laws of Settlement—whose object was to petrify the existing mould of society.

R.F., P. 35

MAN AND LANGUAGE

Man was a social being long before he became human. What marked the dividing point was the creation and use of language. It seems very probable that it was the development of language which lay behind the intellectual discoveries of the Neolithic Age. For the next great leap forward man had to wait not so much for literacy itself but for its extension beyond its original hieratic limits. Once a society has a middle class freed from agricultural shackles and equipped with a script it understands, it is poised for cultural adventure.

E.S., P. 7

MANKIND

Certainly, mankind without Christianity conjures up a dismal prospect. The record of mankind *with* Christianity is daunting enough . . . The dynamism it has unleashed has brought massacre and torture, intolerance and destructive pride on a huge scale, for there is a cruel and pitiless nature in man which is sometimes impervious to Christian restraints and encouragements. But without these restraints, bereft of these encouragements, how much more horrific the history of the last 2,000 years must have been!

H.C., P. 517

Mankind and Totalitarianism

The history of mankind can be seen as a series of attempts to impose a moral order on our somewhat chaotic natures. In a sense this is not only right but admirable; the search for moral order is of the very essence of civilisation, even more crucial to its emergence than the building of cities. The mistake we constantly make is to construct a moral order which is far too detailed—and so open up for ourselves the savage pit of ideological conflict, into which we repeatedly tumble.

R.F., P. 80

Mao Tse-Tung

He was not a millenarian, religious-type revolutionary like Lenin, but a fierce and passionate romantic, with a taste for crude and violent drama; an artist of sorts, cast from the same mould as Hitler, and equally impatient. Like Hitler, he was first and foremost a nationalist, who trusted in the national culture. From the philosopher Yen Fu he derived the idea that "culturalism," the pursuit of "the Chinese Way," was the means to mobilize her people into an irresistible force. He read and used Marxism-Leninism, but his fundamental belief was closer to the axiom of his ethics teacher . . . Yang Chang-chi. . . . "Each country has its own national spirit just as each person has his own personality . . . if you take it apart it dies."

M.T., P. 197

While he used the Marxist formulations, and indeed considered himself a great Marxist thinker, much superior to Stalin's contemptible successors, he never in practice attempted to apply objective Marxist analysis. He did not believe in "objective situations" at all. . . . He seems to have believed all his life that the true dynamic of history was not so much the maturation of classes (that

[214]

might be the outward expression) as heroic determination. He saw himself as the Nietzschean superman made flesh.

M.T., P. 546

In his artistic longings, in his romanticism and in his belief that will is the key not only to power but to accomplishment, Mao was an oriental Hitler. . . . The most important respect in which Mao recalled Hitler was in his imminent eschatology. Mao was, above all, a violently impatient man. He lacked the unhurried stoicism with which Stalin remorselessly pursued his objectives and his hatreds. Mao, like Hitler, wanted to speed up history. He thought his successors would prove poltroons and faint-hearts and that unless things were done in his own lifetime, they would not be done at all.

M.T., PP. 546–47

Like Hitler, Mao loved politics as theatre. . . . Mao never made the transition from revolution to administration. He lacked Stalin's bureaucratic appetite. For him, history was a cosmic play, a succession of spectacular episodes, in which he was actor, impresario and spectator. No sooner had the curtain come crashing down on one scene—"the Long March," say, or "the Fall of the KMT"—than he clamoured for it to rise again. . . .

M.T., PP. 546–48

. . . Mao's reign was . . . always, in the deepest sense, a tragedy: for what he caused to be enacted was not theatre but a gigantic series of experiments on hundreds of millions of real, living, suffering people. [The early 1950 land reform] would mean executions of 22,500 a month, a high rate even by Stalin's worst standards . . . The total number of killed during this first post-war drama of Mao's may have been as high as 15 million. . . . This gigantic piece of social engineering was also accompanied by Mao's first shot at mental engineering, or brainwashing, which he termed "thought reform." It was designed to replace traditional family piety with

filial piety to the state as the central moral value of the nation and
to elevate Mao into a substitute father-figure.

M.T., P. 548

MADISON, JAMES

Madison, like Jefferson, could not emancipate himself. In 1834,
aged 83, he sold 16 able-bodied slaves to a kinsman for $6,000,
they giving "their glad consent" because of "their horror of going
to Liberia"—so much for the African solution. Despite his many
promises to free his slaves, the will he drew up the next year did
not set them free; to do so would have impoverished his widow.
Thus another well-meaning man went to his grave with a guilty
conscience.

B.M., P. 305

MAGNA CARTA

It is a document without a unifying viewpoint. Nor is this surprising, granted the circumstances of its creation. The parties involved were too numerous, the physical forces behind them too
evenly balanced, to produce any other result. [The barons] sucessfully
. . . inserted a "security clause," appointing a committee of 25
barons as watchdog on the King's behaviour. The Church got in a
clause about its own rights. . . . Virtually all the parties were in
debt, so three clauses were accordingly inserted, the onus of which
fell largely on the Jews. The drafting of the treaty . . . was in the
hands of the . . . Chancery clerks. . . . So many clauses were inserted
to suit the convenience of bureaucracy. . . . Some radical fellow
even succeeded in putting in a bit to protect the rights of villeins.
During these five days of argument and re-drafting, the charter grew
and grew. It became enormous, in its totality quite beyond the
comprehension of any one of the parties.

H.E., P. 121

To appeal to Magna Carta became the one, great, unanswerable argument which any and every section of society could employ. Within a generation its provisions became largely incomprehensible—some of them remain enigmas even today—but it was none the less the written embodiment of the golden English past, a massive monument of constitutional rectitude. For the first time it made politics respectable, because it made them old. So the English came to see compromise, consultation, the settlement of dispute by argument as opposed to force as their outstanding national characteristics; and in time shaped their habits to conform with this image. The history of Magna Carta is a triumph of English hypocrisy—always one of our most useful assets.

H.E., P. 122

MARCUSE, HERBERT

Being a pseudo-scientist, a myth-maker, he uses language like a witch doctor or high priest, as a magical incantation. He is not interested in the objective facts, as he is putting forward a conspiracy theory, into which all human phenomena must be squeezed; but, of course, once the essential suspension of rational disbelief has been achieved, all conspiracy theories work, all the time, and in all circumstances. . . . One mark of the pseudo-scientist is his imprisonment in his time: Marcuse's writing is essentially the product of the culmination of the long post-war boom in the 1960s; by the later 1970s, events had conspired to make his assumptions seem remarkably dated.

E.S., P. 156

MARRIAGE

The modern Western concept of the binding bourgeois marriage and the legitimate offspring is a very valuable piece of social furniture, which it took a long time to fashion. Such a concept is the mark of an advanced civilization. Legal confusion over the form of marriage, and varieties of marriage, is the mark of a primitive or immature society, just as the absence of marriage is the mark of a savage society—indeed of an existence which can scarcely be called a society at all. The stable monogamous marriage is one of the most fundamentally creative inventions of Judeo-Christian civilization.

P.P.J., P. 138

. . . the rise of the West is due in great part to its ability to define the law with certitude, and to uphold it against all-comers—for legal certainty is the basis of investment and capital formation. At the heart of any stable law of property is a clear and universal legal doctrine of marriage, legitimacy and inheritance. The clarification of marriage law in the sixteenth century, and the consequential elucidation of the law of inheritance which followed in the seventeenth century, leading in turn to vital developments in the law of entails and patents, created the stable, sure and enlightened legal structure on which the Industrial Revolution was based, and without which it could not have taken place. It was the monogamous bourgeois family structure, centred upon a clear definition of marriage, which provided the social framework within which the capitalist lift-off was achieved, and the rapid ascent to late-twentieth-century living standards was made possible.

P.P.J., P. 139

MARRIAGE AND LAW

If marriage as a legal contract conveys no more privileges, and imposes no more duties, than concubinage—or any other social and sexual arrangement which human ingenuity may devise, from homosexual unions to polygamy and sex-communes—then we have a legal vacuum right at the heart of our social arrangements. Where the law leaves a legal vacuum, there is an inevitable tendency that force and anarchy will fill it. No system of law can long endure which implies that informal arrangements are no more or no less binding than formal and legal ones. To destroy marriage law is a step towards destroying the rule of law itself.

P.P.J., P. 145

MARY, QUEEN OF SCOTS

Mary's problem was not just that she was a woman; she was also an ideologue. Where her grandfather had been an empirical conservative in matters of religion, where her father had been . . . an Erastian, where her half-sister was to be a *politique* and a sceptic, Mary was a convinced and inflexible papalist . . . indeed determined to accept the authority of Rome in all its plenitude. She was the only Tudor sovereign to set herself a fixed and dramatic purpose—the reunion of England with Rome—and to pursue it at all costs. Therein lay the failure of her reign, whose conclusive note, as Pollard observed, was sterility. Elizabeth was to learn, from Mary's bitter experience, that England could be effectively governed only by the fusion of ideas, and that there was no alternative but to search for the consensus, and abide by its decisions.

E., P. 38

She was chaste by choice, and virtuous by policy and inclination. The mystique of her court—the cult of the Faerie Queen, the sexual favourites, the pretend love-affairs, the political minuets she danced with the popinjays who surrounded her—was an elaborate and calculated exercise in royal diplomacy, designed to replace the licensed gangsterism of masculine chivalry by a non-violent system which a woman could manipulate. It seems to us in retrospect shameful that this noble and virtuous queen, whose intelligence soared above her courtiers', and whose ability and sense of responsibility rivalled that of even her most devoted and accomplished advisers, should have felt it necessary to demean herself to this masquerade. But there was no other way.

H.E., P. 131

MARX, KARL

His mature theory was a superstition, and the most dangerous kind of superstition, belief in a conspiracy of evil . . . [one] extended to embrace a world conspiracy theory of the entire bourgeois class.

H.J., P. 252

. . . he was not really a scholar and not a scientist at all. He was not interested in finding the truth but in proclaiming it.

I., P. 54

In fact his greatest gift was as a polemical journalist. He made brilliant use of epigrams and aphorisms. Many of these were not his invention. Marat produced the phrases "The workers have no country" and "The proletarians have nothing to lose but their chains." The famous joke about the bourgeoisie wearing feudal coats-of-arms on their backsides came from Heine, as did "Religion is the opium of the people." Louis Blanc provided "From each according to his abilities, to each according to his needs." From Karl Schapper came "Workers of all countries, unite!" and from Blanqui "the dictatorship of the proletariat."

I., P. 56

. . . neither Marx himself nor Jenny had any interest in money except to spend it.

I., PP. 74–75

The truth is Marx was an intellectual crook. He was so far from being a scientific writer that absolutely everything he wrote which relies on "factual" data has to be treated with scepticism. He can never be trusted.

S., FEBRUARY 17, 1990

MARX AND ANTI-SEMITISM

Marx, the self-elected scourge of all superstition, religious or secular, the paladin of rationality, who set out to sweep away all the cobwebs of the past from the face of the world, and to reveal it as it really was, might not Marx of all people—himself descended from long lines of rabbis on both sides—have disposed of this particular superstition once and for all, and finally rid the world of its two-thousand-year-old burden of anti-Semitic fantasy? In fact he did the opposite. He reinforced it. He gave it a whole new lease on life, and new, respectable garments of pseudo-rationality, calculated to appeal to the young of successive generations.

C., APRIL 1984

Marx's form of anti-Semitism was a dress rehearsal for Marxism itself. August Bebel would coin the phrase, much used by Lenin: "Anti-Semitism is the socialism of fools." . . . only a fool blames the Jews alone. The socialist has grasped the point that the Jews are only the symptoms of the disease, not the disease itself. The disease is the religion of money, and its modern form is capitalism. Workers and peasants are exploited not just by the Jews but by the bourgeois-capitalist class as a whole—and it is that entire class, not only its Jewish element, which must be destroyed. . . . To reverse Begel's epigram, if anti-Semitism is the socialism of fools, socialism is the anti-Semitism of intellectuals.

C., APRIL 1984

MARX ON PROMETHEUS

Marx's presentation of Prometheus is . . . based upon a misreading of Aeschylus's *Prometheus Bound*, an error perpetuated by Marxist scholars to this day. The comparison with Christ is further misleading, since Marx is confusing myth with history. . . . Prometheus serves him as a launching-point for an attack on religion itself, as a pseudo-science. It is a false and obsolete science, refuted by true, empirical science; a false metaphysic, too, since it is dualistic, admitting an "other" world, beyond and above nature. It denies the possibility of an earthly paradise and distrusts human reason by revolving around mysteries which are inaccessible to man's understanding. Its moral values are false since it presents salvation as individualistic, [egotistic and] personal rather than social. As salvation is presented as beyond, rather than on, earth, it inhibits man from performing his appropriate social duties here. . . . By presenting God as the absolute, religion is anti-humanistic, denies man his Promethean vocation, and degrades him into the mere tool or plaything of a superior being.

P.W., P. 67

MARXISM

Capitalism seems to have recovered its entrepreneurial vigor. Marxist socialism appears to be dying, except perhaps in that home of lost causes, the university campus.

F.A., JANUARY 1989

It is not enough to say that Marxism is false because the Soviet Union has failed to create the stateless, perfect and classless society. Marx is not to be judged by "Utopian Socialism" or what is now temed "Vulgar Marxism." It is a wise element in Popper's methodology that, just as a valid-seeming theory should be constantly tested at its weakest point, so a pseudo-scientific theory should be tested at its strongest. If Marx's scientific theory of socio-economic laws is treated with intellectual seriousness, a number of factual predictions emerge . . . all of which prove to be false. Thus: only fully developed capitalist countries can go Communist; the revolution would have to be based on the industrial proletariat; the industrial proletariat must get poorer, more class-conscious, more numerous and more revolutionary under capitalism . . . and so forth. Virtually all Marx's predictions of what must happen, on the basis of his "laws of iron necessity," have been falsified by events. Hence, his theory is not scientific . . . but a form of prophecy.

E.S., P. 151

. . . . intellectuals, especially academics, are fascinated by power, and the identification of Marxism with massive physical authority has tempted many teachers to admit Marxist "science" to their own disciplines, especially such inexact or quasi-exact subjects as economics, sociology, history and geography. No doubt if Hitler, rather than Stalin, had won the struggle for Central and Eastern Europe in 1941–45, and so imposed his will on a great part of the world, Nazi doctrines which also claimed to be scientific, such as its race-theory, would have been given an academic gloss and penetrated universities throughout the world. But military victory ensured that Marxist, rather than Nazi, science would prevail.

I., P. 53

The undertone of violence always present in Marxism and constantly exhibited by the actual behaviour of Marxist regimes was a projection of the man himself.

I., P. 69

The original Marxist thesis was that capitalism would collapse. That had not happened. The first fall-back position (Khrushchev's) was that the "socialist bloc" would overtake the West in living standards. That had not happened either. The second fall-back position, used from the early 1970s onwards, which was sold to the Third World and became the UN orthodoxy, was that high Western living standards, far from being the consequence of a more efficient economic system, were the immoral wages of the deliberate and systematic impoverishment of the rest of the world.

M.T., P. 691

At the root of all Soviet difficulties was a theory based on dishonest use of statistical evidence, compounded by sheer ignorance.

M.T., P. 726

No Marxist ever seems to have held sensible views on agriculture, perhaps because neither Marx nor Lenin was really interested in it. Marxism is an essentially urban religion.

M.T., P. 726

MARXISM AND ANTI-SEMITISM

Modern theoretical anti-Semitism was a derivative of Marxism, involving a selection (for reasons of national, political or economic convenience) of a particular section of the bourgeoisie as the subject of attack. It was a more obviously emotional matter than analysis purely by class, which is why Lenin used the slogan that "Anti-Semitism is the socialism of fools." But in terms of rationality there was little to choose between the two. Lenin was saying, in effect, that it was the entire bourgeoisie, not just Jewry, which was to blame for the ills of mankind. And it is significant that all Marxist regimes, based as they are on paranoid explanations of human be-

[223]

haviour, degenerate sooner or later into anti-Semitism. The new anti-Semitism, in short, was part of the sinister drift away from the apportionment of individual responsibility towards the notion of collective guilt—the revival, in modern guise, of one of the most primitive and barbarous, even bestial, of instincts.

M.T., PP. 117–18

MARXISM AND GENOCIDE

Marxist theory cannot . . . make absolute distinctions between violence against a race and violence against a class. . . . As he saw it, races, peoples and nations were subjected to the same Hegelian processes as classes. [Marx] often discussed with Engels the notion of inferior . . . races. . . . Engels liked to quote a saying of Hegel's that "residual fragments of peoples" always become "fanatical standard-bearers of counter-revolution." Thus you could have a reactionary people as well as a reactionary class—a thought which appealed strongly to Stalin as well as Hitler, and indeed to Mao Zedong . . . when he dealt . . . with that reactionary little people, the Tibetans.

C., APRIL 1984

MARXISM AND MERCY

There is, indeed, no place for mercy in determinist systems such as Marxism. Mercy, like free will, is an anti-determinist idea. . . . So-called "history," as the dynamic of Marxism, has no mercy becauase it is an impersonal idea and mercy implies a person. The notion of "socialism with a human face," though superficially attractive, is self-contradictory in terms of Marxism. Mercy is thus greater than justice and it can be so because it is non-deterministic and embodies free will.

P.J., P. 82

Marxist Utopianism

In South-East Asia today the victims of Marxist Utopianism number millions, perhaps tens of millions. They will never figure in a Foxe's *Acts and Monuments*, any more than there can be a martyrology of Auschwitz; there are too many of them. And the vast majority simply have no idea why they are being killed. In a way, that is the most horrific thought of all.

R.F., P. 85

Mass

Whenever I attend mass in the morning, I feel an access of strength to help me during the day. For a religious service is an extraordinary occasion when men and women come together for the sole purpose of honoring God, measuring themselves, not by standards of success or failure, but by the yardstick of eternity. They ask themselves, "Am I fit for it? If not, how can I become so?" It is important to ask these questions daily, which is most unlikely without the regular discipline of church attendance.

R.D., JUNE 1985

McCarthy, Senator Joseph

McCarthy was a radical Republican; not a right-winger. . . . The Senator smelt an issue and brandished it. He was not a serious politician but an adventurer, who treated politics as a game.

M.T., P. 459

The damage inflicted by McCarthy on individual lives was due to two special factors. The first was the inadequacy of American libel laws, which permitted the press to publish his unsupported allegations with impunity, even when they were unprivileged. It was the press, especially the wire-services, which turned an abuse into a scandal, just as in the 1970s it was to magnify the Watergate case into a witch-hunt. Second was the moral cowardice shown by some institutions, notably in Hollywood and Washington, in bowing to the prevailing unreason. Again, this is a recurrent phenomenon, to be repeated in the decade 1965–75, when many universities surrendered to student violence.

M.T., P. 460

McLuhan, Marshall

What is surprising is that McLuhan should ever have been taken seriously by the educated. His theory bears all the hallmarks of a pseudo-science in their most unmistakable form: the feverish search for "confirmatory" evidence culled from every possible context, however irrelevant; and a parallel blindness to the multitude of facts which contradict it. It also has the giveaway built-in defences against criticism, since when falsifying facts are . . . thrust unavoidably under his nose, he feels himself able at any point in the argument to drop an example or "proof," on the grounds that it was a "scientific probe" that has not survived empirical experiment. His methods, in fact, are a travesty, almost a caricature, of the way in which the real scientist works.

E.S., PP. 149–50

Media

. . . the violence of print is often the prelude to the violence of blood.

H.J., P. 475

Media power today, though growing, is essentially blind, negative, destructive and irresponsible. It is exercised not so much by ambitious individuals as by a volatile, undirected, collective journalist consensus as to what constitutes news and how to play it. It tends to be anti-authority and to cling to such left-liberal luggage as slops about in the bilgewater of the western ship of state, but the sense of purpose and intelligence which directs its efforts are no higher, as a rule, than those which animated the Gadarene swine.

S., NOVEMBER 1, 1986

[There is] the increasing tendency of the media to make news rather than simply report it—especially in the field of politics. The trend is there on both sides of the Atlantic. The outstanding example was the Watergate Case, where a democratically elected president was overthrown by what, in effect, was a media *putsch*. In the United States there are high-minded journalistic *caudillos* who see themselves as the ultimate custodian of constitutional legitimacy, just as the army does in some Latin-American states.

S., NOVEMBER 1, 1986

Britain has never been a democracy as such, in the way that the United States tries to be. Its unwritten constitution has always contained a strong element of elitist guidance. Constitutional experts have recognised this by referring to Britain as a "parliamentary democracy." Now I begin to wonder whether we shouldn't call it a "media democracy." The selection and presentation of events, and in some cases their creation, have become more important in the political process than the original events themselves.

S., NOVEMBER 1, 1986

The media goes where it thinks the money is. Up till a few years ago it was widely believed young people had all the ready cash. Now the conventional wisdom is that the old, who have paid off their mortgages, dominate the purchasing power. Hence, at a time of acute advertising famine, it is grey hairs that glitter. So the Centre for Policy on Ageing has got it all wrong. But then what can you expect of an organisation which wants to replace Shakespeare's "Seven Ages of Man" with the "Four Sociological Ages," beginning "Childhood and Socialisation" and ending "Decline and Dependence"?

S., JULY 13, 1991

. . . the media favours neither youth nor age; what it likes is extremities. A youth who defrauds shareholders of millions at the age of 16, a girl who whacks a Wimbledon champ at 15, an old lady who "routs masked intruders" in her nineties, or alternatively is raped, robbed and murdered by them—these are the staple fare of newspapers and television alike.

s., JULY 13, 1991

The adversarial culture of the past—our side and their side—has gone too. Saddam Hussein gets at least as much time on television news bulletins as Mrs. Thatcher. If the second world war had been fought in the television age, would Hitler have been battling with Churchill to have the last word on the *Nine O'Clock News?* I fear so, and getting it, often enough.

s., AUGUST 16, 1990

MEDIA BIAS

There is another way in which television coverage is bent: the constant use . . . of what I call the Tendentious Dynamic, otherwise known as the Mounting Syndrome. . . . It is a very general media failing [which uses] . . . verbal devices, in reporting the news, not merely to describe what *has* happened but to assert what is *going* to happen, and indeed *ought* to happen. It is an old Agitprop device springing from the Marxist concept of historical inevitability.

s., AUGUST 26, 1986

In Britain . . . political and religious advertising is unlawful on television, and . . . religious groups are forbidden by law to operate cable stations or channels . . . to reinforce the position of existing incumbents. . . . In fact it would be . . . the programme hierarchies (largely left-wing) and above all the hatred of the established religious bodies for any form of advertising which would today prevent Jesus from being heard. The truth is, freedom of commercial speech is the essential basis of a much more fundamental right—the right to propagate ideas.

s., AUGUST 30, 1986

As for the notion of left-wing writers finding it difficult to get their voices heard, that too is humbug. . . . Indeed one gets the impression that a little bit of left-wing talent seems to go further than any other kind. . . . On the BBC and ITV they are paramount on every current-affairs, discussion, arts and books programme that matters. They award each other the prizes. They are always on the plug for fellow-toilers in the radical vineyards. . . .

S., NOVEMBER 15, 1988

MEDIA DEMOCRACY

Democracy comes in many forms, and today we are witnessing the birth of a phenomenon that I call "media democracy" because the press now plays so strong a role in decision making. This raises very serious problems because the elected element is missing.

U.S.N., JUNE 22, 1987

MEDIA DISTORTION

. . . television has a much stronger inherent tendency than print journalism to distort or even fake violent events. For many years now, and in innumerable free countries, the organisers of demonstrations likely or deliberately calculated to end in violent conflicts with the police, have worked closely with television to giganticise these planned—one might almost say pitched—battles for the edification of a universal audience. The demonstrators want to make propaganda, or to convey to the public a sense of growing crisis, which may be wholly artificial. The television networks want violent, real action to grab viewers and raise ratings. So both parties have a common interest in the breakdown of order.

S., NOVEMBER 9, 1985

MEDIA DUOPOLY

But of course the people who run the BBC-ITV duopoly—the people who make the speeches and collect the titles and gongs—are not concerned with the public interest as you and I conceive it, dear reader. They are concerned with the public interest as they conceive it: rounding a nice, cosy establishment set-up, keeping the duopoly afloat and imposing their view of society and culture on the British people. I believe this duopoly to be one of the greatest evils in Britain today.

S., JULY 20, 1985

MEDIA AND FREEDOM OF INFORMATION

. . . during the late 1960s and 1970s . . . *The New York Times* and *The Washington Post* led the way in promoting what might be called the hypertrophy of one particular . . . far from preeminent aspect of the journalist's work until it virtually took over the rest. The result was disastrous. The publication of the "Pentagon Papers" (and other secret material) led to government defensive measures which produced the Watergate Affair, and this in turn undermined the authority of the presidency, producing the loss of South Vietnam and the Khmer Rouge massacre of between one-fifth and one-third of the population of Cambodia.

S., MAY 17, 1986

MEDIA AND INFORMATION

Contemporaries of, say, Herod the Great, Louis XIV, or Napoleon could be forgiven if they hero-worshipped monsters. How could they get access to the truth? Now was it difficult . . . for Hitler to impose himself on the Germans, and Stalin to present himself to the Russians, as guardians and savior-figures. By contrast, those of us who live in media democracies theoretically know all the facts about our elected leaders and can make informed judgments about their views . . . and characters. In practice, alas, we are as easily

[230]

deceived as ever; indeed, in some ways the existence of the all-powerful media actually abets the process of deception.

A.S., SEPTEMBER 1991

MEDIA AND PATRIOTISM

There is a cultish code of honour among people who work in it, especially in the television networks, which insists that patriotism is not merely outdated but actually evil. . . . Such attitudes are part of that arrogant and destructive pseudo-religion, media triumphalism, which allots to producers, editors and reporters—some of whom have little education and alley-cat morals—the role of a deity, sitting in judgment on the world, especially the country they happen to live in. It is this misplaced professional pride, founded on nothing more than the sheer power of the media today, which produces the kind of paradox in which the British television networks, in a holier-than-the-public mood, insist it is morally right for them to give air time to IRA mass-murderers and make it easier for them to blow up innocent men, women and children.

S., JANUARY 19, 1991

MEDIA AND VIOLENCE

The great lesson of our age, hammered home in the media day after day, is that violence usually gains its ends—and is always worth a try. Almost every day the media report a victory for violence or display people in senior positions giving moral support to those who practise it.

S., MARCH 22, 1986

MEDIA AND VIOLENT NEWS

The overdue decision to stop television providing a platform for IRA mass-murderers has been denounced by apologists for the media as censorship (though with not much conviction). The public sup-

[231]

ports the ban, considering that human lives are more important than the self-esteem of media people. My view is that limitations on television coverage of Ulster violence-culture, such as IRA funerals and Orange marches, should be extended.

s., JUNE 24, 1988

MEETINGS

The human race is divided into two groups: those who like to get on with it and those who like to attend meetings.

s., AUGUST 16, 1986

MEN AND COSMETICS

This phase in human history, when ordinary males put up with presenting their beauty unaided, has lasted about 150 years and was bound to end. Television has played a potent part in the change. Since politicians and other celebrities discovered the improvement make-up could bring to their appearance, they have been tempted to make discreet use of it even off the box. It is spreading rapidly, in my observation, along with the more obvious use of bright colours, glitter and jewellery among young males. It is only a matter of time before traditional male evening dress goes for good, and we are back among the silks and satins. And, when mousse and moisturiser march for men, can wigs be far behind?

s., SEPTEMBER 21, 1991

MESSIANISM (TWENTIETH CENTURY)

[In place of religious belief] Nietzsche rightly perceived that the most likely candidate would be what he called the "Will to Power," which offered a far more comprehensive and in the end more plausible explanation of human behaviour than either Marx or Freud. In place of religious belief, there would be secular ideology. Those who had once filled the ranks of the totalitarian clergy would become totalitarian politicians. And, above all, the Will to Power would produce a new kind of messiah, uninhibited by any religious sanctions whatever, and with an unappeasable appetite for controlling mankind. The end of the old order, with an unguided world adrift in a relativistic universe, was a summons to such gangster-statesmen to emerge. They were not slow to make their appearance.

M.T., P. 48

MIDDLE CLASS

It would not be correct to say that there is an absolute law which associates the emergence of a middle class with the flowering of civilization. All one can say is that, pursuing the technique of proof by falsification, it is impossible to produce a case in which the necessary freedoms have been established without the assistance of such a class. What seems equally established is that, when the status and power of the middle class is eroded or destroyed, political and economic freedom is lost, and civilization is in consequence diminished. For the only alternative to a social structure in which a middle class can survive and prosper is the harsh division, familiar to all totalitarian states, between rulers and ruled, between the *honestiores* and the *humiliores*. . . . Indeed, without the bridge of a middle social group, the distinctions between the two halves of society must become more fundamental, and the legal rights of the *humiliores*, whether in the Roman empire or in modern Fascist-Communist systems, gradually approximate to those of slaves.

E.S., P. 185

Throughout history all intelligent observers of society have welcomed the emergence of a flourishing middle class, which they have rightly associated with economic prosperity, political stability, the growth of individual freedom and the raising of moral and cultural standards. The middle class, stretching from the self-employed skilled craftsman to the leaders of the learned professions, has produced the overwhelming majority of the painters, architects, writers and musicians, as well as the administrators, technologists and scientists, on which the quality and strength of a culture principally

[233]

rest. The health of the middle class is probably the best index of the health of society as a whole; and any political system which persecutes its middle class systematically is unlikely to remain either free or prosperous for long.

E.S., P. 253

. . . there is nothing morally unhealthy about the existence of a middle class in society. No one need feel ashamed of being *bourgeois*, of pursuing a *bourgeois* way of life, or of adhering to *bourgeois* cultural and moral standards. That it should be necessary to assert such a proposition is a curious commentary on our age.

E.S., P. 258

MIDDLE EAST

. . . a complicated place embittered by countless archeological layers of savagery and barbarism, especially since the end of Western dominance—for whose understanding a cool head, an absence of prejudice, and, above all, disbelief in conspiracy theory are all essential.

A.S., OCTOBER 1990

MILLENARIANISM (SECULAR)

More recently, the specifically Christian element, always the first victim when millenarianism lurches into terror, had tended to recede into the background or disappear altogether. Yet millenarians, from Tertullian on, had nearly always been anti-clerical—a characteristic they share with modern non-Christian prophets and apocalyptics, like Marx, the Paris communards of 1870, Trotskyites, Maoists and other seekers for an illusory perfection in this world. The secular Daniels of the twentieth century have scriptural credentials and their lineage is Christian.

H.C., P. 264

[234]

MISSION

Basically, there are two possible forms of proselytization of a society. One is to evangelize the lowest and least privileged elements, capture their allegiance in huge numbers, and so work upwards from the base. This was the method followed by the first Christians within the Roman empire. The second is to aim at the élite, or even at the individuals at the head of the élite, obtain recognition or adoption of the faith as a matter of state policy, and then work downwards, by authority, example or force (or all three). . . . The religious instinct of the missionaries was to go for the masses, for, in the absence of military and state sanctions, Christianity is most successful when it appeals to the underdogs and the deprived, and so comes closest to its earliest pastoral attitudes.

H.C., P. 410

MISSOURI COMPROMISE

The compromise itself served to postpone any threatened breakup of the Union for the best part of three decades. . . . But the agreement, by drawing an actual geographic line between slavery and freedom, seemed to lay down the frontier of a future conflict. . . . By postponing the showdown, however, it did something of great historical importance. If the Union had broken up in the early 1820s, the North would not have possessed the physical power to coerce the South, especially a South allied to Britain. The outcome would have been two Americas, and the history of the entire North American continent—and so the world—would have been quite different.

B.M., PP. 316–17

MOB

. . . it was rare for more than a few hundred people to engage in serious violence. Nor was it difficult to organize a mob for any purpose in a population in which the average age was 16 and vast numbers of people of all ages were underemployed and hung about the streets. . . . But those who had been mobbed might raise one of their own. People brought up in these times were used to it. Hence, Mr. Pickwick's remark: "It's always best on these occasions to do what the mob do." "But suppose there are two mobs?" suggested Mr. Snodgrass. "Shout with the largest," said Mr. Pickwick.

B.M., PP. 386–87

MODERN WORLD

What is true is that, for the first time in history, every single nation in Western Europe is now, theoretically at least, a democracy under the rule of law, and there has been a strong movement toward political and economic freedom in Eastern Europe, too. But with some exceptions, much the same could have been said of Europe in 1918–19, and look what followed.

C., MARCH 1992

The modern world began on 29 May 1919 when photographs of a solar eclipse, taken on the island of Principe off West Africa and at Sobral in Brazil, confirmed the truth of a new theory of the universe . . . for most people, to whom Newtonian physics, with their straight lines and right angles, were perfectly comprehensible, relativity never became more than a vague source of unease. It was grasped that absolute time and absolute length had been dethroned; that motion was curvilinear. All at once, nothing seemed certain . . . it was as though the spinning globe had been taken off its axis and cast adrift in a universe which no longer conformed to accustomed standards of measurement. At the beginning of the 1920s the belief began to circulate, for the first time at a popular level, that there were no longer any absolutes: of time and space, of good and evil, of knowledge, above all of value. Mistakenly but perhaps inevitably, relativity became confused with relativism.

M.T., PP. 1–4

MODERNISM

Nearly all the major creative figures of the 1920s had already been published, exhibited or performed before 1914, and in that sense the Modern Movement was a pre-war phenomenon. But it needed the desperate convulsions of the great struggle, and the crashing of regimes it precipitated, to give modernism the radical political dimension it had hitherto lacked, and the sense of a ruined world on which it would construct a new one. . . . The cultural and political strands of change could not be separated, any more than during the turbulence of revolution and romanticism of 1790–1830.

M.T., PP. 9–10

Marx, Freud, Einstein all conveyed the same message to the 1920s: the world was not what it seemed. The senses, whose empirical perceptions shaped our ideas of time and distance, right and wrong, law and justice, and the nature of man's behaviour in society, were not to be trusted. Moreover, Marxist and Freudian analysis combined to undermine, in their different ways, the highly developed sense of personal responsibility, and of duty towards a settled and objectively true moral code, which was at the centre of nineteenth-century European civilization. The impression people derived from Einstein, of a universe in which all measurements of value were relative, served to confirm this vision—which both dismayed and exhilarated—of moral anarchy.

M.T., P. 11

MODERNITY

[Nietzsche] wrote in 1886: "The greatest event of recent times— that 'God is dead,' that the belief in the Christian God is no longer tenable—is beginning to cast its first shadows on Europe." Among the advanced races, the decline and ultimately the collapse of the religious impulse would leave a huge vacuum. The history of modern times is in great part the history of how that vacuum had been filled . . . the most likely candidate would be what he called the "Will to Power" . . . a far more comprehensive . . . and more plausible explanation of human behavior than either Marx or Freud. In place of religious belief would be secular ideology.

M.T., P. 48

The historian of modern times is made constantly aware of the increasingly rapid interaction of political events over wide distances. It was as though the development of radio, the international telephone system, mass-circulation newspapers and rapid forms of travel was producing a new conception of social and political holism corresponding to new scientific perceptions of the universe and matter. According to Mach's Principle, formulated first at the turn of the century and then reformulated as part of Einstein's cosmology, not only does the universe as a whole influence local, terrestrial events but local events have an influence, however small, on the universe as a whole. Quantum mechanics, developed in the 1920s, indicated that the same principle applied at the level of micro-quantities. There were no independent units, flourishing apart from the rest of the universe.

M.T., P. 102

MONK

It can be argued that, in the long run, civilization has benefited from the intellectual self-abasement of [the eighth and ninth] centuries. Much of the ancient world survived because of the intense reverence of a handful of men for the literary relics of the past. Monks put the preservation of the surviving texts above their own lives, and regarded their reproduction as infinitely more important than their own creative labours. . . . The monks argued that the more copies they succeeded in making, the more likely it was that one at least would survive; and they were right. In the eighth century, the *scriptorium* of St. Martin of Tours transcribed a fifth-century Livy; the copy survived, the original is lost.

H.C., P. 156

MONNET, JEAN

Monnet was small, mousy, quiet, colourless, rhetoric-hating: in appearance and manner the exact opposite of de Gaulle. What the two men shared was huge persistence and will; and, equally important, the ability to inspire and lead the young. De Gaulle bred Gaullists; Monnet, the Eurocrats.

M.T., P. 591

MONOPOLY

I am often reproached for my criticism of the BBC and accused of being hostile to public service broadcasting as such. But I do not necessarily reject the principle. . . . The objections to television bias—especially its hatred of authority in any shape—come by no means exclusively from the Right of the spectrum.

S., OCTOBER 15, 1988

MONROE, JAMES

A case can be made for describing the Monroe presidency . . . as the first great era of corruption in American history. Indeed, the word itself was used with increasing frequency. Many Americans came sincerely to believe that their government, both administration and Congress, was corrupt, and this at a time when, in Britain, the traditional corruption of the 18th-century Walpoleian system was being slowly but surely extruded from public life. . . . by corruption Americans of the 1820s did not mean simply the use of bribes and stealing from the public purse. They also meant the undermining of the constitutional system by secret deals, the use of public office to acquire power or higher office, and the giving of private interests priority over public welfare. But they thought there was plenty of simple thieving, too.

B.M., P. 906

[239]

MOORCRAFT, WILLIAM

. . . he set in motion that delicate form of paranoia, known as the Great-Game mentality, which was to be part of the British Raj until the very instant of Britain's withdrawal in 1947 and which, in the form it took on the other side of the hill, was to obsess Russian policymakers as late as 1979, incite them to invade Afghanistan, and so bring the mighty Soviet empire crashing down in the next decade. It was quite an accomplishment for a veterinarian who set out to buy horses.

B.M., P. 716

MOORE, G. E.

G. E. Moore (1873–1958) achieved a world-wide reputation as the specialist of "common-sense" philosophy, but to the non-academic his claim to the title is not immediately apparent. In 1926, he contrived to draw a distinction between "meaning" and "analysis," which led to a fierce debate, on both sides of the Atlantic, about "the meaning of analysis," "the analysis of meaning," "the meaning of meaning" and "the analysis of analysis": a debate still going on.

E.S., P. 13

MORAL

The only valid source of moral life is a living God.

R.D., JUNE 1985

MORAL LEADERSHIP

. .. generous-minded Victorians, who took big risks by publicly expressing their concern for the poor, did not pretend that they knew everything about the problem or propose specific solutions. They had no Boards of Social Responsibility or heavily-financed commissions producing massive studies . . . But they did understand the nature and value of moral leadership, and provided it according to their lights. As a result they were listened to and occasionally heeded: indeed, their collective impact was considerable and salutary. But of course they had a considerable advantage over their successors today: their belief in God was still solid and they had no need to turn to political dogma as a substitute.

s., july 18, 1987

Moral Order

For the construction of a moral order must start with a recognition of the limitations of political (and religious) action. Perfection cannot be organised. Happiness cannot be planned or engineered. Even justice is an aim and an ideal, rather than an actual condition to be brought about by legislation. A society under the rule of law is a plausible, and attainable, objective. But a Just Society is a Utopia. The piecemeal solution may lack divine symmetry but there is about it a huge humanity. Not only is the best the enemy of the good: a totalitarian moral order is bound to be an enemy of justice, and so in the end destructive of order itself.

r.f., pp. 83–84

Moral Order (Totalitarian)

It would . . . be a mistake to see the new Tyranny of Politics simply in terms of its murdered victims. A totalitarian moral order is not merely a way of death; it is a way of life too. In Grosseteste's Lincoln or Calvin's Geneva the most notable feature was not the persecution of dissidents but the daily oppression of ordinary people. Even outside the totalitarian structures of our age, there is the same risk of enforced conformity in societies—albeit nominally free . . .

r.f., p. 85

MORAL RELATIVISM

Hitler . . . appealed to the moralistic nature of many Germans, that is, those who had a keen desire for "moral" behaviour without possessing a code of moral absolutes rooted in Christian faith. Himmler, the conscientious mass-murderer, the scrupulous torturer, was the archetype of the men who served Hitler best. He defined the virtues of the SS, the embodiment of Nazi "morality," as loyalty, honesty, obedience, hardness, decency, poverty and bravery. The notion of obeying "iron laws" or "a higher law," rather than the traditional, absolute morality taught in the churches, was a Hegelian one. Marx and Lenin translated it into a class concept; Hitler into a race one. Just as the Soviet cadres were taught to justify the most revolting crimes in the name of a moralistic class warfare, so the SS acted in the name of race—which Hitler insisted was a far more powerful and central human motivation than class. Service to the race, as opposed to the Marxist proletariat, was the basis of Nazi puritanism.

M.T., P. 296

MORALITY (SOCIAL)

Any government which conducts a deliberate assault on standards of moral conduct is asking for trouble, not least in the economic field. The successful working of a modern economy in a free society where . . . trade unions are privileged under the law, must depend to a large extent on the degree of self-restraint exercised by powerful groups within society. When self-restraint is lowered, that is, when large groups of workers with economic power lay claim to the national product, in such a way that the sum total of those claims exceeds the capacity of the economy, the result must be inflation. When this abdication of a sense of responsibility spreads from the industrial unions to the middle class, and so becomes . . . collective, the result can only be hyperinflation. The level of social morality is directly linked to the performance of the economy. Hence it follows

. . . that the proletarianization of middle-class morality leads to economic catastrophe.

E.S., P. 191

MORALS

One of the most striking phenomena revealed by the scientific study of history is the astonishing stability of sexual morals. In this respect, at least, we do not get better or worse: we have sinned evenly across the centuries. On the public surface of life, of course, attitudes change sharply. . . . But beneath these torrents of words and threats, the great mass of the ordinary people follow patterns which seem to be immutable. . . . The one reliable index of morality—the statistics of illegitimate births—suggests that the volume of sin varies only with the size of the population.

S.N., P. 31

MORES

I have been thinking about prelatical *mores* because, a fortnight ago, my wife had her handbag stolen in an Angelican church café. . . . You ask: they did it in a *church* café? What more likely these days? When parts of the North-east were reduced to anarchy recently, with . . . in fact professional criminals ram-banging and looting shops, burning houses, assaulting police . . . our friend George Cantuar blamed it all on social deprivation in general and the Government in particular. No doubt the two young men who stole my wife's bag would say it's the Government's fault too.

S., NOVEMBER 23, 1991

MUGGERIDGE, MALCOLM

No man of his generation, except the late Evelyn Waugh, has cherished words so deeply, or used them with such fastidious exactitude. He has made his living by the word, written and spoken; but he longs for a world in which the word, grand, true, eloquent, dramatic, elegant, is wholly divorced from commercial rewards.

S.N., PP. 69–70

MURDOCH, RUPERT

There is nothing of a Hearst or a Northcliffe about him, no power-madness. He is one of those people whose lurid image bears little relation to reality. He is essentially a working newspaperman who itches to run static or fading properties better. That is his prime motive and it seems to me an excellent one.

S., MARCH 28, 1987

MUSIC

Music is the intellectual queen of the arts, the one whose theory and practice is closest to the workings of the sciences, and where the impulsions of logical dynamism are most forceful. But it is also much closer to our human essence than is usually supposed. Like speech, it is a characteristic of humanity even at the most primitive level. A study, for instance, of the Veddas, a pygmoid people of primeval hunters living in the interior of Ceylon at the very lowest layer of culture, reveals that, though they have no instruments of any kind, they possess a musical system, with intervals, rhythm, recurring melodical turns and characteristic terminal cadences. Such prototypes of music in its most elementary form bear no relation whatever to even the most complex bird-calls and other animal noises.

E.S., P. 226

MUSIC AS RELIGION

. .. the new kind of transcendent music Beethoven wrote, and the new importance he gave to music in the intellectual and moral cosmos, did constitute a secular substitute for religion: There was a new faith, and Beethoven was its prophet. It was no accident that, about this time, new concert halls were being given temple-type facades, thus exalting the moral and cultural status of the symphony and chamber music (as opposed to the opera). New theaters were Greek, churches themselves Gothic, museums Egyptian—but the concert hall was the setting for the new high priest, the composer.

B.M., P. 121

N

Napoleon, Age of

Behind the ostensible *Zeitgeist* pressing for change, there was a hidden but more powerful *Zeitgeist* anxious for stability. After two decades of wars . . . and privation, most people, whatever their class, wanted to return to the civilized values and the absence of violence which they, or their parents or grandparents, could vaguely remember. In this sense "repression" was a welcome phenomenon . . . for those whom a later age would call "the silent majority," and one achievement of the years 1815–1830 was that they saw, by and large, a return to stability and the civil settlement of disputes, thus laying the foundations of a century which was to witness enormous improvements in the human condition brought about primarily by the absence of war and civil disturbance.

B.M., P. 116

Napoleonic Code

In France, the Revolution initially brought some relief to women. . . . But . . . Bonaparte himself was hostile to women's claims. "Women in these days require restraint," he laid down. "They go where they like, they do what they like. It is not French to give women the upper hand. They have too much of it already." . . . a man could sue for divorce on grounds of simple adultery, the wife only if the husband's concubine was brought into the home . . .

(an adulterous wife could be imprisoned for three months to two
years . . . while an adulterous husband was simply fined . . .)

B.M., P. 475

NASSER, GAMAL ABDEL

[Nasser's] *Philosophy of the Revolution* was a frothy mixture of Marxist
tags, western liberalism and Islam: good, flatulent stuff. He was an
archetypal member of the "Bandung generation": adept at words,
but not much else. Like Sukarno, he was brilliant at devising slogans
and titles: he often changed the name of the party he created and
of the gimcrack Arab federations he negotiated. His particular spe-
ciality was crowd-manipulation. His windy rhetoric went down well,
especially with the students, and he seems to have been able to goad
the Cairo mob into chanting any slogans he wished, often changing
them from day to day.

M.T., P. 488

Nasser went to Bandung. It completed his corruption, as it did for
other young nationalist politicians. Why sweat at the thankless task
of keeping a poor country fed and clothed when the world stage
beckoned? Bandung opened Nasser's eyes to the opportunities the
age offered to an expert publicist and sloganizer, especially one
prepared to play the anti-colonialist card. And he had been holding
one in his hand all the time: the Jews! Israel was easily rationalized
into a general imperialist conspiracy theory.

M.T., P. 489

NATIONAL SOCIALISM

Hitler's regime . . . was marked by constant bilateral and multi-
lateral struggles between its component parts, what Hobbes called
"a perpetual and restless desire for power after power, that ceaseth
only in death." Goering tapped his colleagues' telephones from his
"research office" and acquired such useful treasures as a set of love-

letters from Alfred Rosenberg to a comely Jewess. Bormann spied on all. So, of course, did Himmler and Heydrich. Virtually everyone was in a position to blackmail everyone else, and as each sought to win Hitler's goodwill by betraying what he knew of the others, the Führer was kept well informed.

M.T., P. 292

There is no evidence whatever that Hitler was, even to the smallest degree, influenced by big business philosophy. He bowed to business advice only when convinced that taking it would forward his military and external aims. He regarded himself as a socialist, and the essence of his socialism was that every individual or group in the state should unhesitatingly work for national policy. So it did not matter who owned the actual factory so long as those managing it did what they were told.

M.T., P. 293

The real antithesis to National Socialism was individualism, a society where private arrangements took priority over public, where the family was the favoured social unit and where the voluntary principle was paramount. A society in which the family, as opposed to the political party and the ideological programme, was the starting-point for reconstruction, was the answer to the totalitarian evil.

M.T., P. 581

NATIONAL SOCIALISM AND CHRISTIANITY

[Adolf Hitler] hated Christianity and showed a justified contempt for its German practitioners. Shortly after assuming power, he told Hermann Rauschning that he intended to stamp out Christianity in Germany "root and branch." "One is either a Christian or a German. You can't be both." He thought the method might be to "leave it to rot like a gangrenous limb." Again: "Do you really believe the masses will ever be Christian again? Nonsense. Never again. The tale is finished . . . but we can hasten matters. The parsons will be made to dig their own graves. They will betray their God to us."

H.C., P. 485

NATIONAL SOCIALISM AND LAW

The lawlessness of Hitler's Germany, beneath a thin veneer of legal forms, was absolute. As Goering put it, "The law and the will of the Führer are one." Hans Frank: "Our constitution is the will of the Führer." Hitler worked entirely through decrees and ordinances, as opposed to law, here again resembling Lenin, who never showed the slightest interest in constitution-making. In any matters which were of interest to the Nazis, the Ministry of Justice did not function. . . . But Hitler did not even like removable or subservient judges. Like Marx and Lenin, he hated lawyers—"a lawyer must be regarded as a man deficient by nature or deformed by experience," he said— and he eventually superimposed on the ordinary juridical system the Nazi "People's Courts," a Leninist device which achieved its sombre apogee under the ferocious Roland Freisler in 1944–45.

M.T., PP. 289–90

NATIONAL SOCIALISM AND RELIGION

Hitler's plans for Christianity were more draconian than anything envisaged by the Russians. He told his entourage on 13 December 1941: "The war will be over one day. I shall then consider that my life's final task will be to solve the religious problem. . . . The final state must be: in the pulpit, a senile officiant; facing him, a few sinister old women, as gaga and poor in spirit as anyone could wish." Anti-Christian activities undertaken in Poland and elsewhere were more ferocious than anything contrived by the Russians, and applied equally to Catholic, Protestant and Orthodox churches. Himmler said: "We shall not rest until we have rooted out Christianity." . . . The plan involved not merely the separation of Church and State but the progressive and systematic destruction of religion.

H.C., PP. 492–93

[249]

NATIONALISM

. . . during the process of settlement in eastern and central Europe, from the fourth to the fifteenth centuries, and during the intensive phase of urbanization which took place from the early eighteenth century onwards, about one-quarter of the area had been occupied by mixed races (including over ten million Jews) whose allegiance had hitherto been religious and dynastic rather than national. The monarchies were the only unifying principle of these multi-racial societies, the sole guarantee (albeit often a slender one) that all would be equal before the law. Once that principle was removed, what could be substituted for it? The only one available was nationalism, and its fashionable by-product irredentism, a term derived from the Italian *Risorgimento* and signifying the union of an entire ethnic group under one state. To this was now being added a new cant phrase, "self-determination," by which was understood the adjustment of frontiers by phebiscite according to ethnic preferences.

M.T., P. 20

NEHRU, JAWAHARLAL

The arguments Nehru used to defend China were identical with those used on Hitler's behalf in the mid-1930s: Nehru was not only the last of the Viceroys, he was also the last of the Appeasers.

M.T., P. 475

What Nehru really enjoyed was holding forth about international morality on the world stage. In the 1950s he became the leading exponent of the higher humbug. At home he practised acquisitiveness.

M.T., P. 475

THE NEW DEAL

The notion that Roosevelt's "New Deal" raised the U.S. from the abyss is largely mythology: the American economy was beginning to recover some months before he took office, and his efforts to involve the state probably retarded and enfeebled the process.

P.P.J., P. 180

NEWMAN, JOHN HENRY CARDINAL

. . . it is a permanent characteristic of Christianity that emphasis on one of its matrices always leads to the development of a rival. In the 1820s, Oxford, and notably Oriel College, was undergoing an intellectual revival. The Oriel fellows included John Keble, John Henry Newman, Edward Pusey, the Regius Professor of Hebrew, and R. H. Froude. . . . It is notable that whereas in the Reformation, the first Protestants had appealed to the early Church against papal triumphalism and mechanical Christianity, this new group of Christian reformers employed the early Church to illumine a path back to Rome. . . . Newman began to drift away from Anglicanism when he worked on his book about Arianism in the fourth century. He discovered on his own account how serious a threat history was to Protestantism because of its biblical fundamentalism. He wrote: "To be deep in history is to cease to be a Protestant." He saw history as an asset to Catholicism in that its study reminded the believer of the incredible richness of its past, which Rome alone seemed fully to represent in the nineteenth century.

H.C., PP. 377–78

NEWS

What is news? To a great extent it is what the consensus within the national newspaper confraternity decides is news (television tends to follow suit), and that decision often reflects traditional attitudes and values which are now out of date.

S., SEPTEMBER 13, 1986

NEWSCASTERS

They are technically more competent than ever before, even if their English lacks elegance and often grammar and syntax; and they have a broader knowledge of the world than earlier generations of communicators. What makes me tremble is the evident lack of moral training, their semi-detachment from the Judaeo-Christian system of ethics which, more than ever before, is now the only sheet-anchor for a world adrift on an ocean of doubt and fear. Too many people in the media find it difficult to make principled and systematic distinctions between right and wrong because they have simply never been taught how to do so.

S., AUGUST 31, 1991

NEWSPAPERS

All big firms need strong, confident leadership, and in newspapers that means one-man leadership. No great national newspaper can be run except as an autocracy.

S., JULY 21, 1984

Unfortunately, vice is generally supposed to sell newspapers, even quality ones.

S., OCTOBER 18, 1986

A newspaper is rather like a Victorian maidservant—it cannot afford to lose its character.

S., DECEMBER 13, 1986

Manners maketh man but they do not, alas, make for mass-circulations.

S., NOVEMBER 26, 1988

Newspapers love to go for people but are liable to become paranoid the instant they are subjected to the mildest chastisement themselves.

s., february 10, 1990

Newspapers (Local)

Many thousands of words are devoted to detailed "Community Calendars," which reflect the extraordinary range of activities in which Californians engage. . . . Most of the meetings take place in churches and these listings testify to the huge, active power of religion in American life but still more the American obsession with bodily health.

s., june 4, 1988

Local papers take you close to the real America in all its touching and neurotic diversity. Despite all the critical fuss about Nancy Reagan's astrologer, I notice that virtually all U.S. papers give space to star-guides. . . . Reading local newspapers suggests that in this, as in countless other respects, the Reagans are a typical American family.

s., june 14, 1988

Newspapers (Modern)

The significance of the high-tech revolution is that it is bringing us more papers, and so more opinions. Soon, we shall all be able to find one we consider intelligent.

s., march 15, 1986

The *Today* papers have broken free of the old Fleet Street system but, having done so, find themselves rebels without a cause. They have handsome high-tech bodies but no heart and no soul, and not very much mind either. My spirits always sink when a paper announces it is giving politicians from all parties space to say their piece. Then I know that it has no ideas and few convictions.

s., JUNE 17, 1986

NEWSPEAK

Modern euphemism, which Churchill rightly termed as giving people the name if they cannot have anything else, rarely if ever works. . . . The language suffers, but the pains of the deprived are not thereby lessened. Yet the practice is on the increase, and no list could now hope to be exhaustive. A backward child is a late-developer; a cripple is handicapped; the poor are lower-income groups or under-privileged; the deaf are hard of hearing; slums are sub-standard houses; the insane are mentally ill, and drunkards alcoholics; a subject becomes a citizen or a national, and old people are senior citizens, or, worse, geriatrics. Eggs are not big or small but large, medium or standard; cheap becomes budget, thrifty or economy; a second-hand or used car is owner-tested; dustmen (or binmen in the North of England) become refuse-collectors, night-watchmen security officers. . . . In fact, the capacity of ordinary persons to accustom themselves to, and so discount, euphemism is almost infinite.

E.S., PP. 104–5

The ineffectiveness of happiness linguistics (except in the damage it inflicts on language) is seen in the fact that one euphemism must soon be replaced by another. There is no final euphemism that satisfies. In the United States, the poor were officially reclassified as needy, then deprived, then underprivileged. The last term is open to the real objection that a privilege ceases to have any meaning if everyone is given it, the supposed object of the welfare operation. As one philologist has pointed out, a true definition of an under-privileged person is one, for example, who is not allowed to join the Communist Party in a Soviet-type state, or a trade union in a western one. In any case, underprivileged soon became pejorative in turn, and was followed by disadvantaged—open to the same objection in terms of strict meaning.

E.S., P. 105

As all totalitarian rulers have discovered, once you have hacked away the logical and rational foundations on which the edifice of civilisation rests, it is comparatively easy to invert the process of ratiocination, dress up the results in verbiage, and sell them to thousands of apparently well-educated people.

R.F., P. 29

NEW TESTAMENT

. . . even if we were to have the perfect and original texts of the gospels, they would not protect us from the efforts to create "constructive truth" made by the evangelists themselves.

H.C., P. 27

It was an instrument which had been fashioned by the Church, rather than vice versa.

H.C., P. 55

NEW YORK'S PRESS

In my view New York could do with a more varied press. The stage-army of liberals which dominates the media there gives everything a uniform and predictable tone, *The Wall Street Journal* and the editorial page of the *Post* excepted. *The New Yorker* exudes the upper-middle-class progressive consensus of the Forties and Fifties, *The Village Voice* the strident radicalism of the Sixties and early Seventies, while *New York* magazine tries to be more contemporary left, with articles on such subjects as the way in which rich Yuppies are taking over the Upper West Side and driving out the deserving poor.

S., MAY 25, 1985

THE 1980S

The period was notable for a sharp and sustained decline in anti-Americanism. It seems to have largely disappeared except on the university campus where, like Marxism, it lingers on, a curious survival from the past. Elsewhere it has proved remarkably difficult for the far left to assemble a rent-a-mob and march on an American embassy.

F.A., JANUARY 1989

The 1960s were a decade of illusion and baseless fantasies of utopia; the 1970s were a decade of disillusion, shattered hopes and rising fears. The 1980s have been a decade of realism, in which the affairs of the world, and of the West in particular, have been placed on a firmer, more concrete foundation.

F.A., JANUARY 1989

The 1980s formed one of the watersheds of modern history. The spirit of democracy recovered its self-confidence and spread. The rule of law was re-established in large parts of the globe and international predation checked and punished. The United Nations, and especially its Security Council, began for the first time to function as its founders intended. Capitalist economies flourished mightily and, almost everywhere, there was growing recognition that the market system was not merely the surest but the only way to increase wealth and raise living standards. As an intellectual creed, collectivism collapsed and the process of abandoning it got under way even in its strongholds. Stalin's empire, the last of the colonial conglomerates, disintegrated.

M.T., P. 697–98

The Eighties have been a disastrous decade for the Left intelligentsia. One by one, cherished communist regimes are throwing up the ideological sponge. All over the world Social Democrats are hoisting flags of doctrinal surrender. Marxism is discredited, except . . . [on] the university campus.

S., FEBRUARY 4, 1989

. . . we are crossing another great historical watershed, like the Peace of Westphalia in 1648. That key event did not end war. But it ended the wars of religion. Thereafter alliance and wars were motivated by secular greed rather than doctrinal rectitude. So it is today.

S., NOVEMBER 11, 1989

1989

Thus the year 1989, which the Left throughout the world had planned as a celebration of the bicentennial of the French Revolution—the beginning of modern radical politics, as it was argued—turned into something quite different: a Year of Revolutions indeed, but of revolutions against the established order of Marxism-Leninism.

M.T., P. 758

THE 1950S

The Fifties [were] the decade of affluence, a word popularized by the fashionable economist J. K. Galbraith in his 1958 best-seller, *The Affluent Society*. The book attacked the old "conventional wisdom." In doing so it created a new one. Galbraith and his school argued that the . . . world was abundant in resources. The advanced economies had mastered the difficulty of producing goods. The economic problem was solved. What remained was a political one: distributing them equitably. The state should play a creative role by employing "private affluence" to end "public squalor" and cure dangerous imbalances in wealth not only within nations but between them. . . . it was notable that, unlike in the Twenties, it was not the Right but the Left who now believed that prosperity would go on for ever and who turned the Sixties into the decade of illusion.

M.T., P. 613

THE 1990s

. . . greed may not be very elegant, but it has two merits. It is the same everywhere. And it is basically rational. So, as Russia becomes "normal," it may continue to be dangerous and perhaps even aggressive. But it will speak the same language as anyone else. We are leaving the Age of Doctrine. We are entering the Age of Deals. That is progress.

S., NOVEMBER 11, 1989

THE 1970s

The 1970s [were] a decade of exceptional anxiety and disillusionment when concern about the environment and the exhaustion of raw materials [was] added to the spread of Cold War competition throughout the world and the ravages of collectivism in Eastern Europe, most of Africa and large parts of Asia and Latin America. Everywhere, democracy and the rule of law that gave it meaning appeared on the defensive, even in its heartlands.

M.T., P. 697

THE 1960s

It was a decade of illusion, in which eager spirits were led by long-continued prosperity to believe and propagate many Utopian notions: that poverty could be abolished, cruelty and violence legislated out of existence, every freedom infinitely extended and voraciously enjoyed, and some kind of democratic and egalitarian paradise established on earth. The vast and unconsidered expansion of higher education was both a product and accelerator of these illusory forces, pouring on to the scene countless armies of young graduates, who shared these fantastic hopes and set about elbowing aside the obscurantist and authoritarian elders who alone, it was argued, prevented their realization.

P.J., P. 54

It is one of the most fundamental fallacies of the post-Sixties Left that there is no such thing as objective truth.

s., october 11, 1986

THE 1930s

Self-delusion was obviously the biggest single factor in the presentation of an unsuccessful despotism as a Utopia in the making. But there was also conscious deception by men and women who thought of themselves as idealists and who, at the time, honestly believed they were serving a higher human purpose by systematic misrepresentation and lying. . . . The Thirties [were] the age of the heroic lie. Saintly mendacity became its most prized virtue. Stalin's tortured Russia was the prime beneficiary of this sanctified falsification. The competition to deceive became even more fierce when Stalinism acquired a mortal rival in Hitler's Germany.

m.t., pp. 276–77

The ramifying influence of Thirties totalitarian terror was . . . immense, in space and time. But at that epoch, the ultimate consequences of Hitler and Stalin seemed unimportant. What mattered was what their regimes would do in the immediate future, not merely to their helpless subjects, but to their neighbours near and far. The advent of Stalin and Hitler to absolute power dealt a decisive blow to a world structure which was already unstable and fragile. Both had limitless territorial aims, since both subscribed to imminent eschatologies, one of class, one of race, in the course of which their rival power-systems would become globally dominant. Hence the arrival of these two men on the scene introduced what may be termed the high noon of aggression.

m.t., p. 308

THE 1920s

. . . the view that the 1920s [were] a drunken spree destructive of civilized values can be substantiated only by the systematic distortion or denial of the historical record. The prosperity was very widespread and very solid. It was not universal: in the farming community particularly it was patchy, and it largely excluded certain older industrial communities, such as the textile trade of New England. But it was more widely distributed than had been possible in any community of this size before, and it involved the acquisition, by tens of millions, of the elements of economic security which had hitherto been denied them throughout the whole of history.

M.T., P. 223

NIXON, RICHARD

It is impossible to predict how historians a hundred years from now will judge Nixon, a man whose career testifies both to the positive power of will and endurance in public life and to the destructive power of the East Coast establishment—his mortal enemy.

C., OCTOBER 1988

Fallen statesmen rarely rise again. But it pays them to live long. Nixon, like Herbert Hoover before him, has survived nearly all his enemies. . . . Few men have been more successful at putting the past behind them and looking firmly into the future.

C., OCTOBER 1988

NOMENKLATURA

It was a standing grievance of all the U.S.S.R.'s satellites, and all its republics, that they were the victims of Russian exploitation; it was equally the passionate conviction of the Russians themselves that they were being milked by satellites and republics alike: "We poor Russians pay for all," as they put it. The fact, of course, was that Russians, republics and satellites alike had been the victims of an incorrigibly inefficient system. In so far as anyone did the exploiting, it was the *nomenklatura*, the privileged caste of high Communist Party officials and army officers, which existed in all of them. . . . The Gorbachev family enjoyed the perks as much as anyone; in New York, during the Gorbachev-Reagan summit in Washington in December 1987, Mrs. Raisa Gorbachev went shopping with an American Express Gold card, illegal in Russia and punishable with a long prison term. But she was above the law: a *nomenklatura* wife.

M.T., P. 766

NORTH, COLONEL OLIVER

. . . whose only real crime was patriotism.

S., JANUARY 16, 1988

NOVEL (ENGLISH POLITICAL)

Even in England, no activity arouses a higher degree of passion and ambition than politics. Westminster brings out the best and worst in a man more faithfully than any other institution. Yet few novelists have gone there in search of material, and fewer still have succeeded in finding it.

S.N., P. 83

NUCLEAR POWER

Because nuclear reactors are mysterious things, difficult to understand, they are regarded with the superstitious awe George Eliot described in *Silas Marner*, where the old-style farmworkers treated the indoor machinery of the weavers as inhuman, wicked and devilish. The fear of nuclear power is not based upon a rational calculation but on superstitious dread of a ray-like emanation, akin to a diabolic force.

S., FEBRUARY 14, 1987

Nuclear Weapons

The old free enterprise Merchants of Death looked innocent by comparison with modern states, competing to sell destruction by the megaton.

M.T., P. 685

. . . precisely because war is so infinitely corrupting, and because the means at the disposal of those so corrupted are now of such colossal magnitude, the need to prevent war becomes absolutely paramount. It must therefore dominate the moral debate. And, though nuclear weapons introduce no new principle, they do embody staggering novelties of scale. They thereby produce a moral paradox: they destroy the economy of war, and so make it easier to prevent. The axis of war theology, therefore, now revolves around the notion of peace by deterrence.

P.P.J., P. 164

The existence of nuclear weapons does not . . . introduce a new moral principle. If we apply the criteria of discrimination and proportion it is obvious that the unrestrained conventional bombing of cities was wrong, and it follows naturally and *a fortiori* that the unrestricted use of thermonuclear warheads against cities is wrong. I do not see how any Christian can dissent from this view.

P.P.J., P. 164

Nudism

A nudist colony, I imagine, is a bore's paradise: it's awfully difficult to give anyone the brush-off if both you and he are stark naked.

S.N., P. 259

The fact is that nudism is not natural, unless you are doing something such as swimming, where clothes are a nuisance. In any other situation, the nudist is a joke, and often an unfunny joke.

S.N., P. 260

Watching their behaviour, on the rocks, in the sea, in the village street, in the cafés and shops, I came to the firm conclusion that most of them are obsessed by sex. The men come [to the colony] to look at naked girls, and spend most of their time doing so, quite unequivocally; while the girls come there to be looked at, and quite manifestly enjoy it.

S.N., P. 259

O

O'CONNELL, DANIEL

He was the first Irishman to see that nationalist objectives were more likely to be achieved not through the Protestant elite, nor through a revolutionary mob, but by the legal and organized use of Catholic power, based on professional political agents and the parish priests.

ID., PP. 91–92

O'Connell's programme was simple. First, he would organize a legal mass campaign to secure Catholic emancipation and the vote. Then, on the basis of the political power thus secured, he would campaign for repeal of the union. He tried to keep within the law: no easy matter, for with the Convention Act, various Coercion Acts and the periodic suspension of Habeas Corpus, there were only four or five years of normal government in the whole period from 1796 to 1823. Twice O'Connell had to dissolve and refound his organization in order to comply with the law. To remain legal was essential to him, for his power rested on his superb ability to enthuse and control great mass meetings. He had no time for the secret oath and the arms cache: Irish freedom, he said, was not worth the shedding of a single drop of English blood.

ID., P. 92

O'CONNOR, JOHN CARDINAL (AND POLITICIANS)

The Cardinal rightly reminds them that Catholicism is not about political horse-trading but about truth, faith and morals and that the Church has the duty to expel those who reject its beliefs. Needless to say, in the United States telling the blunt, awful truth in public is a rare event and what the Cardinal said has excited fearful cries of rage, fear and pain among the hedonistic multitudes of the City of Gotham. He has already been accused of seeking to revive the Spanish Inquisition.

S., JUNE 23, 1990

OIL SHORTAGE

The oil panic—the unplanned switch from low- to high-cost energy—was a disaster of the first magnitude for our civilization. Almost overnight, it turned a routine slow-down of the world economy into a major depression, by far the worst since the 1930s. It brought to a bitter end the thirty-year Keynesian boom, resurrected the spectre, indeed the reality, of mass-unemployment in the advanced states, cut growth-rates to nil, or even to reverse growth, and induced a new and highly destructive crisis of confidence in the free economy and in free societies everywhere. What made the Middle East price-revolution even more effective in bringing western growth to an end was the fact that another campaign by the eco-lobby had succeeded in delaying the introduction of the vast new oil fields on the North Slope of Alaska. The fanatics, as it were, brought down the West with both barrels.

E.S., P. 100

OLD TESTAMENT

What makes it unique is that the context, or setting, in religion and history, continues to expand and acquires its own momentum. The law-code remains the core, but in a sense it becomes an excuse for writing the history of a people, a civilization and its divine

[265]

patron. The Hebrews were great lawyers but they were superlative historians. As an antique law-code, the Old Testament is only one, albeit the best, of many; as a work of history it is unsurpassed, for even the achievements of the classical Greeks are fragmentary by comparison. The sense of history is an important stage in the development of civilization.

C.H.L., P. 81

OPINION

Neil Ascherson wrote in his column . . . "It is always, everywhere, wrong to kill people for their opinions." Ascherson is an intelligent man, but that struck me as a foolish remark. If Hitler had been killed for his opinions at *Mein Kampf* stage, six million Jews would not have been murdered. If Kerensky had shot Lenin for his opinions, before he had a chance to put them into practice, 20 million Russians might have lived out their lives naturally, and Ascherson's Polish friends would be free men and women today.

S., MARCH 15, 1986

OPINION POLL

[In the early nineteenth century] city dwellers expressed their approval of a public event by putting candles in their windows at night—"illuminating" as it was called. They might also refuse to do so. "Illuminating" was the earliest form of public opinion poll. In times of social unrest, however, mobs would sometimes order householders to illuminate, to celebrate the acquittal of a radical hero by a Middlesex jury, for example, on pain of having their windows broken if they failed to comply. Such orders were often cravenly carried out, but they were bitterly resented. People disliked being put in fear by social inferiors they despised.

B.M., PP. 385–86

OPUS DEI

Opus Dei has been the most successful Catholic movement of the twentieth century, and it has aroused intense suspicion and jealousy, not least within the church itself. Like the Dominicans, another order of Spanish origin, it is accused of fanatical doctrinal zeal and intolerance. As with the Jesuits, before their recent radicalization, Opus Dei is said to be ultra-conservative and to have exercised enormous political influence . . . It is also accused of educational imperialism, and fights running battles with Catholic chaplains in some universities. Like the reformed Carmelites of St. John of the Cross and St. Teresa of Avila, it is said to subject young recruits to intolerable mental conditioning and excessive physical rigour, including the use of self-inflicted corporal chastisement. Like the medieval Benedictines, it is accused of possessing incalculable wealth.

P.J., PP. 182–83

ORATORY

. . . oratory engenders myths, and myths, in turn, breed realities.

M.T., P. 253

ORWELL, GEORGE

Orwell . . . was an almost classic case of the Old Intellectual in the sense that for him a political commitment to a utopian, socialist future was plainly a substitute for a religious idealism in which he could not believe. God could not exist for him. He put his faith in man but, looking at the object of his devotion too closely, lost it.

I., P. 306

Orwell had always put experience before theory . . . Theory taught that the left, when exercising power, would behave justly and respect truth. Experience showed him that the left was capable of a degree of injustice and cruelty of a kind hitherto almost unknown, rivalled only by the monstrous crimes of the German Nazis, and that it would eagerly suppress truth in the cause of the higher truth it upheld.

I., P. 309

The truth is that the literary conceits elaborated in both *Animal Farm* and *Nineteen Eighty-Four*, though excellent in their time, are too fragile to carry the weight of all the ideological overkill they are now receiving. The Orwell industry will end by destroying Orwell's work. He has already been turned upside down and stood, as it were, on his short-back-and-sides head.

S., JANUARY 7, 1984

Certainly poor old Orwell could not have foreseen that, by the time his fatal year was reached, the clergy would be in the van of verbal totalitarianism and that the people most in need of watching could be the Right Reverend Peace and Big Monsignor.

S., JANUARY 7, 1984

OXFORD MOVEMENT

Newman believed that there must be a cut-off point beyond which human inquiry was not allowed to penetrate. Up to that point, thought and argument were free; after it, prohibited. But who was to determine that point? And who was to decide what was to be believed beyond that point? Only one Church was really prepared to take on such responsibilities, and their draconian consequences, and that was Rome. Hence in the 1840s and 1850s, Newman and others crossed to Rome in the quest for authority.

H.C., P. 378

P

PAINTING (MODERN)

. . . art must excite or it fails and becomes functional like furniture.

S., JUNE 28, 1988

PAPACY

A man comes to the throne of St. Peter at an age when most public officials are seeking retirement. He is brought from comparative obscurity to startling world prominence, and his previous career, which usually embraces most of his working life, is quickly embellished with pious anecdotes and edifying inventions. . . . It is not always clear to the historian when his policies are shaped by his own judgment, and when they are directed by the relationship he claims with Providential forces; his reign thus defies normal political analysis. His actions have to be seen not merely in their contemporary context but *sub specie aeternitatis*; he directs a global organization whose temporal functions are often in conflict with its deeper spiritual purposes, and whose successes or failures cannot be identified by the criteria of secular society.

P.J., PP. 3–4

The popes of modern times have varied enormously in personality: . . . Leo XIII, the diplomat with the grand manner and the imperious phrase: Pius X, the handsome giant with the bitter conservatism of the successful peasant; Benedict XV, shy, crippled, gentle and perceptive; Pius XI, the dull bourgeois pedant, who grew more sharp

[269]

and interesting as he aged; Pius XII, the solitary ascetic and poly-
math . . . and dictatorial. Yet their characters tend to be merged
in the anonymous solemnity of their office . . . the stereotyped *pietas*
with which they are presented by the ecclesiastical apparatus to the
hundreds of millions of Catholics throughout the world. They become blurred: holy men dressed in white, remote from the world,
distant figures . . . Only the insiders are capable, at the time, of
judging the nuances of papal statesmanship; the real significance of
a pontificate is often understood, if at all, only after—sometimes
long after—the subject is dead.

P.J., PP. 116–17

Does power corrupt and absolute power corrupt absolutely? Certainly, in theory, there is no power so absolute as that of "Christ's
Vicar on Earth." But in practice it is a different matter.

S.N., P. 64

Papal Law

The legal revolution enormously strengthened the hands of the papacy because to be able to dispense justice effectively was, to medieval man, a chief sign of power. The growth of papal law was
both a cause of the papacy's claim to total sovereignty, and the
means whereby successive emperors were humbled or smashed. On
the other hand, it gradually turned the papacy, and so the Church
as a whole, into a totally different kind of institution. It became
not so much a divine society, as a legal one; and a legal society
increasingly divorced from the total society surrounding it. . . . As
Roger Bacon bitterly remarked, for every theologian in Innocent
IV's entourage there were twenty lawyers.

H.C., P. 206

Papal State

For a world-wide organization, in contact with 750 million people,
the Catholic Church has an extraordinarily small central base. The

papal state consists only of the 109 acres of the Vatican City, most of which is taken up by the basilica of St. Peter's and the Vatican gardens and museums . . . John Paul possesses few of the physical instruments of government. Paul VI abolished the papal gendarmerie and the Noble and Palatine Guards. Only a hundred or so Swiss guards are left. There is a daily newspaper, a powerful radio station run by the Jesuits and a printing house. The pope has his own bank and mints his own coins. There is a small railway system for goods and a helicopter pad. But in most other respects the state, which has about 450 actual citizens, is a legal and constitutional device to guarantee the sovereignty of the papal absolutism, rather than a physical entity.

P.J., P. 169

PARLIAMENT

The English parliament has had more influence in the world than any other political institution. Yet its history remains to be written.

S., APRIL 1, 1989

PAUL, ST.

Paul did not invent Christianity, or pervert it: he rescued it from extinction.

H.C., P. 35

Paul insisted [Jesus Christ] was God: it is the only thing about him which really matters, otherwise the Pauline theology collapses, and with it Christianity. But equally, Paul is an obstacle to those who wish to turn Christianity into a closed system. He believed in freedom. For him, Christianity was the only kind of freedom that matters, the liberation from the law, and the donation of life. He associated freedom with truth, for which he had an unlimited reverence.

H.C., P. 40

PAUL VI

If Pope Paul's decision on contraception provoked a crisis of conscience in the radical wing of the church, the ruthlessness of the liturgical changes has produced comparable strains at the other end of the spectrum of opinion. It could be argued, in fact, that Pope Paul contrived to get the worst of all possible worlds and on different issues alienated both progressives and conservatives, leaving the authority of the papacy on a very narrow basis of support in the center.

P.J., P. 239

PEACE

Peace has always been a vote-winning issue in the United States. Yet there is an instructive contrast in Democrat and Republican records. Wilson won in 1916 on a promise to keep America out of the war; next year America was a belligerent. Roosevelt won in 1940 on the same promise and with the same result. Lyndon Johnson won in 1964 on a peace platform (against Republican "warmongering") and promptly turned Vietnam into a major war. Eisenhower in 1952 and Richard Nixon in 1972 are the only two Presidents in this century who have carried out their peace promises.

M.T., P. 460

PERMISSIVE SOCIETY

What characterised the cultural progeny of the Permissive Society was its sheer exorbitance, its passion for excess. Clearly, useful political debate becomes impossible when a democratically elected prime minister is dismissed as a Hitler. Such a comparison itself suggests a violent approach to public affairs. Violence is now an omnipresent feature of much of our cultural output, especially what is directed at the young, which rests on an unholy tripod of brutality, crude sex and radicalism.

S., JANUARY 21, 1989

[272]

PERÓN, JUAN

Perón's career illustrated the essential identity of the Marxist and the fascist will to power, for at times he borrowed from Lenin, Mussolini, Hitler, Franco and Stalin. He had great personal charm; a superb speaking voice; a gift for ideological verbiage. He spoke of his labour followers as "the shirtless ones" (they were in fact well paid). He called his philosophy *Justicialismo*, the first of the bogus "isms" of what was to become the Third World. Perón could claim to be the prototype not merely of a new kind of Latin-American dictator but of all the post-colonial charismatics of Africa and Asia. He was the link between the old-style mountebank dictator and the new Bandung model. He showed how to manipulate head-counting democracy.

M.T., P. 617

Perón gave a classic demonstration, in the name of socialism and nationalism, of how to wreck an economy. He nationalized the Central Bank, railways, telecommunications, gas, electricity, fishing, air-transport, steel and insurance. He set up a state marketing agency for exports. He created Big Government and a welfare state in one bound . . . He had no system of priorities. He told the people they would get everything at once. In theory they did. . . . By 1951 he had exhausted the reserves and decapitalized the country, wrecked the balance of payments and built wage-inflation into the system.

M.T., P. 617

PHILOSOPHY (TWENTIETH CENTURY)

. . . Ludwig Wittgenstein, one of the key figures of our period, . . . tended to destroy confidence in philosophy as a guide to human reason. For half a century Wittgenstein's influence on academic philosophy was immense. By the early 1990s doubts were raised about his sanity: was he a genius, or simply a madman? But by then much damage had been done. A leading Logical Positivist like Sir A. J. Ayer, who at the time of his death in 1989 was widely regarded as the world's leading philosopher, remarked with some complacency that philosophy demonstrated that man was ignorant rather than knowledgeable. . . . Empirical popular knowledge, usually termed "common sense," had been dismissed contemptuously by Bertrand Russell as "the metaphysics of savages." But if academic philosophers thought the world was peopled by fools, most made little or no attempt to enlighten them on the great issues of the day. . . . The negative and destructive nature of twentieth-century philosophy, its obsession with the inadequacies and failures of language, above all its failure to address itself to the immense problems confronting humanity, was a source of shame to the few who tried to grapple with them, notably Karl Popper: "I cannot say that I am proud of being called a philosopher," he wrote.

M.T., P. 699

PHOTOGRAPHERS (NEWSPAPER)

I have always thought photographers to be rather cold-blooded creatures, clicking away while the wounded moan and the dead lie unburied. No doubt they would claim this is the only way they can transact their professional business. But they are positively warm-hearted compared to television cameramen and those who direct and egg them on. The need to get "good pictures" is so paramount in their minds that they will stolidly, unsmilingly go about their complex trade in conditions of such appalling human misery as to overwhelm decent people with compassion and an irresistible urge to help in some way. But television crew do not help. They film. And then they concentrate on getting their film back to base for transmission.

S., MARCH 30, 1985

PHOTOGRAPHY, INVENTION OF

[In the early 1800s, artists] were intrigued by the technology of the effects of light and made increasing use of the refined *camera oscura*

. . . (They were not the only ones; in the 1820s a version of this machine was used to detect pickpockets at horse races.) [Henry] Brougham characteristically boasted in his old age that the paper on optics he wrote at age 16, portions of which were read to the Royal Society in 1796, anticipated the invention of photography, and it was only the scientific establishment's willful omission of this key passage which "withheld from humanity" the invention for decades.

B.M., P. 606

PICASSO, PABLO

His ability to overawe and exploit both men and women—some of them highly intelligent and uneasily aware of what he was doing to them—was by far the most remarkable thing about him.

S., JULY 9, 1988

He said that for him women were divided into "goddesses and doormats"; and his object was to turn each goddess he captivated into a doormat. He was both predatory and intensely possessive. He would steal a friend's wife, then tell him he was doing him an honour by sleeping with her. He discarded at will, but to desert him was treason. He told one mistress: "Nobody leaves a man like me." There was, indeed, a streak of monomania in Picasso which confirms Jung's view that his paintings were the work of a schizophrenic. "I would rather see a woman die," he told Françoise Gilot, "than see her happy with someone else."

S., JULY 9, 1988

Picasso [was] an intensely superstitious atheist—he had his own barber so that no one could collect his hair-clippings and "get control" of him . . .

S., JULY 9, 1988

[275]

PIUS XII

Pius was a Tridentine pope. To him, the Greek Orthodox were simply schismatics, and the Protestants heretics. There was nothing more to be said or discussed. He was not interested in the ecumenical movement. The Catholic Church already was ecumenical in itself. It could not change, because it was right and always had been right.

H.C., P. 504

Pius's whole analysis of Christianity and the world implied a long period of waiting. It would take time before heretics and schismatics came to their senses, and Marxists abandoned their godless materialism. The Church could wait, as it had waited before. It would remain in its fortress, avoiding contact with the evils of compromise, and from time to time lifting its admonitory voice. It was a policy of splendid isolation; or, if the isolation was not splendid, it was at least holy.

H.C., P. 505

One might say that Pius, seeing his inability to create a perfect world, wanted a world which was frozen and immobile. Motion was dangerous: experience showed it invariably led in the direction of evil. Change must therefore be resisted at all costs: God, in his infinite wisdom, had condemned his church to fight a perpetual rearguard action, and every inch yielded must be bitterly contested. At the same time, while resisting change, the church must never for an instant allow her claims to be obscured and diminished. On the contrary, they must be constantly asserted in all their plenitude.

P.J., P. 95

POETS (BRITISH ROMANTIC)

We often forget how young this generation of English poets were when they transformed the literature of the English-speaking world; how young indeed when they died—Keats twenty-five, Shelley twenty-nine, Byron thirty-six. When Byron, having fled England for good, first met Shelley . . . Shelley was twenty-four; Mary and

[276]

Claire a mere eighteen. Mary's novel *Frankenstein* . . . was, you might say, the work of a schoolgirl. Yet if they were in a sense children, they were also adults rejecting the world's values and presenting alternative systems of their own, rather like the students of the 1960s.

I., P. 41

POLAND AND THE CATHOLIC CHURCH

The Catholic Church is the most respected institution in Poland precisely because, on essentials, it is seen to be unbending, unchanging and sure of itself.

P.J., P. 19

POLICE (SECRET)

The notion of a state political police, composed of plainclothes officers operating in secret, was an importation from the totalitarian system Bonaparte set up in France after the coup d'état of November 1799. To have a secret police became, for the Habsburgs and for most European ruling houses who could afford one, the sign of a "modern" monarchy. Once the force was set up, it soon found enemies to observe.

B.M., P. 108

POLITICAL CAMPAIGNS (MODERN)

Smart politicians tell you that nowadays, and especially at election times, there is no point in wasting too much energy on actual political meetings, attended by the faithful. Of course you have to go through the motions and pretend they are important. But what wins votes now is what happens on the air waves and especially on television. All the rest is traditional mummery.

S., APRIL 6, 1985

POLITICAL CARTOONIST

Most of them are products of art schools during a period when
drawing had ceased to be taken seriously.

S., AUGUST 6, 1988

POLITICAL CONVENTIONS

Increasingly . . . [they are] . . . media events rather than real ones.

S., NOVEMBER 4, 1986

POLITICAL CORRECTNESS

. . . intolerance is its essential characteristic. It is the current and
so far the most dangerous form of liberal fascism.

S., OCTOBER 19, 1991

Political Correctness itself is a modern variant of the old American
Puritan tradition, once directed against witches, fallen women, the
poems of Walt Whitman and burlesque shows. The woman academic
at Penn State who recently objected to a print of Goya's "Naked
Maja," and obliged the university to remove it, speaks for this
tradition. A hundred years ago she would also have objected, but
on religious grounds: the Maja's nakedness would then have been
an affront to "decency," an insult to the "purity of women." Now
she uses the cant term of the 1990s: it is a case of "sexual harassment."

S., NOVEMBER 30, 1991

The currently correct use of escape-words is a matter of some concern
for governments. Words or expressions like dole, relief, unemployment benefit, National Assistance, many already obsolete or obsolescent, are gravestones on ancient political battlefields. Much
official thinking went into attempts to avoid the word "slump";
thus we had depression, recession, business-cycle; and a good deal
of dishonest juggling took place with unemployment, high em-

[278]

ployment, underemployment, full employment and overemployment, leaving a state of genuine confusion over the exact meaning of official "unemployment figures," with the risk of popular misinterpretation and thus of dangerous consequences for economic policy.

E.S., P. 107

POLITICAL HEARINGS (TELEVISED)

. . . if newspapers (whoever owns them) tend to work against authority, I have a hunch that televising Parliament will operate in rather the opposite direction. For the first time the journalist no longer stands between the public and the politicians . . . Now, suddenly, we not only hear but see all the members of the House of Commons as they actually are in their daily legislative and interrogatory work. . . . Now we can indeed see them uninterpreted, as though we were in the same room, and it is only a matter of time before a channel becomes available for transmitting Commons proceedings *in toto*. Needless to say, a great deal will be uninteresting, but the point is that the telecast will always be there if there is something we care about and wish to see.

S., DECEMBER 23–30, 1989

POLITICAL MORALITY AND GRESHAM'S LAW

By early 1933 . . . the two largest and strongest nations of Europe were firmly in the grip of totalitarian regimes which preached and practised, and indeed embodied, moral relativism, with all its horrifying potentialities. Each system acted as a spur to the most reprehensible characteristics of the other. One of the most disturbing aspects of totalitarian socialism, whether Leninist or Hitlerian, was the way in which, both as movements seeking power or regimes enjoying it, they were animated by a Gresham's Law of political morality: frightfulness drove out humanitarian instincts and each corrupted the other into ever-deeper profundities of evil.

M.T., P. 296

POLITICAL PARTY PLATFORMS

Policy programmes are supposed to answer unspoken questions from the electorate about what a party intends to do in office. In fact there is no evidence that voters ask these questions, until provoked into doing so by the publication of policies.

S., JUNE 2, 1990

POLITICAL PROCESS

Most men and women, going about their daily affairs, do not choose to devote much time or effort to political matters, except in periods of acute national crisis. They have more interesting or worthwhile preoccupations. That is perfectly natural and proper. God forbid that the majority of mankind should devote themselves to the political process: life would then indeed become intolerable; nasty, brutish and short too, in all likelihood. But the indifference of the majority opens wide the doors of power to dedicated minorities, who give the pursuit of political power absolute priority in their lives. Such men and women, almost by definition, are ill-suited to exercise it wisely. Representative institutions, however, by the very nature, enable fanatics to acquire power disproportionate to their numbers.

H.E., P. 425

POLITICAL RESTRAINT

. . . the experience of the twentieth century indicates that self-imposed restraints by a civilized power are worse than useless. They are interpreted by friend and foe alike as evidence, not of humanity, but of guilt and lack of righteous conviction.

M.T., P. 636

POLITICIANS

Recent legislation makes it increasingly hard for Congressmen to add to their salaries by activities outside politics. . . . The ban is well-intentioned, but it tends to create a class of professional politicians who go into politics for life and who know no other kind of occupation. Such a class is inimical to the spirit of the Constitution. It creates a cast of mind remote from the real life of the country, and the isolation is increased by living in an artificial federal capital whose only activities are politics and government.

That is one reason why the United States has such a huge budget deficit, its rulers spending vast sums they do not dare to collect from the taxpayers, so mortgaging the future.

C., DECEMBER 1991

The French Revolution had lowered the threshold of abuse at which men rose. It proved that cutting off royal heads was easier than had previously been thought and did not bring down the heavens. That undoubted fact was now a permanent temptation to every enemy of society who wished to acquire moral respectability for his crimes. . . . In the past, men with a grievance had suffered in silence or taken to the hills and robbed. Now the hitherto resigned joined secret societies, and the bandits called themselves politicians.

B.M., P. 662

. . . the great human scourge of the twentieth century; the professional politician.

M.T., P. 510

"We believe," said a speaker, "in the Democracy of the Committed." Of course, the speaker does not believe in democracy at all. He believes in oligarchy, an oligarchy of political activists and zealots who impose their views on the rest of the community by their ability to manipulate the democratic machinery. All men are equal, but the Committed are more equal than others.

R.F., P. 102

[281]

Where the financiers go, the politicians will be well advised to follow. They have never been more unpopular because they have never been less successful in persuading ordinary people that their policies are sensible. Just as financial men need the adman to communicate with shareholders, so politicians will have to employ him more.

S., MAY 17, 1986

I distrust politicians, especially Ministers, who talk too freely and are willing to divulge information "off the record." In the first place such information is often untrue, or hopelessly subjective, or deliberately slanted. In the second place, if it is true, it can usually be discovered by other means which do not prevent publication.

S.N., P. 15

A politician should never flinch from office, or relinquish it lightly. Too many of our greatest political talents have spent most of their lives in sterile opposition.

S.N., P. 100

POLITICIANS (ENGLISH)

England was for long the best (since least) governed country on earth because its politicians were amateurs. I use the word in its true sense: they loved politics but did not imagine it to be the sole or even the chief purpose of their existence.

P.P.J., P. 243

POLITICIANS (PROFESSIONAL)

I believe these amateur politicians were more representative of ordinary people than their professional successors, who tend to move in a limited circle of activists—work, indeed, in the "politics industry," sharing its jargon, preconceptions, trade secrets and remoteness. The fact that many of them work ridiculously long hours

[282]

makes the results worse, not better; the *déformations professionelles* they develop become more pronounced and incurable.

P.P.J., PP. 243–44

POLITICIANS AND RETIREMENT

[Thatcher is] . . . 65—say some, retirement age. That is nonsense. The world would be in a tragic state today if other outstanding leaders had taken this advice. Winston Churchill was almost exactly [65] . . . when a desperate country called on him to save it from Nazi conquest in 1940. He was 78 when he was summoned again to clear up the mess of Attlee's Britain in 1951. Konrad Adenauer was no less than 73 when he began his monumental task of creating the West German democratic state and bringing his country back into the ranks of the civilised nations. He didn't think himself too old, and indeed served for another 14 years . . . Charles de Gaulle likewise was 67 when he returned in 1958 to save France from civil war, solve the Algerian problem and get his country solidly on its feet again—a job which took him ten years. And don't forget . . . Ronald Reagan was almost 70 when he first entered the White House to give the United States back its self-respect and pride.

S., JUNE 29, 1991

POLITICS

. . . disastrous consequences . . . flow when men use the politics of force because they are too impatient for the politics of argument.

M.T., P. 123

. . . by the year 1900 politics was already replacing religion as the chief form of zealotry. To archetypes of the new class, such as Lenin, Hitler and Mao Tse-tung, politics . . . was the one legitimate form of moral activity, the only sure means of improving humanity. This view, which would have struck an earlier age as fantastic, even insane, became to some extent the orthodoxy everywhere: diluted

[283]

in the West, in virulent form in the Communist countries and much of the Third World.

M.T., P. 784

One of the great themes of the modern age is the way in which political emotions have replaced religious ones as the main driving force of the idealistic elite.

P.P.J., P. 173

This is the time of year when, traipsing round the party conferences, I reflect on the sheer, barren sameness of politics and wonder how any sensible man or woman can choose to spend a lifetime in such a wasteland. This prompts a further reflection. Is there not something peculiar about a person who not only elects for such a life but enjoys it, finds it an indispensable drug?

P.P.J., P. 243

A characteristic of the tyranny of politics is that the political activists present themselves as more estimable than the rest of us. Militancy is a virtue *per se*. It is a new priesthood, whose ritual lustrations and phylacteries endow its members with peculiar claims on our approbation. It is then only a small step to claim privilege, as of course all priesthoods have done throughout history. With privileges necessarily goes the power to oppress.

R.F., P. 87

Most civilised people find time for a great many other things.

S., AUGUST 23, 1986

Disillusionment with politics is probably the widest-spread intellectual phenomenon of the late 20th century.

S., SEPTEMBER 17, 1988

. . . there is, to put it no more strongly, a general scepticism about the value of politics. Those who put their faith in it, the academics, philosophers and writers as well as the practitioners, have pitched

[284]

their claims too high; the results have been meagre even when not actually disastrous . . .

S., SEPTEMBER 17, 1988

The notion that politics could transform or improve every aspect of society—that there is a political solution for every human problem—dates only from Rousseau. But the idea was eagerly taken up because it is as attractive in its own way as the vision of life after death, and it provided a powerful substitute for declining religious faith. Politics as panacea underlay all the great utopian philosophical systems of the 19th century, especially Marxism, and has been responsible for all the calamitous experiments in social engineering which have made the 20th century the bloodiest in human history. . . . All our century has proved is that, while politics cannot make things better, it can sometimes make them considerably worse.

S., SEPTEMBER 17, 1988

Politics is ultimately about the everyday lives of ordinary people, which are infinite in their variety.

S.N., P. 17

. . . politics has little to do with perfection: it is the art of balancing comparative good—and evil. The experience of the last sixty years or so shows that unity is the most precious gift a political party can possess. It is, in fact, the key to electoral victory. But it cannot be purchased without certain sacrifices of doctrine and principle. We can be purists, yes—but only by living, like hermits, in the wilderness.

S.N., P. 99

No wise man, I think, would dispute . . . [the] contention that self-interest is a healthy political guide. But it is precisely in exposing and propagating self-interest that the art of politics lies.

S.N., P. 110

[285]

POLITICS, AGE OF

One of the great transformations of history has been the replacement of religion by politics as the prime emotional concern of elites. It encompassed two centuries, in phases of a century each. But the age of politics, like the age of religion, is now drawing to a close. Politics has failed; politicians have not delivered.

P.P.J., P. 185

. . . the political zealot offered New Deals, Great Societies and welfare states; at the totalitarian end, cultural revolutions; always and everywhere, Plans. These zealots marched across the decades and hemispheres: mountebanks, charismatics, *exaltés*, secular saints, mass murderers, all united by their belief that politics was the cure for human ills: Sun Yat-sen and Ataturk, Stalin and Mussolini, Khrushchev, Ho Chi Minh, Pol Pot, Castro, Nehru, U Nu and Sukarno, Perón and Allende, Nkrumah and Nyerere, Nasser, Shah Pahlevi, Gaddafi and Saddam Hussein, Honecker and Ceausescu. By the 1990s, this new ruling class had lost its confidence and was rapidly losing ground, and power, in many parts of the world. Most of them, whether alive or dead, were not execrated in their own homelands, their grotesque statues toppled or defaced, like the sneering head of Shelley's Ozymandias.

SMM.T., P. 784

POLITICS (AMERICAN)

In America scandal politics have been institutionalized [and] certainly deter the honest from seeking office. What is not clear is whether the new climate of mistrust is making public life cleaner. . . . if honest men and women will not run for office, their places will be taken by the less scrupulous. And fear of exposure has never deterred real adventurers.

C., DECEMBER 1991

[286]

POLITICS, COLLECTIVE MORALISM OF

We now face the threat of an assault on our personalities and privacies by the collective moralism of politics—which is nothing more than a mask for the egotism and ambition of tiny bands of bigots. We must erect constitutional defences here also, and say: "Thus far may politics enter, and no further. Within these frontiers let scepticism flourish and the private non-political being be left in peace!" In short, let us make a corner of the world safe for the Erasmian majority, who have the refreshing modesty to wish "to define as little as possible."

R.F., P. 88

POLITICS AND ECONOMICS

The political process has had little more impact on world economic growth than it has had on the weather. Even at the level of the individual national unit, political decisions have rarely had more than a marginal effect, at any rate for good. They have been most productive when they have removed man-made obstacles to the free play of industrial capitalism.

P.P.J., P. 178

POLITICS AND THE MEDIA

[There is] a lurking antipathy to what is seen as media attempts to set the agenda and determine the outcome of the American political process. Ordinary voters are aware that one reason the 1988 choice between Bush and Dukakis was so poor is that many able American politicians were unwilling to enter the presidential race because they did not want themselves or their families savaged by reporters. They see the claims of the U.S. media that this was the dirtiest campaign on record as untrue and hypocritical. Untrue because the amount

[287]

of dirt thrown on both sides was not large; hypocritical because most of it was first unearthed and exploited by the media.

S., NOVEMBER 12, 1988

POLITICS AND MORALS

The truth is that no political cause is worth the abandonment of elementary morality. Whether terrorism works varies with the case, but it can never serve an ideal.

R.F., P. 195

POWER

. . . the corruption by power takes many forms. One kind of power is exercised by a great man, a seer, a prophet, over his followers, and he is corrupted by their adulation, subservience and, not least, flattery.

I., P. 131

. . . power is not to be despised but used, not to be overrated but justly considered.

P.J., P. 17

PRAYER

If someone asks me, "Does it make sense to pray to a God in whom I do not believe?" I answer, "Yes, indeed it does." It is a matter not of intellectual theory but of simply turning in the right direction, a plea for help.

R.D., JUNE 1985

PRESIDENT OF THE UNITED STATES

[In the early 1800s] American presidents were expected to be more available than European heads of state and heads of government. . . . "The succession of visitors," [Adams] recorded, "from my breakfasting to my dining hour, with their variety of objects and purposes, is infinitely distressing." . . . Many cases which would now be dealt with cursorily at a low bureaucratic level were then dealt with by the president face to face. . . . Adams had to receive a Mr. Arnold, who said he had been traveling and found himself in Washington without money; he would be "much obliged" to the president for a loan to see him back home to Massachusetts, "which I declined."

B.M., PP. 388–89

PRESIDENTIAL ELECTION (U.S.)

In theory, the presidential election is an exhaustive effort to discover the best available talent. It is open to any man or woman born in America. It progressively winnows out the unsuitable through the state primaries, through the party conventions, and finally through the universal election itself. It is designed to ensure the survival of the fittest. In fact it does nothing of the sort. How can it be said to do so when it eliminates, even at the stage of candidacy, such formidable contenders as Nelson Rockefeller or Henry Jackson, yet nominates lightweights like Goldwater or McGovern? When it re-elects, overwhelmingly, men of proven mendacity like Johnson and Nixon? When it confronts the elector with the hopeless alternative of Ford or Carter?

R.F., P. 226

PRESS

The press, indeed, was the new dynamic force in the 1820s, setting the pace of political change in all the advanced societies. It was associated with the latest technology, a process begun in 1813 when John Walter of the London *Times* bought the first two double presses worked by steam. . . . To avoid a strike and possible violence, Walter devised a strategy for introducing steam printing which in some ways anticipated Rupert Murdoch's when he introduced new computer technology in the 1980s and won "the Battle of Wapping." . . . What was also noticeable was the tendency of journalists to lean toward radicalism and against the established order, whatever it might be.

B.M., PP. 948–49

It was not long before Macaulay, referring to the parliamentary gallery, coined the phrase "the Fourth Estate." . . . Indeed, in the Restoration, 1815–30, despite all the efforts to curb them, journalists probably exercised more power than in any other country. It was writers—journalists and historians, but, above all, journalist-historians—who destroyed the Bourbons in the 1820s. During these years, it has been said, "only a hyphen separates the journalist and the historian."

B.M., PP. 950–51

The truth is that it never pays to have a row with the press. You may hate them and think their behaviour intolerable, but quarrelling with the press makes no more sense than abusing the voters. The thing to remember about journalists—Harold Wilson in his prime never forgot it—is that what they want from you is fresh information they can turn into a tasty story. If you are hostile, they will turn that into a story too. To use the press, to exploit them as they try to exploit you, requires intelligently contrived positive offerings.

S., MAY 2, 1987

. . . if the Press teaches [the public] to treat [politicians] with contempt, it will in time get contemptible politicians.

S.N., P. 17

PRESS, FREEDOM OF

There is a common supposition—common simply because it is put about by those skilled with words—that freedom of print and speech, of satire and criticism, should be virtually unlimited; that such is the hallmark of a healthy society. I do not agree. Its abuse in the Weimar Republic, for instance, was one of the factors which provoked many ordinary, inarticulate Germans into voting for the Nazis. The cruel use of words and images is no more justifiable than the cruel use of physical force, and just as likely to provoke a breakdown in society.

S., JUNE 28, 1986

Journalists assume that freedom of the press is a popular cause. They are mistaken.

S., JULY 19, 1986

The British media has an incorrigible habit of sneering at the American way of doing things. But America is the only country in the world where the institutional structure is geared to taking press freedom as seriously as the journalists do themselves. When an American journalist is arrested by the Soviets, the whole establishment, from the President down, pulls out all the stops.

S., NOVEMBER 4, 1986

When an editor weeps for a vanishing press freedom, you may likewise be easy: those tears will soon be dried. The present . . . scourge of libel damages flailing the backs of the guilty and innocent alike, is a much greater threat to press freedom than a well-drafted statute: there are plenty of snoring aldermen as it is. Nor does the *Times*, or any other newspaper opposing a privacy law, produce a defence of the extraordinary proposition that the only judge of the public interest is an editor, elected by nobody and responsible to no one, other than Mr. or Lord Moneybags. The obvious truth is that the only reliable judge of the public interest is the public—

operating both through Parliament, in enacting a statutory definition, and through juries, in interpreting it in specific cases.

S., DECEMBER 2, 1989

PRESS AND RACE

The black community wants race/colour suppressed in court cases and reports of riots and violent assaults, but stressed where its mention is favourable to its members, for instance in sports stories. . . . The Press Council itself is also inconsistent. . . . It does not, in practice, apply its own relevancy rule consistently. In a ghastly case involving a man who drank 18 pints of Guinness and ten brandies, then set fire to his house and killed his four sons, the Council ruled that the *Sun* was entitled to describe him as Irish because it was not "pejorative or prejudicial." But the context certainly was, and this is supposed to be the basis of the Council policy. In an equally appalling case involving a black youth who murdered one girl and raped five others, the Council condemned four papers for calling him "black." Is the Council drawing a categorical distinction between "Irish" and "black"? If so, it should explain why.

S., DECEMBER 20, 1986

PRIDE

The mechanism of the fall is the same even in the most spiritually sophisticated and learned persons. At the root there is always excessive self-confidence, a rash reliance on one's own chosen path, a refusal to submit to the judgement of him who holds God's place (the ecclesiastical superior), an awareness of being favoured by God in terms of insight, intelligence and acquired merit.

P.J., P. 153

PRIEST (POLITICAL)

A priest who treats the pulpit as a political soap-box and, instead of sticking to faith and morals, tries to make contentious party points on issues of current controversy should be treated like any other tub-thumper, and heckled.

s., FEBRUARY 16, 1991

PRIVACY

Editors, in particular, must be made to realise that abuse of the press's freedom may involve risking their own. There is nothing more calculated to instil a few moral values into an editor than the anticipatory clang of a cell door.

s., JULY 19, 1986

The truth is, everyone, from the Queen to the dustman, has a right to some privacy. The press will not admit this obvious, human fact.

s., JUNE 18, 1988

The press insists: "We have a right to invade privacy whenever it is in the public interest to do so. Who decides when it is in the public interest? Why, we do, of course." Believing in this principle, newspapers think they can do more or less what they please, subject to the existing law and libel risk. Methods vary of course. The downmarket tabloids conspire with prostitutes. The qualities hire "investigative journalists" to harass the families of public figures.

s., JUNE 18, 1988

The most brutal invaders of privacy are usually the most careful to get their facts right. So the victim has no redress. Juries know this. They also know that, even in cases where there are grounds for a libel action, ordinary people flinch at the financial risk of suing.

s., JUNE 18, 1988

We live in a treacherous world where confidentiality is a joke and privacy almost a thing of the past. It is a world full of spies, sneaks,

[293]

document-thieves and cads—and of people ready to defend anything they do . . . But for how much longer will ministers be able or willing to do so in private? It is already dangerous for them to put down anything frank in writing, however high the classification of the document. The next stage will be secret tapes, and then even private conversations at the top will be risky. That is what happens in a police state. But here the threat to freedom of private discourse comes from the media itself and the first victim is good government.

s., JULY 21, 1990

PRIVACY LAW

The absence of a privacy law in this country has many sad consequences. Among the worst is the way in which it allows the media to wreck the marriages of prominent persons by making public tittle-tattle which might otherwise die a natural death and by setting aggrieved spouses against one another and thus sending a rocky but retrievable union into the ditch—then licking its greasy chops over the result.

s., AUGUST 3, 1991

PRIVACY, RIGHT TO

The right to privacy is one of the most important human rights because it protects one of the deepest human needs. Even famous public figures, from prime ministers to pop stars, should be given some privacy. It is particularly important to protect the privacy rights of those fortuitously involved in the glare of public life—the spouses and children of those in the news.

s., JULY 19, 1986

PROHIBITION

Spirit drinking was much more a problem in the United States than in Europe; by the late 1820s, American men were drinking, per capita, a yearly average of four gallons of pure, 200-proof alcohol. This, in turn, produced a reaction. The American temperance movement dates back to 1810, but it was in 1826, with the foundation of the American Temperance Society, that the drive for prohibition first acquired national dynamism, a portent of the future. By 1840, the temperance movement had already reduced per capita consumption from 4 gallons to 1.5.

B.M., P. 760

. . . if wholehearted in intention, it was not so in execution. It was another testimony to the ambivalence of American society. America willed the end in ratifying the Eighteenth Amendment; but it failed to will the means, for the Volstead Act was an ineffectual compromise—if it had provided ruthless means of enforcement it would never have become law. . . . Moreover, the Utopianism inherent in Prohibition, though strongly rooted in American society, came up against the equally strongly rooted and active American principle of unrestricted freedom of enterprise. America was one of the least totalitarian societies on earth; it possessed virtually none of the apparatus to keep market forces in check once an unfulfilled need appeared.

M.T., PP. 209–10

Prohibition, far from "Americanizing" minorities, tended to reinforce minority characteristics through specific patterns of crime: among Italians, Jews, Irish and, not least, among blacks, where from the early 1920s West Indians introduced the "numbers game" and other gambling rings, forming powerful black ghetto crime-citadels in New York, Chicago, Philadelphia and Detroit. . . . The truth is, Prohibition was a clumsy and half-hearted piece of social engineering, designed to produce a homogenization of a mixed community by law. It did not of course involve the enormous cruelty of Lenin's social engineering in Russia, or Mussolini's feeble imitation of it in Italy, but in its own way it inflicted the same damage to social morals and the civilized cohesion of the community. The tragedy is that it was quite unnecessary.

M.T., P. 212

PROPAGANDA

If there is an enemy in our midst—and who can doubt it?—must not that enemy be fought with all the means at our disposal? Those means include, to give it its real name, propaganda.

S., AUGUST 11, 1984

PROPHET (BIBLICAL)

The importance of the prophet in Israel's political history is that once such a man established himself in the public estimation as a seer who felt "the hand of the Lord," he was an alternative source of divine guidance to the monarch and therefore a check on the monarch's activities. He presented . . . the populist tradition. Of course the kings tried to win over the prophets by giving them an honoured place at court and by putting up with their contradictions and verbal chastisements. Even so, prophets of any status were not easily neutralized by royal patronage and they remained angular figures even in the Presence Chamber. They were a reminder that the king, like everyone else, was under the Law. In this respect Israel can always be correctly described as a state under the rule of law, with the prophets forming an unofficial constitutional court.

C.H.L., P. 52

PROSPERITY

The 1820s is . . . the first decade in history in which it is possible to point to a connection between general prosperity, which produced a rise in living standards among all classes, and the process of depoliticization. This was to become a familiar phenomenon in the history of the advanced countries, with political activity subsiding during the upswing in the trading cycles and resuming during the downswing. But prosperity had a ratchet effect: From the early 19th century onwards, the level attained at the end of each complete cycle was always higher than at the beginning, so the politics of desperation began to be succeeded by the politics of aspiration; hunger passed out of the equation.

B.M., PP. 872–73

PROTESTANT ETHIC

In putting forward the theory of the "Protestant ethic," Max Weber and his followers argued that Protestant theology, with its heavy emphasis on justification by faith and predestination, generated "a salvation panic" among believers. This, in turn, led to the methodical practice of good works (thus developing in economic terms habits of industry and capitalism). Good works were useless as a means of attaining salvation, since that was already determined, but they were indispensable as a sign of election, to get rid of the fear of damnation, and induce what Luther called "the feeling of blessed assurance"—an inner conviction that you were saved.

H.C., P. 313

PSYCHOANALYSIS

As Sir Peter Medawar has put it, psychoanalysis is akin to Mesmerism and phrenology: it contains isolated nuggets of truth, but the general theory is false. Moreover, as the young Karl Popper correctly noted at the time, Freud's attitude to scientific proof was very different to Einstein's and more akin to Marx's. Far from formulating his theories with a high degree of specific content which invited empirical testing and refutation, Freud made them all-embracing and difficult to test at all.

M.T., P. 6

PUBLIC OPINION

Ordinary men and women favor freedom of speech and movement; all want the right to sell their labor in the highest market, to spend their money as they please; they welcome the right to vote, and

[297]

most support freedom of the press, and even religion. But the more sophisticated forms of liberalism are less popular, and some are downright unpopular. If countries like the United States and Britain had government by referendum—something which is now technically possible on a day-to-day basis—they would become radically less liberal in a short time. Over a huge range of issues, from what is taught in the schools and how, to the treatment of criminal offenders, public opinion, so far as one can see, would insist on a harder, harsher society, but also one which would become more industrious, and safe. Such are the orders of human priorities in the mass.

C., MARCH 1992

PUBLIC RELATIONS

Electoral victories are only a means to an end: the end is good government. And good government is impossible today without intelligent, professional and sustained public relations. It is tragic to see an administration which, in essentials, is well-founded, hastening towards disaster for lack of the skill to put its case.

S., JUNE 30, 1984

. . . the effectiveness of a government does depend in some measure not just on getting its legislation through Parliament but in persuading the public it is right.

S., AUGUST 5, 1989

PUBLIC SECTOR CULTURE

This sector includes the subsidised theatre, national and local, the public galleries . . . Public sector culture or PSC scarcely existed before 1914; it is now the dominant element in our cultural life, for not only can writers and artists pursue their entire careers within it, but the power its privileged financial position bestows gives it a predominant influence on the way our culture is heading. More important, until now it has controlled the broadcasting element completely. The long-term impact of television on our national culture cannot yet be fully measured—40 years is too short a testing-span—but it clearly has been, and is, enormous.

s., NOVEMBER 6, 1990

PUBLISHERS

I score publishers according to ten criteria: (1) generosity over advances and terms; (2) quality of editing; (3) quality of production, especially proof-reading, illustrations, indexing, binding and jackets; (4) pricing policy; (5) salesmanship; (6) overseas rights and other subsidiary rights; (7) skill in handling publicity; (8) long-term vision; (9) general honesty; (10) and, not least, friendliness to authors. No publisher, in my experience, will score ten. But he ought not to be below six. Decent publishers will rate seven or eight . . . But there is also an 11th quality, what constitutes the "x factor," and which I term enthusiasm.

s., AUGUST 26, 1989

PURITAN

One of the characteristics of the Puritans was the extraordinary violence of their language. They made, indeed, a positive virtue of crude phraseology, especially in their castigation of women, whom they regarded (on the supposed authority of the Bible) as natural vessels of iniquity and, in matters of state, vain and foolish.

E., P. 256

PURITAN (LEFT-WING)

. . . [one] who objects to people enjoying anything.

s., APRIL 23, 1988

PURITAN SERMONS

The Puritans disliked public performances of any kind because they drew the rabble away from their sermons.

E., P. 363

R

Racism

The 19th century was the great age of racism, prompted probably by the huge and visible increases of population. . . . But whereas in the Far East, the "elect nation" racist ideologies of China and, now, Japan were clothed in the priestly robes of religious cosmogony, in Europe they tended to wear rationalist and philosophical garments. Underneath, however, were the same flesh and bones of gullible men, easily persuaded by their rulers and intellectual guides that they were, in essence, and could be in reality, supermen, ruling the world.

B.M., PP. 808—9

Race-poisoning was a comparatively common obsession in the time of Hitler's youth, rather as ecological poisoning became an obsession of many in the 1970s and 1980s. The notion of ubiquitous poisoning appealed strongly to the same type of person who accepted conspiracy theories as the machinery of public events. As with the later ecologists, they thought the race-poison was spreading fast, that total disaster was imminent, and that it would take a long time to reverse even if the right policies were adopted promptly. Hitler calculated it would need a hundred years for his regime to eliminate racial poisoning in Germany.

M.T., PP. 342—43

RACISM IN BRITAIN

One reason why racism of all kinds continues to flourish in Britain is precisely that the subject is protected from the free winds of public exposure and debate. The result, quite apart from anything else, is that the public is grievously mis- or under-informed, and disbelieves such "facts" as are allowed to trickle through. This is the fertile ground from which racial prejudices and harassment spring. Hence we have the paradox that in Britain today racial antagonism is increasingly the work of the race relations industry itself.

s., APRIL 21, 1990

RAPE

Rape, in its essence, is not primarily a sexual activity but a gross and cruel act of violence. It is in the spread of violence that we should seek the causes of its increase. Titillation in the media helps to arouse sexual desires, but the media presentation of violence is more likely to persuade the potential rapist that he can satisfy these desires by force.

s., MARCH 22, 1986

RAT RACE

We hear constant appeals that human beings must escape from "the rat-race" of free-enterprise society. Here is a case of verbal prestidigitation obscuring manifest reality, since it is a matter of universal knowledge that neither rats, nor any other animals, take part in races, unless compelled and trained to do so by men. Men, unlike animals, are immensely competitive, ambitious and aggressive creatures. The "rat-race," or rather "man-race" is a normal and necessary part of human existence. If social and other restraints are removed, human societies will tend to organize themselves into infinitely graded hierarchies . . . always changing, whose minute distinctions are marked by that most flexible and accurate of all indices—money. Thus, as human beings . . . attempt to realize their capacities, the middle grades of society . . . will develop, unless massive and deliberate steps are taken to restrain them. The evolution of a middle class seems to be both a cause and a measure of the development of civilization.

E.S., PP. 186–87

REAGAN, RONALD

It is impossible to imagine the 1980s without him. Future historians may call it the Thatcher Decade; they may even be tempted to call it the Gorbachev Decade. But it is far more likely, in my view, that they will settle for the Reagan Years. For it is the genial character of this unusual man, reflecting his attractive blend of naivety and wisdom, which has given an unmistakable coloring to a decade in which the peoples of the West felt better off and more secure.

F.A., JANUARY 1, 1989

He appeared a man of few but strong and simple ideas, firmly held and confidently executed. Unlike Carter, Reagan had both a political philosophy and a world outlook, both of them quite clear, in relation to which Europeans could orient themselves. He did not hesitate, he acted. He was consistent. He was usually predictable.

F.A., JANUARY 1, 1989

Kennedy mesmerized the elites (or some of them) and especially the intellectuals, who were the group least pervious to Reagan's charm. But Reagan was liked by ordinary people, especially those anxious to get on and better themselves.

F.A., JANUARY 1989

Reagan's dominance during the 1980s was by no means mainly due to changing demographics. Better than any other politician except Margaret Thatcher herself, he caught the spirit of the age. He was undoubtedly inspired by her victory and example—she was his John the Baptist or, to put it another way, he was her aptest pupil—

and for eight years, with one exception, they formed a mutual admiration society of two.

M.T., P. 749

America's growing self-respect went a long way to erase the masochism generated by the Vietnam débacle, and enabled Reagan, who had no inhibitions about the legitimate use of America's enormous power, to perform on the world stage with growing aplomb. He was not a rash man, and certainly not a bellicose man, but he was a staunch believer in absolute values of conduct with a clear view of the difference between right and wrong in international affairs. When he felt the need to act, he acted; not without careful deliberation, but without any feelings of guilt or *arrières-pensées*.

M.T., P. 750

REAGAN, RONALD, AND REARMAMENT

At a deeper level, however, Reagan's rearmament program, accompanied as it was by a resurgence in the U.S. economy, had a demoralizing effect on the Soviet elite. . . . Without American dynamism in the 1980s it is highly unlikely that the Soviet leadership would have set out on . . . a potentially disastrous road of reform. . . . This American challenge, and Soviet response, may well turn out to be the leading development of the last decades of our century. If so it will indicate once again the importance of will in politics. For the Reagan Administration's decision to rearm was essentially an act of will—the will of one simple, single-minded man.

F.A., JANUARY 1989

REFORM (BRITISH)

The pioneers make a proposal; a quarter of a century later it is generally accepted by enlightened opinion; chance and accident, financial cuts and economic crises, the churches, the Lords and other obstacles to progress delay it for another quarter-century; implementation takes 10 years or so. By then the reform is universally accepted as obvious common sense, and pious regret is expressed that it was not accomplished sooner. Meanwhile, the rest of the world has moved on. . . .

H.E., P. 402

REFORM (CHRISTIAN)

The Jesuits were a striking case of a highly educated and strongly motivated élite allowing the stresses of religious conflict to confuse their moral values. They were not isolated. Indeed, the problem was general. It is a tragic but recurrent feature of Christianity that the eager pursuit of reform tends to produce a ruthlessness in dealing with obstacles to it which brings the whole moral superstructure crashing down in ruins. The Gregorian papacy, so zealous for virtue, fathered some of the worst crimes of the Middle Ages.

H.C., P. 305

RELIC

The popularization of this cult by Ambrose in fourth century Milan was a decisive event in Christian history. Relics rapidly became, and for some 800 years remained, the most important single element in Christian devotion. . . . Pilgrimages to the sites of important relics, common since the fourth century, became the chief motive for travel for over a thousand years, and determined the communications-structure and often the shape of the international economy. It was not just that towns expanded around relics: so did regional, national and even international fairs, which were timed to coincide with the annual parade of key relics. A major factor in the prosperity of northern France, for instance, was the great fair which originated as a joint procession of the relics of St. Denis and Notre Dame. Relics were much more valuable than any precious metal. They were in fact the most important focus for the highest metallic art of the Dark Ages.

H.C., PP. 161, 163

RELIGION

What the world witnessed, during the late 1970s, throughout the 1980s and into the 1990s, was a widespread retreat from the churches and established religious bodies which had sought to rationalize their beliefs and come to terms with societies which in general were non-religious; and simultaneously, the growth of fundamentalism, which bypassed rationalism, stressed the overwhelming importance of faith and miraculous revelation and rejected the idea of compromise with institutions based on non-belief.

M.T., PP. 704–5

RELIGION (MODERN)

. . . modern pseudo-religions. What we may call . . . Christianity without Christ, tends to leave out the obligatory element in either conduct or belief. The idea of inflexible commandments, or the categories of specific sins, are . . . re-presented as modes of approach to moral problems, and the difference between right and wrong ceases to be objective, imposed from without, and becomes wholly subjective, and a matter for personal decision. Hence the readiness with which this type of moral theology accepts sexual promiscuity (and aberration) and individual acts of terrorism . . . on the doctrinal plane, the Resurrection, the very core of Christian belief, is not presented as an external event but is "translated" in terms of phenomena existing in the mind of the believer. Thus religion, both in its moral and in its doctrinal aspects, exists entirely within the individual and nowhere else. Christianity ceases to be a community of believers, animated by an external impulse, and becomes a multitude of separate personal universes, each revolving on its own doctrinal and moral axis.

E.S., P. 120

RELIGION (PSEUDOSCIENTIFIC)

One of the most important developments of our time, I would argue, is the growth, as a consequence of the rapid decline of Christianity, of irrationalist substitutes for it. These are not necessarily religious, or even quasi-religious. Often they are pseudoscientific in form, as for instance the weird philosophy of the late Teilhard de Chardin. The ecology panic is another example. It is akin to the salvation panic of sixteenth century Calvinism. When you expel the priest, you do not inaugurate the age of reason—you get the witch doctor.

R.F., P. 162

RELIGION (SECULAR)

Power-religions . . . encompass a variety of ideas . . . which have been forged into ferocious instruments of state tyranny. They ascribe to Nature, Biology, History or other abstractions many of the attributes which Christian theology ascribes to God. These abstractions are then presented as irresistible forces which the new state incarnates. Hence the Nazis deified the blood-force of the German race, which had an irresistible historical role to play for the next thousand years. They retained the old ruler-God worship of Hitler . . . For the Nazi baptism service, a room was decorated with Nazi flags, the Tree of Life, . . . and candles and a centre-altar contained a photograph of Hitler and a copy of *Mein Kampf*. For Nazi weddings, there were runic figures . . . and a fire-bowl; the married couple received bread and salt under a picture of Hitler and the Nazi flag, swore oaths and listened to appropriate Nazi music and readings.

E.S., P. 126

REPORTING

. . . reporting can be, and at its best ought to be, a sophisticated art in which it pays to be fair. . . . Readers know that life is rarely simple. Indeed they relish complexity, as the success of rococo story tellers, from Dickens to Chandler, testifies. It is also safer. One of Johnson's laws is: more details, fewer writs.

S., AUGUST 13, 1988

RESEARCH (HISTORICAL)

Historical research tends to move in circles. A traditional view is inherited from the actual protagonists, and becomes orthodox, textbook history. In time, an enterprising historian comes along, subjects it to critical analysis, and produces a significantly new version. He breeds pupils, who form a revisionist school, and push his conclusions much further. With the advent of a new generation, there is a counter-revolution: the revisionist theory is itself assaulted. . . . Sometimes the matter is now seen to be too complex to admit of any firm explanation, and the reader (who has followed the historians thus far) is left confused. More often, a modified version of the traditional view is re-established. Much academic blood is split, and little progress achieved.

H.E., P. 7

RESEARCHERS

. . . my experience teaches: put not your faith in researchers. American magazines employ them in large numbers and, when you write for one, they are liable to send you telexes with 50 or more queries, most of them unhelpful. ("What is your evidence the Queen prefers tea made from Malvern Water?") Moreover, they . . . insert errors as well as remove them.

S., OCTOBER 19, 1989

RESOURCES

. . . inanimate resources, important though they are, are not the raw material of the higher wisdom. The most vital development of the next ten years will be the improvement in the use of our human resources.

N.R., DECEMBER 14, 1992

REVOLUTION

In our time we have had our fill of revolutions. The cult of revolution is, indeed, one of humanity's great self-inflicted wounds. One can think of few that have achieved anything positive for the common-weal which could not have been secured by peaceful means.

S., JULY 15, 1989

REVOLUTION, PROLETARIAN

. . . the whole philosophy of the proletarian revolution was based on the assumption that the Jew, as such, did not exist except as a fantasy promoted by a distorted socio-economic system. Destroy that system and the caricature Jew of history would vanish, like an ugly nightmare, and the Jew would become an ex-Jew, an ordinary man. It is hard now for us to get back inside the minds of highly intelligent, well-educated Jews who believed this theory. But many thousands of them did. They hated their Jewishness, and to fight for the revolution was the most morally acceptable means to escape from it. It gave to their revolutionary struggle a peculiar emotional vehemence, because they believed its success would involve a per-sonal liberation from their Jewish burden, as well as a general lib-eration of humanity from autocracy.

H.J., P. 450

REVOLUTION, AMERICAN

What is tremendously significant and new about the American Rev-olution is that its victory for religious freedom and the separation of Church and State was won not so much by left-wing millenarian sects revolting against magisterial churchmen, but by the denom-

[309]

inational leaders and statesmen themselves, who saw that pluralism was the only form consonant with the ideals and necessities of the country.

H.C., P. 428

REVOLUTION, FRENCH

. . . the French Revolution and its aftermath brought not progress but retrogression.

B.M., P. 462

The French Revolution had opened an era of intense politicization. Perhaps the most significant characteristic of the dawning modern world, and in this respect it was a true child of Rousseau, was the tendency to relate everything to politics. In Latin America, every would-be plunderer or ambitious bandit now called himself a "liberator"; murderers killed for freedom, thieves stole for the people.

B.M., P. 662

. . . what happened was a combination of England's experience in the 1530s and the 1640s, a revolution directed not only against the crown and the possessing classes, but against the clergy as a whole, and against Christianity as such. Thus the idea of the modern secular State came into existence, and the concept of Christendom as a total, international society, already damaged by schism, finally dissolved. The process had its roots deep in the Enlightenment which in France . . . developed outside, rather than within, a Christian framework, and portrayed reason and religion pulling in opposite directions rather than (as in England) in harness. But if the roots were deep the flowering of anti-clericalism and atheism was to some extent accidental, one of the great muddles of history. The result was a confrontation between "reason" and "religion" which revealed the limitations and weaknesses of both, and raised a number of fundamental issues which have not yet been solved.

H.C., PP. 356–57

[310]

. . . for the first time a frontal attack was made on Christian institutions. Catholicism was tested to destruction and found to be, at least temporarily, highly vulnerable. But reason, which took its place, was also tested to destruction and found to be inadequate, even ridiculous.

H.C., P. 358

. . . the revolution was not reformist, it was millenarian. It was, in fact, the first modern millenarian revolt. It looked backwards to the Münster of the 1520s, and the Middle Ages, and forward to Karl Marx and Mao Tse-tung.

H.C., P. 359

The French Revolution is the classic demonstration of the capacity of words to kill.

S., JULY 15, 1989

REVOLUTIONARY

If we want to identify a social enemy we need go no further than examine his attitude to truth: it will always give him away; for, as Pascal says, "The worst thing of all is when man begins to fear the truth, lest it denounce him."

E.S., P. 259

Men who carry through political revolutions seem to be of two main types, the clerical and the romantic.

M.T., P. 50

ROBESPIERRE, MAXIMILIEN FRANÇOIS MARIE ISIDORE DE

Robespierre, with his cruel moral relativism, embodied the cardinal sin of all revolutions, the heartlessness of ideas.

S., JULY 15, 1989

ROOSEVELT, FRANKLIN DELANO

The political success of Roosevelt was due to quite other factors than the effectiveness of his economic measures, which were largely window-dressing, transposed by time into golden myth. He demonstrated the curious ability of the aristocratic *rentier* liberal (as opposed to self-made plebeians like Harding, Coolidge and Hoover) to enlist the loyalty and even the affection of the clerisy. . . . Even more important was his appeal to intellectuals, once the news he employed a "brains trust" got about. . . . There was no intellectual coherence to the Roosevelt administration, but it seemed a place where the clerisy could feel at home.

M.T., P. 257

[Roosevelt's] vanity, so reminiscent of Chamberlain's belief that he alone could "handle" Hitler, was compounded by an astonishing naïvety. He did not believe Stalin wanted territory.

M.T., P. 433

ROSSINI, GIOACCHINO

In fact Rossini, while boasting he could set a laundry list to music, was a profoundly serious artist, much given to melancholia and depression. . . . He made possible Verdi just as surely as Beethoven himself made possible not just Weber but Wagner.

B.M., P. 127

ROTHSCHILD, HOUSE OF

From 1815 the Rothschilds led a new movement in international banking. Governments had always financed war on credit. Now the Rothschilds made it possible for them to raise comparable or even greater sums to accelerate peaceful progress. It was, in its own way, perhaps the key factor in the birth of the modern world because it made so many other developments possible. In the decade 1815 –

25 more securities were floated than in the whole of the preceding century.

B.M., PP. 850–51

ROUSSEAU, JEAN-JACQUES

Rousseau was the first intellectual to proclaim himself, repeatedly, the friend of all mankind. But loving as he did humanity in general, he developed a strong propensity for quarrelling with human beings in particular.

I., P. 10

. . . he was the first intellectual systematically to exploit the guilt of the privileged. And he did it, moreover, in an entirely new way, by the systematic cult of rudeness. He was the prototype of that characteristic figure of the modern age, the Angry Young Man.

I., P. 11

The basis on which he negotiated with others . . . was quite simple . . . because of his uniqueness, anyone who helped him was in fact doing a favour to himself.

I., P. 13

Rousseau's reputation during his lifetime, and his influence after his death, raise disturbing questions about human gullibility, and indeed about the human propensity to reject evidence it does not wish to admit. The acceptability of what Rousseau wrote depended in great part on his strident claim to be not merely virtuous but the most virtuous man of his time. Why did not this claim collapse in ridicule and ignominy when his weaknesses and vices became not merely public knowledge but the subject of international debate? . . . It . . . suggests that intellectuals are as unreasonable, illogical and superstitious as anyone else.

I., PP. 26–27

ROYAL SOCIETY

During the twenty years 1640–60 we see the earliest challenge to the belief that knowledge was indivisible. We can observe it in the formative period in the history of the Royal Society. . . . The founder-members of the Royal Society were all sincere Christians, but they were coming to accept that institutional Christianity, with its feuds and intolerances, was an embarrassment and a barrier to scientific endeavour. Hence they decided to concentrate purely on science, and ruled that religious matters were not to be discussed at the Society's meetings. So for the first time we have a deliberate attempt to cut off science from religion, and to treat the two subjects as completely separate spheres of knowledge and lines of inquiry.

H.C., PP. 327–28

RUSSELL, BERTRAND

As a philosopher, Russell constantly insisted that words must be used with care and in their precise sense. As an adviser to humanity, he confessed, in his autobiography, to "the practice of describing things which one finds unendurable in such a repulsive manner as to cause others to share one's fury." This is a curious admission from a man professionally devoted to the dispassionate analysis of problems, who tied his flag to the mast of reason.

I., PP. 211–12

If many of the statements put out under his name seem childish today, it must be remembered that the 1960s [were] a childish decade and Russell one of its representative spirits.

I., P. 221

S

St. Patrick's Cathedral, Desecration of

Not so long ago, a well-organised mob of homo-yobs, assisted by militant lesbians and pro-abortionists, carried out an attack on St. Patrick's Cathedral in New York, the delightful neo-Gothic edifice on Fifth Avenue, which involved seizing the consecrated hosts distributed at Holy Communion and doing unspeakable things with them. There was a good deal of violence too. The authorities seem to have been paralysed by this outrage and the Governor of New York, Mario Cuomo, a Catholic by birth but a Democratic presidential hopeful by conviction, found himself unable to condemn the act of sacrilege, since in his view the lobbies behind it were too important to offend.

s., may 12, 1990

Saint-Simon, Claude Henri

At one time Le Père Enfantin, as he was known, had about 300 full-time women followers in Paris, and another 100 in Lyons, with branches in the United States and Egypt. When he lectured on sexual equality he sometimes attracted over 1,000 people. He began to advocate free love as one form of women's emancipation, and, as might have been expected, his movement degenerated into messianism and sex orgies.

b.m., p. 479

[The Condition] of the 19th century was often seen as the cause both of insanity and of the suicides it so constantly produced. In France this theory appeared to receive confirmation when Henri Saint-Simon, the philosopher most associated with the modern age, particularly with industry, tried to kill himself. In the early 1820s, to finance his new philosophical system, he toured the French provinces [asking industrialists] for 1,000 francs at a time, never small sums. Most slammed the door in his face . . . Saint-Simon loaded a pistol with seven bullets and tried to blow his brains out . . . he took out his watch and spent his last seven minutes on Earth having final thoughts about the organization of society. He managed to fire all seven shots, but they only grazed his skull, though one pierced his eye, which he lost. The suicide attempt, which was much talked about, had the effect of bringing in considerable funds.

B.M., P. 751

SAMUEL, HERBERT

Samuel did not mind Jewish importuning. What he minded was Arab accusations of unfairness because he was a Jew. Samuel always tried to have things both ways. He wanted to be a Jew without believing in God. He wanted to be a Zionist without joining any Zionist organization. Now he wanted to promote a Jewish national home without offending the Arabs. The thing could not be done. It was inherent in the entire Zionist concept that the Palestine Arabs could not expect full rights within the main area of Jewish settlement. But the Balfour Declaration specifically safeguarded the civil and religious rights of the "existing non-Jewish communities" and Samuel took this to mean that the Arabs must have equal rights and opportunities. Indeed, he regarded this phrase as the axiom of his mission.

H.J., PP. 436–37

SANCTIONS

Sanctions rarely work: they damage, infuriate and embitter but they do not deter or frustrate an act of aggression.

M.T., P. 320

SATIRE

It is sometimes argued that satire, even of the most savage kind, is a sign of health in a free society and that no restrictions should be placed on it. Jewish history does not lend support to this view. The Jews have been more frequently the target of such attacks than any other group and they know from long and bitter experience that the violence of print is often the prelude to the violence of blood.

H.J., P. 475

SCHWARZKOPF, GENERAL NORMAN

The Commander-in-Chief, General Norman Schwarzkopf, proved himself not merely an outstanding military supremo in directing one of the most complex international campaigns in history, involving sea, land and air forces, but showed himself well aware of the TV and public-opinion dimension of the operation. Indeed he proved himself an accomplished performer in front of the cameras at his regular briefings. His summary of Allied strategy, after the campaign was completed, immediately became a TV classic: it was as if one had watched the Duke of Wellington describing the Battle of Waterloo the day after it took place.

M.T., P. 772

SCIENCE

By this we mean a true science, based on objectively established and agreed foundations, with a rational methodology and mature criteria of proof—not the multitude of pseudo-sciences which . . . have

[317]

marked characteristics which can be readily detected and exposed. Science, properly defined, is an essential part of civilization. To be anti-science is not the mark of a civilized human being, or of a friend of humanity. Given the right safeguards and standards, the progress of science constitutes our best hope for the future, and anyone who denies this proposition is an enemy of society.

E.S., P. 259

Science is much too serious a business to be left to the scientists. A great scientist, that is one whose work fundamentally changes the explanation of how nature works, has in the long run far more effect on human behaviour than any statesman, economist or general—quite apart from any practical consequences of his discoveries.

P.P.J., P. 253

SCIENCE AND INDUSTRY

. . . modern science and industry [can] turn the luxuries of one generation into the necessities of the next.

B.M., P. 879

SCIENCE (PSEUDO-)

Immature sciences attempt to bolster up their self-esteem by seizing eagerly on any scientific instrumentation they can possibly use. Hence the fondness among social scientists for the computer, and for the elaborate tables and graphs which can be compiled with its assistance. . . . Worse, for social and academic reasons it is usually necessary to give the accolade of publication to innumerable sets of results, and propositions built on them; so the professional journals are useless in creating workable standards of quality. In psychology, for example, it is notorious that "results" used to confirm hypotheses are often no better than random data because significance tests would validate almost anything. Sociology is often no better; indeed, both

[318]

these "disciplines" usually fail Popper's falsification test since their custom is to look only for evidence which validates theory.

E.S., P. 157

SCIENCE AND SCIENTISM

The emergence of Einstein as a world figure in 1919 is a striking illustration of the dual impact of great scientific innovators on mankind. They change our perception of the physical world and increase our mastery of it. But they also change our ideas. The second effect is often more radical than the first. The scientific genius impinges on humanity, for good or ill, far more than any statesman or warlord. Galileo's empiricism created the ferment of natural philosophy in the seventeenth century which adumbrated the scientific and industrial revolutions. Newtonian physics formed the framework of the eighteenth-century Enlightenment, and so helped to bring modern nationalism and revolutionary politics to birth. Darwin's notion of the survival of the fittest was a key element both in the Marxist concept of class warfare and of the racial philosophies which shaped Hitlerism. . . . So, too, the public response to relativity was one of the principal formative influences on the course of twentieth-century history. It formed a knife, inadvertently wielded by its author, to help cut society adrift from its traditional moorings in the faith and morals of Judeo-Christian culture.

M.T., P. 5

SCIENTIFIC THEORY

Most scientific theories, too, originate in myths—the scientist begins by telling a story. But they only become *scientific* theories at the point when it is possible to test them. Marxism and Freudianism remain in the witch-doctor stage of myth because they dodge refutation by reformulation, osmosis and imprecision. They could be useful; what is absurd and dangerous is that political and physical therapies should be based on them.

E.S., P. 149

[319]

SCRIBES

There might be as many as twenty in a *scriptorium*. Each sat on a bench or stool, with his feet on a footstool, and wrote on his knees; a desk in front held the book he was copying, and a side-table his quills, ink, knife, eraser, compasses and ruler. Scribes worked in absolute silence (dictating of original work and letters was done in another room), but they communicated with posterity by marginal graffiti: . . . "Only three fingers are writing: the whole body is in agony"; "This work is slow and difficult"; . . . "The scribe has the right to the best wine." The Irish were great margin-writers. Thus, in a ninth-century Irish manuscript of Cassiodorus on the psalms, we find: "Pleasant is the glint of the sun today on these margins. It flickers so."

H.C., P. 155

[scribes were urged to "write] faster." There was a sense of gloomy urgency about the task, for men believed that, however horrible the period since Rome's decline had been, things would get worse, not better; and there was much evidence to support their belief. One chief reason why King Alfred, at the end of the ninth century, wanted all the essential Latin texts translated into English was that he believed the coming hard times would wipe out Latin scholarship and that, even if the originals were not destroyed, no one would be able to read them.

H.C., P. 156

SECRET SOCIETIES AND THE "THIRD FORCE"

To some extent [the Third Force] was connected with the Renaissance discoveries of lost texts and especially the cabalistic and Hermetic philosophies. This led to the belief, quite common among sixteenth-century liberal intellectuals, that there was a complete and final system of knowledge to be discovered, which embraced all the arts and sciences, and revolved around Christianity. When, in due course, this system was completely unveiled, it would automatically solve all religious disputes and controversies. . . . But it might also be dangerous, so there was a need for secrecy. One idea which constantly crops up is the "invisible college" of learned men—an international network . . . Secret societies as such probably originated among fifteenth-century Italian intellectuals, and may have been brought to northern Europe by the Hermetic philosopher Giordano Bruno. He certainly formed a circle of like-minded men in Lutheran Germany.

H.C., P. 319

SERFDOM

. . . [Tsar Alexander's] own country ran the largest system of forced labour on earth, under the name of serfdom. It had many aspects, not the least interesting of which was the Russian capacity—to become such a feature of the modern world—to present crimes against humanity in the guise of utopianism.

B.M., P. 291

SEX

In this period of sexual confusion, one sometimes has the impression that the girls themselves are trying, instinctively, to formulate a new code of sexual ethics, based on the facts of their predicament. A girl can no longer afford to refuse a young man liberties; but she employs carefully-graded restrictions which she knows to be accepted among her friends. . . . Ideally, of course, the law and the teaching of the churches should be adapted to what the mass of the people think workable. But for the moment there is an immense gap. So long as that gap exists, her virginity will remain a girl's best friend.

S.N., P. 34

SEX EDUCATION

The truth is, the only sensible advice the Government can give the public can be summed up in six words: chastity before marriage, fidelity within it. But that would be to endorse traditional Judaeo-Christian morality, and so is automatically ruled out.

S., DECEMBER 6, 1986

SHAH OF IRAN

The Shah was not overthrown because he was pro-West, or a capitalist, or corrupt, or cruel—most Middle Eastern rulers were cruel and by their standards he was a liberal—and least of all because he was king. The truth is he destroyed himself by succumbing to the fatal temptation of modern times: the lure of social engineering. He fell because he tried to be a Persian Stalin.

M.T., P. 710

The Shah's regime was overthrown, terrorists playing a major part in the process, not because it was too ruthless but because it was not ruthless enough. The effect of such terrorist victories is not the expansion but the contraction of freedom and law. Iran is now a theocratic horror-state, where the rule of law no longer exists; it is also a state from which terrorists can operate with safety and active assistance.

R.F., P. 213

SHELLEY, PERCY BYSSHE

He illustrated Southey's belief that industrialization, by poisoning the traditional social order, injected people—elites as well as masses—with a spirit of destruction presented as "liberty," of course, but in reality leading to chaos and death. Shelley did not mind being ranked on the side of Satan. He smacked his lips over words like *atheism*, *anarchy*, and *assassin*, which were among his favorites. He was particularly attached to the term *demogorgon*, which was supposed to be the name of the infernal powers that the ancients regarded as unspeakable: Just to pronounce it produced colossal evil.

B.M., P. 432

[322]

According to Shelley, imagination, or "Intellectual Beauty," was required to transform the world; and it was because poets possessed this quality in the highest degree, because poetic imagination was the most valuable and creative of all human accomplishments, that he entitled them the world's natural legislators, albeit unacknowledged. Yet here was he, a poet—and one of the greatest of poets—capable, perhaps, of imaginative sympathy with entire classes, downtrodden agricultural labourers, Luddites, Peterloo rioters, factory hands, people he had never set eyes on; capable of feeling for, in the abstract, the whole of suffering humanity, yet finding it manifestly impossible, not once but scores, hundreds of times, to penetrate imaginatively the minds and hearts of all those people with whom he had daily dealings.

I., P. 48

SIDGWICK, HENRY

Henry Sidgwick (1838–1900), who lost his faith and so became Professor of Moral Philosophy, spent many years writing about ethics and eventually reached the conclusion that the notion of moral obligation was impossible to analyse, but anyway ought to be self-evident to any intelligent adult.

E.S., P. 131

SLAVERY

As men are all equally made in God's image, they have equal rights in any fundamental sense. It is no accident that slavery among the Jews disappeared during the Second Commonwealth, coinciding with the rise of Pharisaism, because the Pharisees insisted that, as God was the true judge in a court of law, all were equal there: king, high-priest, free man, slave. . . . The Pharisees rejected the view that a master was responsible for the actions of his slaves, as well as his livestock, since a slave, like all men, had a mind of his own.

That gave him status in the court, and once he had legal status, slavery could not work.

H.J., P. 156

The West's supine attitude toward the horrors of Barbary piracy had long aroused fury in some quarters. Officers of the British navy were particularly incensed since seamen were frequently victims of the trade. They could not understand why the huge resources of the world's most powerful fleet were not deployed to root out this evil affront to the international law of the sea, once and for all. They could not understand why liberal parliamentarians, who campaigned ceaselessly to outlaw the slave trade by parliamentary statute, took no interest in Christian slavery. . . . They were concerned with the enslavement of blacks by whites and did not give the predicament of white slaves a high priority on their agenda, an early example of double standards.

B.M., P. 287

SLAVERY (AMERICAN)

The southern apologists were still, in their hearts, ashamed of slavery. That is why they used a euphemism. To them, it was not slavery—a word they never spoke, if possible—but "the peculiar institution." The use of euphemisms was to become an outstanding characteristic of the modern world which was being born, and nowhere was it employed more assiduously than in the South's defense of unfree labor.

B.M., P. 313

SLAVERY (ANCIENT)

The existence of slavery as a powerful and ubiquitous institution was all the more unfortunate, from an economic viewpoint, in that Graeco-Roman technology lacked dynamism. The civilizations of the Nile and Euphrates had come into existence because of their technical inventions . . . But they did not systematically develop this repertoire; nor, essentially, did the Greeks. . . . Compared to their striking advances in other directions, involving the critical method, their approach to technology was comatose and unadventurous. Why? Because slaves provided the muscle power . . . there was no market demand for technological advance. And this, in turn, tended to shift Greek rationalization in a metaphysical direction. Plato, so characteristic of the Greek approach, was an anti-empiricist. He argued that true science was teleological. It concentrated on the Mind. It was not the function of science to assist vulgar traders and suchlike; it was, rather, to help the soul to contemplate eternal truth.

E.S., P. 15

SMITH, ADAM

He was the first to note a very important distinction: that love of humanity in general (which he termed "public spirit") was often accompanied by indifference to human beings in particular. Up to a point, "public spirit" was necessary and desirable in society. But it was always liable to degenerate into what he terms the "spirit of system," that is, the fanatical commitment to ideology and dogmatism. Smith thought that love of systems and gadgets was one of man's deepest instincts. It was the chief dynamic which created wealth; but, when reflected in the political love of systems, could also destroy wealth, and human happiness too. The "spirit of system" was the insatiable desire of the gadget-lover to construct society like a machine.

R.F., P. 6

He saw mankind, for the first time in history, move from a society dominated by status to one based on contract, a freely signed document by which one man pledged to work for another; a pledge revocable under law. This, to Smith, was real freedom; true justice. Above all, the change benefited most of the lowliest elements in society, those who had hitherto been the invariable victims of all political and social systems. To Smith, the right of a man to work where, when and how he wanted was the most important of all freedoms—far more vital to his well-being than a mere parliamentary vote.

R.F., P. 35

SOCIAL ENGINEERING

. . . [Alexis] Arakcheev's Gruzino has a strong claim to be considered the first modern experiment in social engineering, an attempt to create the New Man who, Rousseau had argued, could be born in the right conditions. The estate was 35 square kilometers and contained 2000 "souls." The general destroyed all the old wooden buildings and put up . . . belvederes and towers, each of which was equipped with a clock. . . . The clocks dictated their work-, meal- and bed-times, something unheard of in Russia. . . . The idea was to get all the peasants to work ten hours every day . . . except Sundays. . . . A note from him on one damsel reads: " . . . if she does not know her prayers by Lent, I shall have her soundly whipped." Therein lay the catch of Arakcheev's utopia . . . the most characteristic and incorrigible aspect of Russian backwardness—the universal reliance on savage physical punishment.

B.M., PP. 291–92

. . . social engineering has been the salient delusion and the greatest curse of the modern age. In the twentieth century it has killed scores of millions of innocent people, in Soviet Russia, Nazi Germany, Communist China and elsewhere. But it is the last thing which Western democracies, with all their faults, have ever espoused. On the contrary. Social engineering is the creation of millenarian intellectuals who believe they can refashion the universe by the light of their unaided reason.

I., PP. 339–40

It is the birthright of the totalitarian tradition. It was pioneered by Rousseau, systematized by Marx and institutionalized by Lenin. Lenin's successors have conducted, over more than seventy years, the longest experiment in social engineering in history, whose lack of success does indeed confirm Chomsky's general case. Social en-

[326]

gineering, or the Cultural Revolution as it was called, produced millions of corpses in Mao's China, and with equal failure . . . [all] originally the work of intellectuals.

I., P. 340

Though applied by illiberal or totalitarian governments, all schemes of social engineering have been originally the work of intellectuals. Apartheid, for instance, was worked out in its detailed, modern form in the social psychology department of Stellenbosch University. Similar systems elsewhere in Africa—Ujamaa in Tanzania, "Consciencism" in Ghana, Négritude in Senegal, "Zambian Humanism," etc.—were cooked up in the political science or sociology departments of local universities. American intervention in Indo-China, imprudent though it may have been, and foolishly conducted as it undoubtedly was, was originally intended precisely to save its peoples from social engineering.

I., P. 340

. . . the century's most radical vice . . . the notion that human beings can be shovelled around like concrete.

M.T., P. 130

On 21 December 1929 Stalin had celebrated his fiftieth birthday, as absolute master of an autocracy for which, in concentrated savagery, no parallel in history could be found. A few weeks earlier . . . he had given orders for the forced collectivization of the Russian peasants, an operation involving far greater material loss than anything within the scope of [the] Wall Street [collapse] and a human slaughter on a scale no earlier tyranny had possessed the physical means, let alone the wish, to bring about. By the time John Strachey wrote of fleeing capitalist death to find Soviet birth, this gruesome feat of social engineering had been accomplished. Five million peasants were dead; twice as many in forced labour camps. By that time, too, Stalin had acquired a pupil, admirer and rival in the shape of Hitler, controlling a similar autocracy and planning human sacrifices to ideology on an even ampler scale. For Americans, then, it was a

[327]

case of moving from a stricken Arcadia to an active *pandaemonium*. The devils had taken over.

M.T., P. 261

. . . the pursuit of Utopia leads the tiny handful of men in power abruptly to assault a society many centuries in the making, to treat men like ants and stamp on their nest.

M.T., P. 270

Like Lenin and Stalin, Hitler believed in ultimate social engineering. The notion of destroying huge categories of people whose existence imperilled his historic mission was to him, as to them, entirely acceptable. The only thing he feared was the publicity and opposition which might prevent him from carrying through his necessary task.

M.T., P. 413

SOCIAL RESPONSIBILITY

Implicit in the Bible is the holistic notion that one man's sin, however small, affects the entire world, however imperceptibly, and vice versa. Judaism never allowed the principle of individual guilt and judgment, however important, to override completely the more primitive principle of collective judgment, and by running the two in tandem it produced a sophisticated and enduring doctrine of social responsibility which is one of its greatest contributions to humanity. The wicked are the shame of all, the saints are our pride and joy.

H.J., PP. 158–59

SOCIAL SCIENCE

. . . physics seemed to have come to the end of its paramountcy during the 1960s. In any case, it could not tell people what they increasingly demanded to know: what had gone wrong with humanity. Why had the promise of the nineteenth century been dashed? Why had much of the twentieth century turned into an age of horror or, as some would say, evil? The social sciences, which claimed such questions as their province, could not provide the answer. Nor was this surprising: they were part, and a very important part, of the problem. Economics, sociology, psychology and other inexact sciences—scarcely sciences at all in the light of modern experience—had constructed the juggernaut of social engineering, which had crushed beneath it so many lives and so much wealth. The tragedy was that the social sciences only began to fall into disfavour in the 1970s, after they had benefited from the great afflatus of higher education. The effect of the social science fallacy would therefore still be felt until the turn of the century.

M.T., P. 776

SOCIALISM

If [the socialist state] does not go forward, the power of the market system, which expresses certain basic human instincts of barter and accumulation, is such that it will always reassert itself, and capitalism will make its reappearance. Then the embryo socialist state will collapse. If socialism is to go forward, it must push ahead with large-scale industrialization. That means surplus food for the workers; and surplus food to export to raise money for capital investment. In short the peasants must pay the price for socialist progress. And since they are unwilling to pay this price voluntarily, force must be used, in ever-growing quantities, until their will is broken and they deliver what is required of them. That is the bitter logic of socialist power which Stalin grasped in the 1920s: there was no stable point of rest between a return to capitalism and the use of unlimited force.

M.T., P. 268

SOCIALISM AND VALUES

. . . if thrift and diligence were, as some left-wing polemicists seem to claim, artificial aids of a social control system alien to the workers, what were "real" working-class values? Were the labouring poor, in their natural, untampered-with state, lazy, profligate and drunken? Or, to put it another way, if hard work, saving, paying debts promptly, clean living and self-respect characterise middle-class capitalist society, what should characterise a socialist one? Should it merely reflect the attitudes of the shiftless poor—in which case must it not be a hell on earth? Or should the socialist state, in its turn, seek to impose the prudential values—in which case how does its social control differ, in essence, from capitalist methods?

s., AUGUST 22, 1987

SOCIETY (FREE)

The essence of a free society is not so much the right to appoint as the right to remove.

s., MARCH 4, 1989

SOCIOLOGY

. . . a great deal of contemporary sociology is precisely the offspring of the marriage between the pseudo-science of Marxism, and the pseudo-science of Freudianism, which produced the writings of Herbert Marcuse . . . the tutelary deity of the student Fascist Left. Everywhere the sociology students, bred in the so-called "discipline" nurtured by the union of two irrational philosophies, assumed the leadership of the student unions. Freudianism is a throwback to pre-scientific myth descriptions of mysterious natural phenomena; Marxism is a system of quasi-religious prophecy. Both, though rationally quite unsound, have undoubtedly insights which prove useful . . . and Marxism, in addition, has a methodology of power-seeking. The combination is almost uniquely qualified to produce twentieth-century witch doctors . . . in reality playing on some of the deepest and darkest human emotions. Here, then, was the second evil force Hobbes warned against—"the incantation of evil spirits."

E.S., P. 169

Sociology Magazines

Sociology magazines like to scrutinise supermarkets to unearth left-wing points. I read an article in one of them recently which claimed that the average income of customers declines steadily from the 9 a.m. opening onwards. The rich can "choose their time" to shop, so go early, "missing the crowds" and "getting the freshest produce." The poor shop late, are hustled and hassled, get battered fruit and veg, sometimes at reduced prices. The theory is insular and collapses completely once you go to America. When I was a Visiting Professor in Washington, the hypermarket I used on M Street was open 24 hours a day, 365 days a year, and the only correlation I noticed between customers and time was that, during the small hours, even more lunatics than usual were at large.

S., DECEMBER 21, 1991

Source Confidentiality

The defence the journalists need to "protect their sources" is wooly-minded nonsense and of course has no basis in law. It can never be a journalist's professional duty to conceal a crime or protect a criminal.

S., OCTOBER 19, 1985

Soviet Union

Soviet internal struggles have always been about ambition and fear rather than policies.

M.T., P. 264

. . . the confusion of moral issues by the end of the war was fundamentally compounded by the presence, in the ranks of the righteous, of the Soviet totalitarian power. There was scarcely a crime the Nazis or the knights of bushido had committed, or even imagined, which the Soviet regime had not also perpetrated, usually on an even larger scale. It ran precisely the type of system which had produced the war and its horrors.

M.T., P. 429

Politically and morally the Soviet regime was a totalitarian society of an altogether different kind: more a self-perpetuating conspiracy than a legitimate form of government. Though the Chicago-style gangsterism of Stalin had been replaced by the low-key Mafia of Brezhnev and his associates, the essential criminality remained. The regime rested on a basis not of law but of force. In economic terms it was, perhaps, best defined by the pseudonymous Fedor Zniakov . . . as "super-monopoly capitalism," with all significant ownership concentrated in a single centre. Brezhnev's political problem was to ensure that the profits of this super-monopoly were distributed among the ruling class.

M.T., P. 677

SOVIET UNION AND TERRORISM

The reason why terrorism has had no impact on Soviet Russia is not the ferocity of the punishments terrorists receive there, but the fact that their activities get no publicity whatsoever. Silence and darkness are the one response of organised society against which terrorists have no weapon. Alas, it is only possible in those regimes which forswear civilised values; regimes which themselves were founded in terror and survive by it.

S., JULY 6, 1985

SPAIN

It was obvious [in 1939] that a European war was inevitable and imminent. Franco's reaction was a brutal attempt to seal off Spain not only from the coming catastrophe but, as far as possible, from the whole of the twentieth century. Spain had a long tradition of crude social engineering and internal crusades. In the fifteenth and

[332]

sixteenth centuries it had expelled in turn vast numbers of Moors, Jews and Protestants. By such macro-persecution it had avoided the Reformation and the horrors of the Wars of Religion. The failure to adopt similar methods of drastic extrusion had permitted the French Revolution to enter and thus crucified the country for fifteen years of civil war . . .

M.T., PP. 338–39

SPINOZA, BARUCH

Spinoza was the first major example of the sheer destructive power of Jewish rationalism once it escaped the restraints of the traditional community. . . . [He] began the process of Biblical criticism which, over the next 250 years, was to demolish educated belief in the literal truth of the Bible and to reduce it to the status of an imperfect historical record. His work and influence were to inflict grievous and irreparable damage on the self-confidence and internal cohesion of Christianity. They also . . . raised new, long-term and deadly problems for the Jewish community.

H.J., PP. 291–92

Spinoza's work represents the hypertrophy of one aspect of the Jewish spirit: its tendency not just to rationalize but to intellectualize. He was one of those who thought it might be possible to resolve all disputes and conflicts of opinion and reach human perfection by a process of logic. He believed the problems of ethics could be solved by geometrical-type proofs. He was thus in the tradition of Maimonides, who argued that perfect worldly peace could be achieved through reason—that was how he thought the Messianic Age would come. But Maimonides imagined this state being reached when the Law was fully observed in all its noble rationality. It would be achieved on the basis of Revelation, through the Torah. Spinoza, however, did not believe in Revelation and wanted to scrap the Torah. He thought the end could be achieved by pure intellect.

H.J., P. 293

SPIRITUAL

The essence of the spiritual life is the quest for balance. The object, goodness, is clear enough. The difficulty lies in steering towards it between the rival rocks of despair and pride. The human soul must retain its sense of humility and fear of failure, without at the same time denying itself the creative encouragement of success.

P.J., P. 119

SPORT

The establishment of the Jockey Club as the accepted controlling institution of a sport which . . . involved enormous sums of money—far more, in comparative terms, than, say, international football . . . today . . . —was of great importance because it set a new pattern of social control. The expansion of mass sport . . . first in Britain . . . was one of the key developments of the 19th century. . . . What the Jockey Club established was that even in a sport like horseracing, which was peculiarly susceptible to corruption, the most effective mode of control was not legislation and police, but the arbitrary rulings of an unelected body whose verdicts went unchallenged because the social status and wealth of its members made them disinterested.

B.M., P. 712

STALIN, JOSEPH

Black humour always jostled with monomania for possession of the cavity in Stalin's spirit.

M.T., P. 454

This ex-seminarist and revolutionary thug was half-gangster, half-bureaucrat. He had no ideals; no ideological notions of his own. . . . Stalin did not have Lenin's ideological passion for violence. But he was capable of unlimited violence to achieve his purposes,

[334]

or indeed for no particular reason; and he sometimes nursed feelings of revenge against individuals for years before executing them.

M.T., PP. 261–62

. . . the way in which Stalin divided and used [Trotsky, Zinoviev, Kamenev, and Bukharin] to destroy each other, and then appropriated their policies as required—he seems to have had none of his own—is a classic exercise in power-politics. It is important to realize that, just as Lenin was the creator of the new autocracy and its instruments and practice of mass terror, so also there were no innocents among his heirs. All were vicious killers.

M.T., P. 262

The moment the Left was beaten and disarmed, Stalin began . . . preparing the means to destroy Bukharin and the Right. The big clash came on 10 July 1928 at a meeting of the Central Committee, when Bukharin argued that while the *kulak* himself was not a threat—"we can shoot him down with machine guns"—forced collectivization would unite all the peasants against the government. Stalin interrupted him with sinister piety, "A fearful dream, but God is merciful!" God might be, but not the General-Secretary.

M.T., PP. 265–66

While goading on the witch-hunting and building up the paranoia and hysteria, Stalin was contriving his own apotheosis as the heir of the deified Lenin. . . . it was the fiftieth birthday celebrations at the end of 1929 which marked the real beginning not only of Stalin's unfettered personal rule but of the Stalin cult in all its nightmare maturity, with names like Stalinabad, Stalin-Aul, Staliniri, Stalinissi, Stalino, Stalinogorsk, Stalinsk, Mount Stalin, sprouting all over the Soviet empire, and with the first appearance of the Stalinist litanies: Man of Steel, the Granite Bolshevik . . . the Iron Soldier, the Universal Genius, a form of ruler-worship which went back to the Egyptian pharaohs.

M.T., P. 267

Communists had always been infuriated by the tendency of facts to get in the way of Marxist theses. One might say that the whole of

Stalin's dictatorship had been a campaign against facts, or rather a superhuman attempt to transform the awkward facts of humanity into new "deep structures," under six feet of earth.

M.T., P. 696

STALIN TERROR

The famine of 1932, the worst in Russian history, was virtually unreported. At the height of it, the visiting biologist Julian Huxley found "a level of physique and general health rather above that to be seen in England." [George Bernard] Shaw threw his food supplies out of the train window just before crossing the Russian frontier "convinced that there were no shortages in Russia." "Where do you see any food shortage?" he asked, glancing round the foreigners-only restaurant of the Moscow Metropole. . . . But Shaw and his travelling companion, Lady Astor, knew of the political prisoners, since the latter asked Stalin for clemency on behalf of a woman who wished to join her husband in America (Stalin promptly handed her over to the OGPU) and she asked him, "How long are you going to go on killing people?" . . . he replied, "As long as necessary." . . .

M.T., P. 278

THE STATE

It is one of the dismal lessons of the twentieth century that, once a state is allowed to expand, it is almost impossible to contract it.

M.T., P. 618

Another political *cliché* that came into fashion in the early 1990s, reflecting the Left's acceptance of the market, was "the enabling state," as opposed to Big Government: the state was there, the argument went, not to do things itself, so much as to make it possible for people to do things on their own behalf. Conservatives were equally content to use this formulation of government's role. To some extent, then, there was a convergence of views in the world's democracies during the 1980s and early 1990s, but it was a convergence on the terms of the Right.

M.T., P. 746

Hugely expensive and probably ineffectual government campaigns against drug-abuse and AIDS saw the modern state in a characteristic twentieth-century posture—trying to do collectively what the sensible and morally educated person did individually. The disillusion with socialism and other forms of collectivism, which became the dominant spirit of the 1980s, was only one aspect of a much wider loss of faith in the state as an agency of benevolence. The state was, up to the 1980s, the great gainer of the twentieth century and the central failure.

M.T., P. 783

The state had proved itself an insatiable spender, an unrivalled waster. It had also proved itself the greatest killer of all time. By the 1990s, state action had been responsible for the violent or unnatural deaths of some 125 million people during the century, more perhaps than it had succeeded in destroying during the whole of human history up to 1900. Its inhuman malevolence had more than kept pace with its growing size and expanding means.

M.T., P. 783

I once regarded the state as a means whereby the less fortunate among us could be enabled to achieve the self-expression and moral fulfilment which is their right as creatures made in God's image. While continuing to desire the end, I no longer have any confidence whatever in the state as the means towards this end. On the contrary, I have come to see it as the biggest obstacle to the individual self-expression and moral maturity of every single one of us, and most of all the poor, the weak, the humble and the passive.

R.F., PP. 2–3

. . . even in the liberal democracies of the Western tradition the Frankenstein state has contrived to establish itself. It is alive, well, living amongst us and flexing its muscles; looking forward with boundless confidence and insatiable appetite to an indefinite career

[337]

of growth and consumption. The monster is at large all over Western Europe. In the United States it is the last, boldest and most insolent of all the immigrants to clamber onto her shores. But it is above all in Britain, the "very pearl of the West," as Solzhenitsyn has called us, once the citadel of privacy and the acropolis of individual freedom, that the spectre of giant government overshadows our lives and threatens the total destruction of liberal values.

R.F., P. 2

The notion of an efficient state is based upon an illusion, that there is a living abstraction called "society," omniscient in its collective judgments, free from human frailty and weakness, and therefore morally justified in its claims to omnipotence, expressed through the state, which is its active agent. "Society needs," "society demands"—so the state must act. But there is no such creature as "society." "Society" is merely the sum of loud voices, the orchestrated chorus of certain fallible individuals. Society is not a being; still less is its agent the state. Society is a thing. It does not have the capacity to think. It lacks the powers of human reasoning. It cannot make calculations of profit and loss and returns on capital. These, indeed, are built into the market: the market is the only kind of collective which conforms to nature and actually works after a fashion, because it is based upon the voluntary principle and remains a free combination of individuals. But the market is not the state: it is the exact opposite to the state. The state has no brain, collective or otherwise; all it has is an appetite.

R.F., P. 7

The object of the social democratic state is to strike, and to hold, the correct balance between the requirements of social justice and the rights of every individual. But alas! That is not the kind of society we are actually creating. Very largely by accident, and certainly without any conscious grand design, we are slipping towards a Leviathan state, in which organised force, violence or compulsion is the prime determinant of politics, and in which, increasingly, the brute power of the group, buttressed by statutory privileges which place it above Common Law, overrides the public and the individual in the pursuit of its sectional interests: a society in which the ordinary person is nothing, and the corporation everything.

R.F., P. 58

With the onset of the war, each belligerent eagerly scanned its competitors and allies for aspects of state management and intervention in the war economy which could be imitated. The capitalist sectors, appeased by enormous profits and inspired no doubt also by patriotism, raised no objections. The result was a qualitative and quantitative expansion of the role of the state which has never been fully reversed—for though wartime arrangements were sometimes abandoned with peace, in virtually every case they were eventually adopted again, usually permanently. Germany set the pace, speedily adopting most of the Russian state procedures which had so scared her in peace, and operating them with such improved efficiency that when Lenin inherited the Russian state-capitalist machine in 1917–18, it was to German wartime economic controls that he, in turn, looked for guidance.

M.T., P. 15

Any state must make enemies; the art is to avoid a conflict with all of them simultaneously.

S.H., P. 118

THE STATE (SECULAR)

The Gregorian reforms had brought the idea of the secular state into existence by stripping the ruler of his sacerdotal functions. . . . In the long run this was fatal to the whole concept of the Christian society. The lay element was initially put on the defensive but it eventually responded by developing its own modes of thought outside the assumptions of the Christian-clerical world. These modes were alien to Christianity, and ultimately hostile to it. . . . But the secular world learnt from its methods. In the twelfth century, royal justice was a generation or two behind canon law, but it soon caught up. The old empire was destroyed, but kings took its place. They learnt to manipulate papal legal and administrative techniques,

[339]

and copy them. The militancy of the clerical interest produced, in the end, the response of the secular interest, represented by the crown. Thus anti-clericalism was born.

H.C., P. 215

STATECRAFT

Human societies are always faced by crises, of greater or lesser magnitude. In dealing with them, the essence of statecraft is to win a breathing space, during which more permanent solutions can evolve through the interplay of many intellects.

E., P. 2

Any state must sometimes use force and sometimes appeasement. The art is to avoid doing both together, and thus losing both respect and popularity.

S.N., P. 118

STATESMAN

. . . statesmen, however much they may think they are guided by the unalterable laws of realpolitik and national self-interest, are in fact as much influenced by cultural trends and fashions as everyone else. Castlereagh, Metternich, Talleyrand, and Alexander lived in the same world as Beethoven and Byron, Turner and . . . Hugo, and felt the same intellectual breezes on their cheeks.

B.M., P. 111

What ordinary voters require from a statesman are a few big, simple ideas which appeal to their sense of justice and common sagacity.

S.N., P. 196

STEAMBOAT

[Robert] Fulton got the [steamboat] service going by virtue of a monopoly privilege in the New York area. Colonel John C. Stevens of Hoboken, barred from New York for this reason, built a steamboat called the *Phoenix* and started to run her commercially between Trenton and the Delaware River in 1809, the first commercial service at sea. The beginnings of competition led to a mass of lawsuits over privilege and over copyrights—the United States was already in the process of becoming a lawyers' paradise.

B.M., P. 196

STOUT, GEORGE FREDERICK

George Frederick Stout (1860–1944), for many years editor of the philosophical journal *Mind*, was also a psychologist-philosopher, and developed a weird system of his own, which few understood then, or trouble to assess now.

E.S., P. 131

STRACHEY, LYTTON

Not for nothing was Strachey the son of a general. He had a genius for narcissistic élitism and ran the coterie with an iron, though seemingly languid, hand. From the Apostles he grasped the principle of group power: the ability not merely to exclude but to be seen to exclude. He perfected the art of unapproachability and rejection: a Bloomsbury mandarin could wither with a glance or a tone of voice. Within his magic circle exclusiveness became a kind of mutual life-support system. He and [Leonard] Woolf called it "the Method."

M.T., P. 168

STRUCTURALISM

[Walter Benjamin] coined the phrase "the creative omnipotence of language" and he showed that texts had to be explored to detect not merely their surface meaning but their underlying message and structure. . . . [He] belonged to the irrational and gnostic Jewish tradition, like Marx himself and Freud, detecting deep, secret and life-explaining meanings beneath the veneer of existence. What he first began to apply to literature, and later to history, was to become in time a more general technique, used for instance by Claude Lévi-Strauss in anthropology and Noam Chomsky in linguistics. Gnosticism is the most insidious form of irrationalism, especially to intellectuals, and the particular variety of gnosticism developed tentatively by Benjamin, expanded into Structuralism, proved a major force among the intelligentsia from the 1950s onwards.

H.J., P. 480

What all the structuralists had in common was the Marxist assumption that human attributes and activities were governed by laws in a way analogous to the way scientific laws governed inanimate nature. Hence it was the function of the social sciences to discover such laws, and then for society to act upon their discoveries. The emergence of this new form of intellectual Utopianism, with its strong suggestion of compulsory social engineering at the end of the road, coincided exactly with the rapid expansion of higher education, especially of the social science disciplines, in the late Fifties and throughout the Sixties.

M.T., PP. 695–96

To structuralists, facts were by definition on the surface, and therefore misleading. To attempt to marshal them in the form of argument was, obviously, nothing more than a shameless defence of the status quo. Structuralism fitted well into the Potemkin world of the United Nations, where facts were unimportant, where North was South, and vice-versa, where wealth created poverty, where Zionism was racism and sin was the White Man's monopoly. The multinational, that sinister infrastructure of international injustice, was a quintessentially structuralist concept. Structuralism, like Marxism,

[342]

was a form of gnosticism, that is an arcane system of knowledge, revealed to the élite.

M.T., P. 696

STUDENT RADICALISM

The notion that the student body is in some constitutional way a depository of humanitarian idealism will not survive a study of the Weimar period. Next to the ex-servicemen, the students provided the chief manpower reservoir of the violent extremists, especially of the Right. Student politics were dominated by the right-wing *Hochschulring* movement throughout the 1920s until it was replaced by the Nazis. The Right extremists proceeded by converting half a dozen students on a campus, turning them into full-time activists, paid not to study. The activists could then swing the mass of the student body behind them. The Nazis did consistently better among the students than among the population as a whole and their electoral gains were always preceded by advances on the campus, students proving their best proselytizers.

M.T., P. 127

. . . some people argue that the spectacle of student mobs shouting down speakers and even driving them off the platform and out of the university should not be taken too seriously. I do not agree. The free exchange of opinions is important everywhere but it is perhaps more important at a university than anywhere else. Students are peculiarly vulnerable to totalitarian ideology . . .

S., APRIL 5, 1986

SUEZ CRISIS

Suez is often said to have dealt the final blow to Britain's status as a great world power. That is not true. The status had been lost in 1947. Suez simply made it plain for all the world to see. The underlying cause was a failure of will, not of strength, and the Suez fiasco merely reflected that failure, of which Eden was a pathetic

[343]

sacrificial victim. . . . The real loser in the long term was the United States. Eisenhower appeared to act decisively, and he got his way fast enough. Britain came to heel . . . But in the process he helped to prepare a mighty scourge for America's own back, in the shape of the tendentious concept of "world opinion" first articulated at Bandung and now, by Eisenhower's own act, transferred to the UN.

M.T., P. 493

SUKARNO, ACHMAD

Sukarno had no more moral mandate to rule 100 millions than Nehru had in India; rather less in fact. He too was devoid of administrative skills. But he had the gift of words. Faced with a problem, he solved it with a phrase. Then he turned the phrase into an acronym, to be chanted by crowds of well-drilled illiterates.

M.T., P. 478

SUPERPOWER

Superpowers in decay are dangerous animals, and Europeans therefore welcomed the return of American prosperity, exuberance and optimism.

F.A., JANUARY 1989

SUPERSTITION

What is notable about . . . modern-style superstitions is that they are held most strongly by people who are comparatively well educated, or think they are. The really passionate opponents of nuclear power are overwhelmingly middle-class, radical, secularist, the sort of people who would sneer condescendingly at the spectacle of someone praying before a statue of the Virgin Mary. Ordinary working people are not over-fond of having a nuclear reactor nearby (unless they work at the plant) but they do not go on about it. Everyone has superstitions, but to be systematically and argumentatively superstitious, to raise a form of superstition to the level of a political issue, requires education.

S., FEBRUARY 14, 1987

SUPERSTITION, AGE OF

If I were asked to categorise Britain today . . . I would term it the Superstitious Society. Faith has gone, to the point that a policeman who utters the old Christian truism that he is an instrument of God is widely denounced as a nut-case and a menace, and forced to come to the Home Office to explain himself. And, since human beings feel they need to know more about existence than their puny reason can supply, the loss of faith has left a huge vacuum, which a variety of superstitions is filling. G. K. Chesterton, the wisest child of his age, predicted this. If men cease to believe in God, he forecast, they will not believe in nothing; they will believe in *anything*.

S., FEBRUARY 14, 1987

SURREALISM

Surrealism, which might have been designed to give visual expression to Freudian ideas—though its origins were quite independent—had its own programme of action, as did Futurism and Dada. But this was surface froth. Deeper down, it was the disorientation in space and time induced by relativity, and the sexual gnosticism of Freud, which seemed to be characterized in the new creative models.

M.T., P. 9

SWIFT, JONATHAN

. . . Swift was the first Irishman (he was born in Dublin and educated at Trinity College there) to express in the English language the Irish consciousness of a separate identity, lit by a burning indignation at English injustice. He called his patriotism the "perfect rage and

resentment, at the mortifying sight of slavery, folly and baseness";
. . . he feared he would die in Dublin in a rage, "like a poisoned
rat in a hole."

Id., P. 67

Swift turned satire into great art, and gave it an edge so keen and
deadly that, alone of his age, he still cuts to the bone as ruthlessly
as in the 1720s.

Id., P. 116

T

TAXATION

. . . the effects of high taxation on national health can be seen in other ways, notably in the rate of inflation, which is a moral as well as an economic disease. In 1945 Colin Clark and Lord Keynes argued that inflation must follow when taxation exceeded 25 per cent of net national income. They have been proved abundantly right, as more and more nations have stepped over the 25 per cent mark, and provided the evidence. Taxation rates, themselves reflecting political hyperactivity, are almost certainly the biggest underlying cause of the inflationary stagnation which has made the present deep recession the most severe in nearly half a century.

R.F., P. 93

TECHNOLOGY

What was clear, by the last decade of the century, was that Alexander Pope had been right in suggesting, "The proper study of mankind is man." For man, as a social being, was plainly in need of radical improvement. He was, indeed, capable of producing scientific and technical "miracles" on an ever-increasing scale. The ability to create new substances further accelerated the communications and electronics revolution that had started in the 1970s and gathered pace throughout the 1980s and into the 1990s. As the number of circuits which could be imprinted on a given area multiplied, calculators and computers grew in capacity and fell in price. The first true pocket calculator, on which mankind had been working since the

time of Pascal in the mid-seventeenth century, was produced by
Clive Sinclair in 1972 and cost £100; by 1982 a far more powerful
model cost £7.

M.T., PP. 780–81

One should not be concerned by the primitive fear, alas too prevalent
even today, that new technology destroys jobs. Even the most meretricious study of the history of the last 200 years shows conclusively
that, whatever their initial impact, all the four great waves of new
technology have, quite quickly, created millions, and eventually
hundreds of millions, of additional jobs.

P.P.J., P. 184

One of the paradoxes of technology is that, the more advanced it
is, the easier it becomes to operate. . . . A secretary accustomed to
a word-processor, as most of them now are, has a degree of sophis-
tication in the electronic arts good enough for the most complex
television transmission console.

S., FEBRUARY 27, 1988

TECHNOLOGICAL LAG

In the second half of the twentieth century . . . there were at last
signs of a unified theory emerging from the laboratory and reaching
to both ends of the spectrum. At the microcosmic end, molecular
biology, neurophysiology, endocrinology and other new disciplines
began to explain such processes as the mechanism of genetic inheritance and programming. The most important of the micro-level
discoveries came at Cambridge University in 1953 when James
Watson and Francis Crick succeeded in decipihering the double-
helix. . . . More striking still was the speed with which this discovery
was given a multitude of practical applications. The gap between
the theoretical basis of nuclear physics and actual nuclear power was
half a century. In the new biology the gap was less than twenty
years.

M.T., P. 778

[348]

TELEVISION

The visual image . . . can be made to lie as effectively as words—more so, in fact. TV is potentially a much more dishonest medium than the press, and is often so in practice, particularly in current affairs documentary.

s., OCTOBER 6, 1984

. . . if everyone agrees that television has unrivalled efficiency at selling goods, services, culture, music, God, politics and fashion, why does the industry continue to claim that the one thing it cannot sell is violence?

s., SEPTEMBER 5, 1987

. . . at the heart of television's opposition to violence-control there is a fundamental dishonesty, a mendacious denial of the power of the medium. On the one hand, the BBC has always sought to justify its freedom and independence, and its licence fee, by insisting that it is a great civilising force in Britain, a central element in our culture. How can it be this without influencing people's habits, thoughts, tastes, enthusiasms, appetites? Equally, ITV sells its screen-time and thus makes itself a good living in the world by persuading highly professional commercial gents that it has a unique power to persuade the public to buy their products; and as it has an advertising monopoly and charges outrageously high prices, its arguments are clearly convincing—what happens on the screen does make people do things they would not do otherwise.

s., SEPTEMBER 5, 1987

Television cameras are tending to be particpants, rather than re-corders, of political unrest all over the world. Rioting is now a carefully organised and deadly game, played with increasingly so-phisticated tactics before a world audience. Whether we sympathise with the aims of the riot-organisers or not, their growing cynicism, not to say hypocrisy, in using the hot medium of television is apparent.

s., SEPTEMBER 9, 1987

[349]

. . . television standards are now on a level with tabloids, if not lower.

S., MAY 14, 1988

. . . the television set is not an echoing stage but a small, intimate extension to the living-room, where a whisper can be more effective than a bellow and acting, to succeed, must be low-key. In this ambiance, authority, which need not shout, because it has power, and which can forgo adjectives, because it possesses the facts, is likely, it seems to me, to fare better than its critics, who must mount dramas to compensate for their impotence and ignorance. Up to this point in history, the intrusion of the media has made government more difficult. Televising the Commons may begin to reverse the process.

S., DECEMBER 23–30, 1989

TELEVISION AND MORALITY

The people who run it are obsessed by technology and ratings to the exclusion of almost any other aspect. So television has not produced its own school of moral philosophers. It has no moral philosophy. Its only watchword, endlessly chanted by such intellectuals as it can muster, is unlimited freedom, and it is that which has made it the willing accomplice of the cruellest and most dangerous criminals of our time.

S., JULY 6, 1985

TELEVISION PRODUCERS

In civil conflicts they have been known to set up acts of violence (or pseudo-violence) for more convenient and effective filming. They sometimes maintain their own contacts with terrorists and refuse to help the legitimate authorities, even though they know horrific crimes will remain unsolved, and others be committed, as a result of their silence. They frequently give terrorist leaders opportunities to air their views to millions, and thus to raise the morale of their followers, and prolong and intensify the slaughter. The effect of intensive and unrestricted television coverage on a civil conflict is always to make it bloodier and more protracted. The television producer is the terrorist's best friend, for he provides the mass-publicity which is the life-support system of terror.

S., MARCH 30, 1985

TELEVISION AND PROPAGANDA

Television is the ideal propaganda medium, a mendacious monster, not primarily out of malice but from its amoral nature. The hostages saying they were well-treated were on tape; so they were shown. The spectacle of the U.S. Marine frogman being beaten to death was not on tape, so it was not shown. Television presentation is not determined by the truth as a whole, but by the partial truth, often the misleading truth—even the untruth—of its selected images. The terrorists know this and that is why they plan their crimes with the networks in mind. Television is the handmaiden of terrorism, the easy lady asking to be raped.

S., JULY 6, 1985

TELEVISION VIOLENCE

I do not believe that the ritual violence of adventure stories, in which good and evil are sharply differentiated, and violence is shown either as the work of evil men or the justified retribution of lawful society, is corrupting. What is dangerous in the imaginative use of violence on television is its presentation without a moral context, when violence is seen as aimless, habitual, inevitable or even, from time to time, commendable. It has to be sadly admitted that many children and adolescents watching television today, often from one-parent families, are virtually without any moral education at all. Television is their mentor and guide; an if television presents violence in an amoral context, the likelihood is that such youngsters will be encouraged to practise it.

S., OCTOBER 19, 1985

[351]

We should have learned from the big American race-riots of the 1960s, a lesson repeated on a smaller scale in British inner cities in the early 1980s, that televised mob-violence produces copycat riots in places where roughly the same conditions exist. It also has the effect of encouraging rioters to be more daring and destructive. But so far as I know no one in a position of authority or influence has ever suggested here or in the U.S. that television coverage of such incidents should be limited to avoid this inherent tendency of incitement to riot.

s., JUNE 24, 1988

Television has an inherent propensity to promote violence, since it must constantly display dramatic action to hold the flagging attention of its wallpaper viewers, and violence is the most easily portrayed form of action. Hence, for the political manipulators who want to increase the level of violence in our society television is the perfect medium, and that is why terrorists cultivate it so assiduously.

s., NOVEMBER 9, 1985

Many . . . argue that television violence does not influence actual behaviour. . . . But most people think otherwise and this is one of those issues where ordinary folk are more likely to be right than academic specialists. Indeed, broadcasters themselves concede the influence argument when they do want to ban something, such as smoking or the merest whiff of "racism." In any case the phenomenal success of television advertising, much of it designed to change patterns of behaviour by playing on the emotions, gives the lie to the assertion that there is no connection between what people see on the box and what they do.

s., MARCH 1, 1986

TERRORISM

The anti-Semitic torrent poured out by the Soviet bloc and the Arab states in the post-war period produced its own characteristic form of violence: state-sponsored terrorism. There was irony in this weapon being used against Zionism, for it was militant Zionists, such as Avraham Stern and Menachem Begin, who had (it could be argued) invented terrorism in its modern, highly organized and scientific form. That it should be directed, on a vastly increased scale, against the state they had lived, and died, to create could be seen as an act of providential retribution or at any rate as yet another demonstration that idealists who justified their means by their ends did so at their peril.

H.J., P. 579

. . . the political terrorism of the Seventies was a product of moral relativism. In particular, the unspeakable cruelties it practised were made possible only by the Marxist habit of thinking in terms of classes instead of individuals. Young radical ideologues who kept their victims . . . blindfolded, their ears sealed with wax, for weeks or months, then dispatched them without pity or hesitation, did not see those they tortured and murdered as human beings but as pieces of political furniture. In the process they dehumanized themselves as well as those they destroyed and became lost souls, like the debased creatures Dostoevsky described in his great anti-terrorist novel, *The Devils*.

M.T., P. 689

The countries which finance and maintain the international infrastructure of terrorism, which give terrorists refuge and havens, training camps and bases, money, arms and diplomatic support—all as a matter of deliberate state policy—are, without exception, totalitarian states. The governments of all these states rule by military and police force. The notion, then, that terrorism is opposed to "the repressive forces" in society is false; indeed it is the reverse of the truth. International terrorism, and the various local terrorist movements it services, are entirely dependent on the continuing good will and active support of police states. The terrorist is sustained by the totalitarian tank, the torture chamber, the lash and the secret policeman. The terrorist is the beneficiary of the Gulag Archipelago and all it stands for.

R.F., P. 213

[353]

Terrorism . . . is no longer a marginal problem for the civilised world, something to be contained and lived with, a mere nuisance. It is a real, important and growing threat to peace and legitimacy of all civilised states, that is all those states which live under the rule of law. It is an international threat: therein lies its power. That power can only be destroyed or emasculated when there is international recognition of its gravity, and international action, by the united forces of civilisation, to bring it under control.

R.F., P. 216

Terrorism has always been a feature of the Muslim world. The first organized group systematically employing murder for a cause were the Assassins (possibly derived from *hashishi*, drugged), who were Shia Muslims. . . . They followed the teachings of Hasan-i Sabbah, and developed a religious justification for murder, which they saw as a sacramental duty. They were truly a prototype terrorist movement of the modern kind, politico-religious missionaries, with their heavy emphasis on popular agitation and secrecy [and] their . . . nationalistic appeal. . . . Thanks to their use of terror, they often controlled local authorities, and forced governments into compliance or impotence. The various Arab terror movements now operating from Lebanon, Syria, Libya and Algeria would have had little to teach them.

E.S., P. 241

So many bastions of civilisation have been surrendered to the enemy without a fight that we have almost forgotten how to arm ourselves against barbarism. We can, in fact, do it in only one way: by stating that terrorism is always and in every circumstance wrong; that it is not only intrinsically wrong but the antithesis of political idealism; that it must be resisted by every means at our disposal; and that those who practise it must not only be punished but repudiated by those who share their political aims. Anyone who cannot assent to these propositions is no socialist, and has no place on the Left. And it is only by affirming them, without equivocation, that the Left can help to guide international society back to the road of humanism and reason.

R.F., PP. 195–96

[354]

TERRORISM AND CENSORSHIP

It is significant that no one has ever contemplated extending the ban to newspapers, since they are highly competitive and readers will not buy them if they provide platforms for mass-murderers. Only in the broadcasting duopoly, where there is little freedom of choice for consumers and where output is controlled by a tiny and unrepresentative élite protected from popular pressure by statutory privilege, did the Government feel obliged to act. Those in the media who object to the ban have been unable to explain why helping terrorists, by allowing them to justify their killings on radio and television, will enlarge freedom. All the evidence shows that terrorism, by provoking society into restrictive counter-measures, reduces freedom, not last for those in the media.

S., FEBRUARY 4, 1989

TERRORISTS

They reject democracy totally. The notion that violence is a technique of last resort, to be adopted only when all other attempts to attain justice have failed, is rejected by them. In doing so, they reject the mainstream of Western thinking, based, like most of our political grammar, on the social-contract theorists of the seventeenth century. Hobbes and Locke rightly treated violence as the antithesis of politics, a form of action characteristic of the archaic realm of the state of nature. They saw politics as an attempt to create a tool to avoid barbarism and make civilisation possible: politics renders violence not only unnecessary but unnatural to civilised man. Politics is an essential part of the basic machinery of civilisation, and in rejecting politics terrorism seeks to make civilisation unworkable.

R.F., PP. 212–13

TERRORISTS AND TELEVISION

More important to him than the gun or the bomb, the terrorist's most potent weapon is the television camera—ours. Terrorists need human victims, but they need publicity even more: publicity for their cause, their arguments, above all publicity to stress their power and their status as a negotiating partner; to confer on them a spurious legitimacy, as though they were a government of a kind. . . . Television gives the terrorists exactly what they want; and in return it gets free drama and high ratings.

s., JULY 6, 1985

TERTULLIAN

Though the first Protestant, he was saved by his art.

H.C., P. 50

THATCHER, MARGARET

The unacceptable truth about Mrs. Thatcher [is] that she is a simple, straightforward woman who, on big issues, expresses the views of most ordinary British people. The Left needs to see her as a political crook who was quite willing to spill a lot of blood in order to stay in power. They have to believe she wins elections by trickery and fraud because otherwise they are obliged to accept that they themselves do not speak for the masses—which, for progressive middle-class intellectuals, is an intolerable thought.

s., SEPTEMBER 12, 1987

. . . it was notable that she aroused much hostility as well as enthusiastic support, and in the three elections she won her party never secured as much as 50 per cent of the votes cast. In many ways, she resembled de Gaulle: like him, she was good at saying no, and meaning it; like him, she restored her nation's self-confidence and pride; she ruled with great authority for almost exactly the same span; and, like de Gaulle, she fell attempting a fundamental reform of local government, in her case seeking to replace the outmoded and inequitable way in which it was financed.

M.T., P. 745

[356]

"Thatcherism" . . . had a global influence during the 1980s which went well beyond the new fashion for privatization and reducing the state sector. The 1980s [were] a radical conservative decade, and even in states where socialist or Labour governments were elected, the drift away from Marxism, collectivism and all the traditional "isms" of the Left was marked.

M.T., P. 745

She does not believe in the irresistible power of collective forces, but in the salience of the individual and the virtues of leadership. She repudiates the pursuit of equality, except (and the exception is vital) equality before the law. She epitomises her philosophy thus: "Conservatism is about skilled people." She believes in contract not status, possessive individualism as opposed to class-consciousness and collective morality, and she stresses duties rather than rights. She is a leader in the old Churchillian mould who won an election by repudiating the consensus and flaunting her convictions. She is the first politician since 1945 to give a new direction to British politics, and the impact of her personality will by no means be confined to the domestic scene.

R.F., P. 228

. . . to drive out a Prime Minister by a kind of putsch in mid-term is very much against the national interest. No one disputes that Mrs. Thatcher was unpopular. But these things go in cycles, and she has met bad patches . . . surmounted them and gone on to win elections. One of her great virtues was that she proved, twice, that unpopular but necessary economic policies need not lead to electoral defeat. This was noted all over the world and encouraged national leaders to administer the right medicine. By staging a coup during the trough of the popularity cycle, the Heseltine camp and the media people who backed it have struck a severe blow at the courageous management of our affairs. For this and for many other reasons . . . future historians will come to regard November 1990 as a black page in our history, and will be severe on some of the individuals involved.

S., DECEMBER 1, 1990

[357]

THATCHER ERA (POST-)

Now that Mrs. Thatcher, who, with all her faults, had will and guts, has left the stage, what a pitiful collection of bit-players remain to step into the roles of Palmerston and Cavour, of Bismarck and Clemenceau! There is Chancellor Kohl, an ignorant philistine, bent on only one thing, personal survival. Or de Michaelis, the man who tried to despoil Venice. Or Mitterrand, the third-rate journalist from the Nièvre, with his glass pyramids and tinsel opera-house, a pigmy . . . Or the gruesome Dutchman, Lubbers. Or Douglas Hurd, grinning fatuously, as he bustles in and out of Downing Street in his ridiculous green overcoat . . . The notion of these dismal creatures putting together something called a "European foreign policy," let alone directing its armed forces, is laughable; or rather, pitiful. They have nothing in common except the narrowness of their conflicting outlooks. Oh yes: and their moral cowardice, dismally demonstrated by their indifference to Croatia's destruction.

S., DECEMBER 14, 1991

THEATRE AND THE CATHOLIC CHURCH

All theatre has its origins in religious ceremonial; from the sacred dances of the Old Kingdom of Egypt, more than two and a half millennia before the birth of Christ . . . Between dramaturgy and liturgy the dividing line is narrow. It remained so until the early modern age. For not only did the European drama evolve from medieval mystery plays, but the theatrical content of the Catholic religion was powerfully and deliberately reinforced during the Counter-Reformation . . . Roman orthodoxy stressed the histrionic not least to differentiate itself from the drabness and austerity of Calvinism. . . . the church encouraged the Baroque; it patronized the theatrical art of Tintoretto, Veronese, Caravaggio, El Greco; it pressed the secular courts within its orbit to finance the burgeoning drama. The Jesuits, the court clerics *par excellence*, were foremost in legitimizing the theatre and encouraging academic performances in their proliferating colleges and universities.

P.M., PP. 6–7

THINK TANK

. . . the reputation and therefore the influence of a think tank increase in direct proportion to the objectivity of its research. There are plenty of institutions on both sides of the Atlantic which (like "investigative journalists") start with conclusions and work backwards to find evidence to support them.

S., SEPTEMBER 3, 1988

The term is fairly recent, American, and probably dates from the 1940s. The institution is older. Perhaps the first was All Souls, since here were clever fellows gathered together without the boring necessity to teach students.

S., SEPTEMBER 3, 1988

THIRD WORLD

The concept [of the Third World] was based upon verbal prestidigitation, the supposition that by inventing new words and phrases one could change (and improve) unwelcome and intractable facts. There was the first world of the West, with its rapacious capitalism; the second world of totalitarian socialism, with its slave-camps; both with their hideous arsenals of mass-destruction. Why should there not come into existence a third world, arising like a phoenix from the ashes of empire, free, pacific, non-aligned, industrious, purged of capitalist and Stalinist vice, radiant with public virtue, today saving itself by its exertions, tomorrow the world by its example?

M.T., PP. 476–77

. . . in the nineteenth century, idealists had seen the oppressed proletariat as the repository of moral excellence—and a prospective proletarian state as Utopia—so now the very fact of a colonial past, and a non-white skin, were seen as title-deeds to international esteem. An ex-colonial state was righteous by definition. A gathering of such states would be a senate of wisdom.

M.T., P. 477

[359]

The term "Third World" became one of the great cant phrases of the post-war period. It was never defined, for the good and simple reason that, the moment anyone attempted to do so, the concept was seen to be meaningless and collapsed. But it was immensely influential. It satisfied the human longing for simple moral distinctions. There were "good" nations (the poor ones) and "bad" nations (the rich ones). Nations were rich precisely because they were bad, and poor because they were innocent.

M.T., P. 692

THIRD WORLD VIOLENCE

The cult of violence in the Third World, taken in conjunction with the mounting frustrations produced by real and inescapable economic obstacles to advancement, constitute a permanent menace to western civilization, for whatever the true explanations of their predicament, the Third World countries blame no one but the West. Indeed, they have no one else to blame, except themselves and their leaders. For violence, preached as a form of righteousness, requires villains. And if the villains do not exist, they must be invented.

E.S., P. 253

TOLSTOY, LEO

When he became a social reformer, the identification with God became stronger. . . . There were times when Tolstoy seemed to think of himself as God's brother, indeed his older brother.

I., P. 108

. . . [who] regarded prostitution as one of the few "honourable callings" for women.

I., P. 117

TORAH

The Jews survived because the period of intense introspection enabled their intellectual leaders to enlarge the Torah into a system of moral theology and community law of extraordinary coherence, logical consistency and social strength. Having lost the Kingdom of Israel, the Jews turned the Torah into a fortress of the mind and spirit, in which they could dwell in safety and even in content.

H.J., P. 149

TORY

It goes without saying that a Tory government cannot be expected to knock away the props which, in the long run, are its own foundation. It exhorts the workers, on the one hand, to exercise restraint, and, on the other, supplies the upper classes with the means to abandon it. But this is to be expected. The fundamental Tory image is not a prosperous Britain, but a prosperous leisured class.

S.N., PP. 21–22

Conservatism, in fact, is an authoritarian church of platitudes, a party of proverbs. "Spare the rod and spoil the child" . . . "More haste, less speed"—such maxims, which seem incontrovertible until one begins to think about them, evoked roars of approval last week. Indeed, a lady delegate even coined a new one: "A flogging today may save a hanging tomorrow"—and this went down well, too. This is England, . . . the English id, magnified out of all proportion, dominating the whole. The Tories, in short, are atrophied Englishmen, lacking certain moral and intellectual reflexes. They are recognizable, homely—even, on occasions, endearing—but liable to turn very nasty at short notice.

S.N., P. 75

Totalitarian

They have sought to subject, not to exalt, the individual; to suppress, not to reveal, truth; to regiment, not to tolerate; to impose verdicts rather than offer choices; to use violence as opposed to argument; to torture, not to heal. Whatever their declared political complexion, they have one thing in common: an unqualified detestation of liberal ideas and the relentless pursuit of those who seek to express them.

H.E., P. 416

This is the first epoch in nearly 2000 years in which most governments have been guided by what might be called post-Christian ethics. . . . These monsters were the prize pupils of thinkers who had deliberately rejected religion. Lenin derived from Marx the notion that Christianity should be destroyed because it inculcated the vice of humility. Hitler learned from Nietzsche that God was dead and had been replaced by "the will of power." While writing *Modern Times*, I formed the unshakable conviction that man without God is a doomed creature. The history of the 20th century proves the view that as the vision of God fades, we first become mere clever monkeys; then we exterminate one another.

R.D., JUNE 1985

Totalitarian State

. . . the elevation of the state is a very common feature in primitive storage cultures . . . as in imperial China, and in civilizations in process of decay. It was the salient principle of the later Roman empire, with its total abolition of economic and political freedom, and its compulsory corporations. Italian Fascism consciously based itself on the Roman model. Nazi Germany was equally frank in imposing control of labour and eliminating all foci of political and economic power other than the party-state. Stalinist Russia was in all essentials a similar creation, though the compulsory workers' corporations were nominally labelled trade unions on the western model. All these totalitarian societies tended towards the total elimination of the middle class from economic or political decision-making, leaving the population, for all practical purposes, divided into an official elite, and the rest—the old *honestiores* and *humiliores* of Rome's decay. . . . In addition, both the Nazi and the Russian systems quickly began to employ slave-labour, thus conforming to the late Roman pattern, with the supposedly free being very little better off, in terms of movement and choice of occupation.

E.S., P. 78

. . . the family is a protection from—is in fact subversive of—the overweening state. I think it is significant that the modern totalitarian state, with all its illegitimate and monstrous claims on the individual, did not come into existence until the family element had been almost entirely eliminated from government.

P.P.J., P. 137

Marx reintroduced the notion of a total society, governed in all its details by moral necessity. Of course this new Utopian society was in theory secular; but in the organising of human societies the distinction between religious and secular is at bottom false. The theocracies of antiquity were political states. The totalitarian states of today are the realisations of quasi-religious theories.

R.F., P. 84

TOTALITARIAN VIOLENCE

There is not much evidence that Marx enjoyed violence for its own sake. But many of his followers did and do. A taste for violence was of the very essence of Trotsky's character, of his methodology and his philosophy of action. Without violence, the man's whole life was meaningless and empty. Indeed, I would argue that it was inevitable that Marx's collectivist determination (or historicism) should breed violence on an unprecedented scale once his teachings spread; as was equally true of Hitler's rather different version of historical necessity. It is always a temptation to the *exalté* to hurry along whatever apocalypse he believes in. That is one of the many reasons why communist and fascist revolutionaries have so much in common; and why their differences are, by comparison, of little

[363]

importance. Hence there have been many important bridge-figures between the communist and fascist ideologies.

R.F., P. 59

TOTALITARIANISM

. . . all totalitarian systems based on conspiracy theory are prone to anti-Semitism, the oldest conspiracy theory of all. It is latent in their ideology and is liable to become active without warning in moments of "crisis," real or imaginary. Socialism, both in its nationalist and its Marxist-Leninist form, cannot escape the deformation of its origins, which lie in a grotesquely oversimplified explanation of how capitalism originated and functions.

C., APRIL 1984

Total politics has produced the death camp and the slave camp, the psychiatric punishment hospital, brainwashing, Newspeak and secret police forces, of which that of the Soviet Union alone is larger than all the armies of Napoleonic Europe combined. A hundred new nations have arisen, exchanging, except in a handful of cases, forms of colonial dependence for tyrannies infinitely more oppressive. Even in its mildest forms, total politics has produced debilitating "welfare cultures," into which unfortunate millions are born, live, breed and die. At the end of a century of total politics its practitioners, whether democratic or authoritarian, continue to promise, in varying degrees, paradise on earth; but their claims carry no more conviction now than the dogmatic theology of their religious predecessors. We are awaiting a new Nietzsche to proclaim: "Politics is dead."

P.P.J., PP. 174–75

The century of total politics which began in the 1880s opened with a utopian prospectus still more ambitious than that provided by the liberal-rationalists of the 1780s. It closed with a record of disasters unparalleled in any previous age. Nationalism, and totalitarian politics driven by the engines of race and class warfare, produced two world wars which made the Napoleonic conflict seem puny: the first

[364]

war cost 30 million lives, the second 50 million; and since then 150 "minor" wars have added a further 30 million to the death toll.

P.P.J., P. 174

Totalitarianism of the Left bred totalitarianism of the Right; Communism and fascism were the hammer and the anvil on which liberalism was broken to pieces. The emergence of Stalin's autocracy changed the dynamic of corruption not in kind but in degree. For Stalin "was but old Lenin writ large." The change in degree nonetheless was important because of its sheer scale. The arrests, the prisons, the camps, the scope, the brutality and violence of the social engineering—nothing like it had ever been seen or even imagined before. So the counter-model became more monstrously ambitious; and the fear which energized its construction more intense. If Leninism begot the fascism of Mussolini, it was Stalinism which made possible the Nazi Leviathan.

M.T., P. 277

Hitler was not in the business of liberation. Like Stalin, he was in the business of slavery. The accident of race made them opponents, and pitted their regimes against each other. But in essential respects they were fellow-ideologues, pursuing Utopias based on a fundamental division of mankind into élites and helots.

M.T., P. 380

. . . in all totalitarian systems, a false vernacular had to be created to conceal the concrete horrors of moral relativism. SS terms for murder included "special treatment," "resettlement," "the general line," "sovereign acts beyond the reach of the judiciary," above all "sending East."

M.T., P. 419

. . . the lesson of Soviet collectivization has been that such schemes, however morally and economically indefensible, can endure, if pursued with sufficient ruthlessness and brute physical power.

M.T., P. 524

[365]

A totalitarian regime does not normally become internally vulnerable until it attempts to liberalize itself.

M.T., P. 678

. . . the engineering of society for lofty purposes . . .

M.T., P. 784

TOTALITARIANISM AND DEMONOLOGY

. . . the erection of a new demonology was one of the most crucial steps in the creation of totalitarian politics, and why it remains a distinguishing characteristic. Jews, capitalists, kulaks were types of evil collective forces. And archetypal individuals were also constructed to epitomise wickedness. . . . And the trouble with political demonology is that, like *odium theologicum,* it is very catching. Those hate-words come so easily to hand—do they not?—and so easily obliterate shades of political discussion in favour of absolute good and absolute evil. Thus a judge who says something which does not square with current race relations orthodoxy is not misguided or foolish: there are zealots outside his court next day screaming at him that he is a Nazi.

R.F., P. 87

TOTALITARIANISM AND INTERNATIONAL RELATIONS

Italy, Japan, Russia and Germany played a geopolitical game together, whose whole object was to replace international law and treaties by a new Realpolitik in which, each believed, its own millenarian vision was destined to be realized. None of these wolf-like states trusted the others; each deceived when it could; but each took advantage of the depredations of the rest to enlarge its booty and strengthen its position. . . . All these totalitarian regimes suffered from internal predation too, the Hobbesian "war of every man against every man." But at least Germany, Russia and Italy had gangster dictatorships. In Japan, nobody was in charge.

M.T., P. 311

[366]

TRADE

. . . We are moving toward a tripartite world system of trade. This is both encouraging and dangerous. Encouraging, because big internal international markets make the creation of a single world market—the fulfillment of the GATT dream—inherently more likely. When customs barriers are abolished over large areas, the way is prepared for removing them everywhere. Negotiations among three parties are easier than among scores. But dangerous too.

N.R., DECEMBER 14, 1992

TRADE WARS

History shows that trade wars have a depressing tendency to erupt into fighting wars.

N.R., DECEMBER 14, 1992

TRANSCRIPTION

Transcription of manuscripts was first practised by monks at Tours, under Martin, in the late fourth century. But most monastic *scriptoria* were based on the model set up by Cassiodorus at Squillace in the mid-sixth century. The dominant material in the West was parchment—the most durable, but also the most expensive and difficult to work. Moreover, its raw materials could be obtained anywhere—from sheepskin, calf or goat—unlike papyrus, which came from Egypt, or paper, shipped from the East but not generally available before the twelfth century. And it could be washed, scraped and used again. . . . A first-class bible would take a monastic *scriptorium* a whole year to produce. When the copying was done, the head copyist assembled all the copy-books, put them in order, re-read and collated them, and then handed over the assembled codex to be bound in skin. . . . And many of these books were made to last. A small seventh-century St. John's Gospel, from Wearmouth or Jarrow, which was once probably Bede's own copy and is

[367]

now at Stonyhurst, survives in superb condition in its original binding of red African goatskin.

H.C., PP. 154–55

TRENT (COUNCIL OF)

Luther died during the first session [of the General Council at Trent] and the fact was scarcely noted except for savage expressions of regret that it was no longer possible to burn him.

H.C., P. 286

TROTSKY, LEON

Trotsky symbolized the violence and daemonic power of Bolshevism and its determination to inflame the world. More than anyone, he was responsible for the popular identification of revolution with the Jews.

H.J., P. 451

Trotsky remained a moral relativist of the most dangerous kind right to the end. . . . He said it was right to murder the Tsar's children, as he had done, because it was politically useful and those who carried it out represented the proletariat; but Stalin did not represent the proletariat—he had become a "bureaucratic excess"—and therefore it was wrong for him to murder Trotsky's children. Trotsky's followers are, or course, notorious for their attachment to this subjectively defined code of ethics and their contempt for objective morality.

M.T., P. 263

Trotsky, who after his fall presented himself as a believer in party democracy and who was apotheosized by his follower and hagiographer Isaac Deutscher as the epitome of all that was noblest in the Bolshevik movement, was never more than a sophisticated political gangster. . . . Trotsky always took the most ruthless line. He invented conscript labor and . . . used unspeakable brutality. . . .

[368]

Like Lenin, he identified himself with history and argued that history was above all moral restraints.

M.T., P. 263

. . . refused to retract his criticism that Stalin was becoming too powerful. But he could not dispute Lenin's condemnation of internal opposition and, like a man accused of heresy by the Inquisition, he was disarmed by his own religious belilef. "Comrades," he admitted, "none of us . . . can be right against the party. The party is in the last resort always right." . . . Since Stalin was already in control of the party, Trotsky's words forged the ice-pick that crushed his skull sixteen years later.

M.T., PP. 264–65

TROTSKYIST

The term "Trotskyist," first used as a term of abuse by Zinoviev, was defined in its mature form by Stalin, who created the distinction between "permanent revolution" (Trotsky) and "revolution in one country" (Stalin). In fact they all believed in immediate world revolution to begin with, and all turned to consolidating the regime when it didn't happen. Trotsky wanted to press ahead with industrialization faster than Stalin but both were, from first to last, opportunists. They had graduated in the same slaughterhouse and their quarrel was essentially about who should be its new high priest. Had Trotsky come out on top, he would probabaly have been even more bloodthirsty than Stalin. But he would not have lasted: he lacked the skills of survival.

M.T., PP. 263–64

TROUSERS

For men, modernity came with the adoption of trousers, perhaps the greatest of all watersheds in the history of men's fashion. Indeed, it might be said that of all the enduring achievements of the French Revolution, the most important was the replacement of *culottes*, or breeches, by the baggy trousers worn by peasants and working men, the *sans-culottes*.

B.M., P. 458

One of the key innovations of George "Beau" Brummell (1778–1840) was to introduce a strap at the bottom of each leg, which went under the shoe or boot and stretched the trousers . . . tighter. . . . The result was that they showed off the male leg to even greater advantage than breeches and satin stockings, which did justice only to the calf. Older men in authority, whose spindle shanks did not benefit from advertisement, denounced them as obscene and Pope Pius VII condemned them outright in a bitter rearguard action which lasted until his death in 1823.

B.M., PP. 458–59

TRUTH

. . . no consideration should ever deflect us from the pursuit and recognition of truth, for that essentially is what constitutes civilization itself. There are many around today who will concede, in theory, that truth is indivisible; but then insist, in practice, that some truths are more divisible than others.

E.S., P. 259

. . . truth is much more than a means to expose the malevolent. It is the great creative force of civilization. For truth is knowledge; and a civilized man is one who, in Hobbes's words, has "a perseverance of delight in the continual and indefatigable generation of knowledge." Hobbes also writes: "Joy, arising from imagination of a man's own power and ability, is that exaltation of mind called glorying." And so it is; for the pursuit of truth is our civilization's glory, and the joy we obtain from it is the nearest we shall approach to happiness, at least on this side of the grave. If we are steadfast in this aim, we need not fear the enemies of society.

E.S., P. 259

TUDOR DESPOTISM

Tudor government has been termed a "despotism" by historians, but it is difficult to identify the physical machinery which made it possible to behave in a despotic manner. Elizabeth was always painfully conscious of the gap between her theoretical sovereignty and her ability to get things done as she wished. It was one reason why she was so opposed to activist policies of any kind. It is true the Tudors exacted some formal signs of reverence which their predecessors had lacked. They were no longer addressed as "Your Grace," but as "Your Majesty"—a verbal inflation not to much purpose. Elizabeth's greatest subjects spoke to her on their knees, though they were allowed to squat on their heels or stand if the interview was prolonged. In practical terms, the Tudors had to observe the law, and the supreme form of law was the parliamentary statute, which made them dependent on an unpredictable and sometimes uncontrollable assembly.

E., P. 152

TURNER, JOSEPH M. W.

He remained faithful always to his belief that painting is a form of language, that it is essentially descriptive, and that its object is to tell the truth about nature, seen objectively. He believed that paintings have a moral purpose, too, to instruct and improve . . . but that they do so by showing the effect of light on objects. In no sense was he an abstract or "uncommitted" painter. . . . The *Literary Gazette* accused him of replacing "the magic of nature" by the "magic of skill," when, in fact, he was trying to do the opposite and use truth to destroy artificial conventions.

B.M., P. 624

TWENTIETH CENTURY

. . . a century of spectacular crimes . . .

I., P. 341

. . . by the last decade of the century, some lessons had plainly been learned. But it was not yet clear whether the underlying evils which had made possible its catastrophic failures and tragedies—the rise of moral relativism, the decline of personal responsibility, the repudiation of Judeo-Christian values, not least the arrogant belief that men and women could solve all the mysteries of the universe by their own unaided intellects—were in the process of being eradicated. On that would depend the chances of the twenty-first century becoming, by contrast, an age of hope for mankind.

M.T., P. 784

The twentieth century has been one of terrifying disturbance and aimlessness. I calculate that well over 100 million people have been killed by state violence in the last sixty-five years. All our efforts to evolve theories of international behaviour and codes of justice and human rights have failed dismally or, worse, degenerated into humbug and propaganda. I can't help thinking that this general breakdown in human behaviour is due, in part at least, to the absence of an agreed cosmology.

P.P.J., P. 254

Today, on both sides of the Atlantic, there are countless millions, born in the late 1940s, now middle-aged, always well educated and well nourished, who have never known what it was like to be without a vote or without redress against the state—and who can now look forward with some confidence to an old age undisturbed by major conflict. Our forebears would have regarded this as indeed a miracle, a fundamental change in the condition and expectations of a huge section of humanity.

N.R., DECEMBER 14, 1992

For many millions, especially in the advanced nations, religion ceased to play much or any part in their lives, and the ways in which the vacuum thus lost was filled, by fascism, Nazism and Communism, by attempts at humanist utopianism, by eugenics or health politics, by the ideologies of sexual liberation, race politics and environmental politics, form much of the substance of the history of our century. But for many more millions—for the overwhelming majority of the human race, in fact—religion continued to be a huge dimension in their lives. Nietzsche, who had so accurately predicted the transmutation of faith into political zealotry and the totalitarian will to power, failed to see that the religious spirit could, quite illogically, coexist with secularization, and so resuscitate his dying God.

M.T., P. 700

One of the most sensible precepts of the Judeo-Christian tradition is "count your blessings," and our most important blessing is that we have survived the twentieth century, perhaps the most dangerous century in the history of humanity. We are leaving it with the international order, which first broke down in 1914 and remained fractured until the late 1980s, at least partially restored and with good prospects of a complete recovery. Looking back, one is appalled to think of the number of occasions when the civilized world was in real danger of extinction.

N.R., DECEMBER 14, 1992

We have survived a terrible century. That is something. We have learned many of its most important lessons. That is more. We are now poised on the verge of a great adventure in international political and economic coming-together, which can turn the twenty-first century into the period when the first global society is forged. The next ten years will see whether this is likely to happen or not. They are going to be invigorating, exciting years, and I am looking forward to them with relish.

N.R., DECEMBER 14, 1992

U

UNDUE INFLUENCE (EVIL OF)

In an article in the *Independent* . . . the chairman of Crac, the Bishop of Liverpool, defending the old system, called for "a sense of responsibility for those who may be vulnerable to undue influence." But that was exactly the case the High Priest and the Scribes and Pharisees had against Jesus. He was so *irresponsible.* He had wild views and caused trouble and, horror of horrors, threatened to embroil them all in a row with the Romans. He had consorted with that other irresponsible fellow John, who dressed in skins and baptised people in the river, in the most unseemly manner. Jesus was always trying to exercise undue influence, by practising faith-healing and performing miracles, on all kinds of vulnerable people—children, women, above all the poor, who couldn't read the scriptures and were exposed to every kind of foolish nonsense, such as "blessed are the meek, for they shall inherit the earth." Then there was that apostate follower of his, Paul, who wrote things like, "Divine folly is wiser than the wisdom of man," and said that God "has chosen things low and contemptible, mere nothings, to overthrow the existing order." You can't get more irresponsible than that, can you? No wonder the High Priest wagged his beard and rent his garments.

S., NOVEMBER 3, 1990

UNION (CLOSED SHOP)

It is evil because it is a form of monopoly achieved by coercion and it has all the anti-social consequences of any other monopoly.

S., OCTOBER 26, 1985

I know it in my intellect, I feel it in my bones. It is, in all circumstances, and whatever the specious justifications of time, place and convenience, morally wrong. It is wrong in the sense that imprisonment without trial is wrong, and conviction without due process. It hands over the individual to the mercy of the kangaroo court and the menace of the militant shop-floor mob.

R.F., P. 69

UNION LEADERS

How are we to describe a band of determined men occupying key positions in society and using their collective power to raise their incomes, regardless of the needs and interests of the rest? Powerful men who conspire together to squeeze the community are gangsters. Let us identify them as such.

R.F., P. 16

The top trade union bureaucrats, irrespective of their political views, are the new elite, a privileged aristocracy enjoying perks and immunities virtually unknown in Britain since the eighteenth century. They are what Disraeli termed, in *Sybil*, a "Venetian oligarchy," like the old Whig grandees, raised above the common herd and enjoying full access to all the sweets and savouries of a juicy and inequitable political system. They toil not, neither do they spin. Some, an increasing number, have never done manual work of any kind; they have been happily fulfilled bureaucrats all their adult lives. The rest have long since forgotten what the shop floor is like. Much of their time is spent travelling abroad, at "international conferences." And abroad, these days, British embassies are expected to jump to attention when the general secretaries heave in sight, howling for free meals, accommodation and the usual flunkeyism.

[375]

They demand that big lunch and dinner parties be given for them to meet their "opposite numbers"—who are, as it happens, increasingly highly educated and intelligent men (and women), who find the average British trade union general secretary an object of ribald amusement.

R.F., P. 41

Not a group of idealists. Not men who devote their lives to the welfare of all. Not even ideologues. But, rather, an ugly factional interest, like any other which has stained the pages of history, operating at the expense of the community, and motivated by an insatiable lust for personal power, and by enormous greed.

R.F., P. 49

Union Monopolies

The result of this unchallenged monopoly is entirely predictable: the commodity—labour—is about four or five times as expensive as it would be if competition prevailed, and the purchaser is obliged to employ it, at the dictation of the monopoly supplier, in all kinds of wasteful ways, and under constant threat that this sole supply will be withdrawn. These costs are all passed on to the public, which in addition has a much smaller choice of end-prodcuts . . .

S., OCTOBER 26, 1985

Union, Trade

The trade union is a product of nineteenth-century capitalism. It is part of that system. Against powerful, highly organised and ruthless capitalist forces, it had an essential, even noble part to play. But when those forces are disarmed; when they are in headlong retreat —indeed howling for mercy—the union has no function to perform. The trade union movement may be dressed up with economic committees and so forth; but its only real purpose is to bargain for better wages within an all-powerful capitalist system. The British trade union movement has now been taken out of that context and placed in an entirely new one. Yet it is still carrying on doing the only thing it knows how to do—ask for higher wages. As it has beaten all its opponents, as it is for all practical purposes the state, it naturally gets them. A subject government prints the money, and the result is inflation on an unprecedented scale.

R.F., P. 16

The trade union is now increasing its economic power and its political influence faster than any other institutions in western society. It is not wholly malevolent, but it has certain increasingly reprehensible characteristics. One is that it claims, and gets, legal privilege; it thus breaks our fourth commandment, the rule of law. Another is that it curbs the elitist urge in man, the very essence of civilization, and quite deliberately and exultantly reinforces the average. As Ortega y Gasset puts it, in *The Revolt of the Masses,* "The chief characteristic of our time is that the mediocre mind, aware of its own mediocrity, has the boldness to assert the rights of mediocrity and to impose them everywhere." Such an actual or potential menace to our culture can be contained, provided we keep this commandment strictly, and protect the individual agianst corporatism.

E.S., PP. 257–58

UNIONS

The union was not a socialist instrument. It was not a political instrument at all. It was an economic function of the capitalist system, a defensive leaguing together of desperate and exploited men to enable them to meet the owners of capital on something like equal terms. Its great weapon, the strike, was essentially negative, destructive and despairing, like the riot. It might fail at appalling cost, or, even if it succeeded, might damage those who wielded it almost as much as its opponents. It was used because there seemed no other way.

R.F., P. 14

The unions have refused to recognise the limits of their historical role. They have not only rejected the idea of a progressive abdication, and the shift of their social and economic function to the political process, but they have flatly declined to allow the smallest diminution of their power to press the sectional interests they represent. Indeed they have steadily, ruthlessly and indiscriminately sought to increase that power.

R.F., P. 15

British trade unionism has . . . become a formula for national misery.

R.F., P. 16

Since 1945, the British working class has been desperately badly served by the trade union movement. Its standard of living has gone up with agonising slowness. Britain's growth rate has been the worst of any major industrial power, indeed of any industrial power. Real wages have climbed *pari passu*. It is an unfortunate fact, which no amount of trade union militancy and rhetoric can alter, that unionism can increase nominal wages—paper money—but not real wages, at any rate over a period. What it can do, however, and what it has done most effectively in post-war Britain, is to slow down the rate of economic growth.

R.F., P. 19

The idea of a vast left-wing conspiracy within the trade union movement is a figment of right-wing imaginations. British trade unionism does not have sinister ideas. The trouble is that it has no ideas at all. Most of its leaders are perfectly well-meaning. Some are very intelligent. But the movement as a whole is dominated at all levels by the complacent, the conservative, the unimaginative, the lazy-minded, men soaked in old prejudices and habits of mind, Bourbons to the core, forgetting nothing, learning nothing, negative, obstructive, slow, dull, long-winded, unadventurous, immensely pleased with themselves and quite determined to resist planned change of any kind.

R.F., PP. 20–21

. . . its deep-rooted distrust of ordinary counting-heads democracy, which it sees, rightly in my view, as absolutely fatal to the objects, methods and claims of the present trade union movement. Indeed,

[378]

it seems to regard any form of activity among industrial workers outside the trade union framework to be dangerous and illegitimate, if not actually illegal. This philosophy crops up throughout the proposals: in the framing of the ballot-question, in the selection of worker-directors, in their removal or reappointment, and in machinery for any changes in the system. The entire majority report can be summed up in one sentence: "Everything for the union, nothing outside the union, nothing against the union." Now, where have we heard *that* before?

R.F., PP. 63–64

UNIONS (NEWSPAPER)

. . . the breaking of the unions continues to make most papers profitable, at any rate if well managed. Not only is the print wage bill under control but management can now respond appropriately to adverse trading conditions by taking tough decisions and introducing yet more technical savings without having to argue with the unions and pay them danegeld. This happy situation in London is one reason why the New York newspapers, led by the *Daily News*, are at last finding the courage to take on the unregenerate unions there.

S., APRIL 28, 1990

UNITARIANISM

Unitarianism was, to a great extent, the religion of the élite—critics joked that its preaching was limited to "the fatherhood of God, the brotherhood of man and the neighbourhood of Boston."

H.C., P. 428

UNITED NATIONS

In a world where real distinctions are being deliberately eroded or inverted by pseudo-science, where reason is derided, knowledge assassinated and the most fundamental principles of civilization assaulted, we must not be surprised to find that the United Nations, the fount of international authority—such as it is—should have become the World Theatre of the Absurd, a global madhouse where lunatic falsehood reigns and the voices of the sane can scarcely be heard above the revolutionary and racist din. Heart of Darkness, indeed!

E.S., P. 253

. . . the United Nations, which in a non-violent world might be a useful forum in which genuine difficulties could be resolved by argument and negotiation, has become a kind of Roman arena, in which the advanced nations of the West are hunted, in the expiation of largely imaginary crimes, past, present and to come. Or, to vary the metaphor, we can use the expression of the former American ambassador to the UN, Daniel Moynihan: "The inmates have taken over the lunatic asylum."

E.S., P. 253

The United Nations has proved not merely a failure, but a positive obstacle to peace and justice, because it has put the principle of one-nation-one-vote above the rule of the law, including its own.

E.S., P. 257

. . . by the 1970s, the UN was a corrupt and demoralized body, and its ill-considered interventions were more inclined to promote violence than to prevent it. Truman's fatal mistake in allowing executive power to slip towards the General Assembly in 1950, compounded by Eisenhower's error in 1956, when he allowed Hammarskjöld to hound Britain and France as aggressors, now yielded a bitter and abundant harvest. The UN was founded by fifty-one states, the great majority of them democracies. By 1975 there were 144 members, with plans for 165, all but twenty-five of them totalitarian or one-party states, mainly of the Left.

M.T., P. 689

[380]

Up to now, the United Nations has never once been able to tackle an African emergency successfully because it treats symptoms, not causes, often indeed the wrong symptoms.

N.R., DECEMBER 14, 1992

Arafat has no more place in the UN than the head of the Mafia, who can match him in successful crime and perhaps has a wider constituency. But Arafat fits more convincingly the mythology of the modern world, which has replaced negotiation and debate by guns and explosives. And in the UN, of course, he finds many agents of his peers: military gangsters and expert racists, men skilled in the politics of torture and butchery, who have devoted their lives to the destruction of democracy and the courts. More and more, the UN begins to resemble, and sound like, a thieves' kitchen. . . . why do the powers still attached to civilised standards continue to give it their countenance?

R.F., P. 192

UNIVERSITY

The prime function of a university in society is to serve as the monitor and custodian of its culture.

E.S., P. 161

. . . If the university now stands in the front line of civilization, it is urgent to point out that this defensive work should not be a Maginot Line, lost for ever once penetrated. It should, on the contrary, constitute a defence in depth; every . . . variety of institution where higher education is available, while linked indeed in one huge defensive confraternity, should each pursue . . . its own self-determined course. The independence and autonomy of each separate university and college . . . is the best fighting posture for academia to adopt today. . . . the university today is not an ivory tower, but a real one; the prime need is to keep its [independence] . . . and above all to ensure that it is not betrayed from within.

E.S., PP. 172–73

The advent of John F. Kennedy introduced an entirely new phase of idealistic youth culture enormously magnified by a vast program of university expansion. This expansion, planned in the 50's and realized in the 60's and early 70's, was a worldwide phenomenon and one of the most important in the entire 20th century. It not only enlarged but radicalized the campus everywhere; a completely new brand of teacher invaded it.

N.Y.T.M., MARCH 4, 1984

It is a myth that universities are nurseries of reason. They are hothouses for every kind of extremism, irrationality, intolerance and prejudice, where intellectual and social snobbery is almost purposefully instilled and where dons attempt to pass on to their students their own sins of pride. The wonder is that so many people emerge from these dens still employable, though a significant minority, as we have learned to our cost, go forth well equipped for a lifetime of public mischief-making.

S., SEPTEMBER 7, 1991

Universities are the most overrated institutions of our age . . .

S., SEPTEMBER 7, 1991

UNREASON, AGE OF

As the intellectual structure collapses, theories degenerate into slogans and arguments are met with abuse and fists. Thus, inevitably, monsters re-emerge from the graves in which (it was thought) liberalism had buried them. Inverted racism is acclaimed. Black Power . . . Arab anti-Semitism, and the ferocious Moslem cult of male supremacy, is made to appear a force for liberation and justice. Real crimes, crying to heaven for vengeance, . . . are ignored or even justified unless they fall within the narrow categories of approved grievances. There seems no point at which the betrayal of mind is to stop. Some preach that truth is only to be found in hallucination, that drugs are the panacea for the disjunction of the times. Not

[382]

opium of the people: opium for the people. . . . Some take the ultimate step, and argue that only the mad are sane.

H.E., P. 418

USAGE

Indeed, many of the educated persistently misuse words. Among words often so abused today are: arguable (instead of uncertain), dilemma (instead of choice), mentality (disposition), authentic (true), vulnerable (weak), differential (difference), entitlement (right) . . . hopefully (. . . "it is hoped"), alibi (excuse), viable (workable), chronic (severe) . . . idiosyncratic (odd), ambivalence (ambiguity), nostalgia (regret), redundant (out of work) and dichotomy (partition). . . . The cause of such misuse is the overweening desire to scare or impress the less educated. Language is one of those fields where social or professional groups tend to set up electrified wire-fences of verbosity or special usage to denote their private territory and to discourage intruders.

E.S., PP. 110–11

UTOPIAN

Once men begin to claim a monopoly of righteousness—and the blueprint for Utopia—they tend to treat those who hinder them, deliberately or not, as evil. The Old Testament is littered with the reviled corpses of men and women who, somehow, found themselves opposite Yahweh in the moral equation, and were accordingly "smitten." As Christianity ceased to be a simplifying religion, and moved inexorably towards the construction of a total moral order, it acquired *odium theologicum* and the terrifying apparatus of hell and eternal damnation. Indeed, once you seek to impose this moral order by force it is necessary to create the concept of men wholly possessed by evil. Then you can destroy opponents without compunction. It is hard to kill the obstinate or misguided, but who hesitates to slay a demon?

R.F., P. 86

[383]

Utopianism

The new politics did not bring Jerusalem or utopia or the millennium. It produced the Terror, succeeded by the quarter-century of the Revolutionary and the Napoleonic Wars, the largest and most costly conflicts in history so far: Continental wars which had some claim to be termed the first world war. Everywhere the pursuit of political utopianism bred a new and intransigent nationalism, expressing itself in huge armaments, in the destructive spirit of irridentism—the demand that frontiers should be based on race lines—in imperialist acquisitions and in fantasies of racial supremacy.

P.P.J., PP. 173–74

In the 1880s liberalism yielded to socialism as the philosophy of the future, and the notion of the rational state was replaced by the idea of the total state, actively promoting utopia. The decade saw the birth of modern trade unionism, and the first mass strikes in most European countries, seeking not only better conditions but collective ownership. Nor was political utopianism confined to the Left of the spectrum: in 1883 Bismarck introduced the world's first comprehensive system of social security.

P.P.J., P. 174

. . . the experience of the twentieth century shows emphatically that Utopianism is never far from gangsterism.

M.T., P. 718

V

VAN BUREN, MARTIN

Van Buren was the first political bureaucrat . . . He demonstrated, in his long struggle with [De Witt] Clinton, that the man who got the details right and controlled the best organization would win in the end. His Tammany men were called Bucktails by their enemies, a sneer at their rustic origins, but he taught them to be proud of the name and to wear the symbol in their hats, just as the Democrats later flaunted their symbolic donkey. Branching out from Tammany, he constructed an entire statewide system of the party.

B.M., P. 934

VANITY

Among the high and mighty, vanity is not the worst sin: one of the most sinister aspects of Lenin, Hitler and Stalin, the three most evil men of the century, was their curious lack of it.

S., MARCH 19, 1988

VATICAN II (EXCESSES OF)

In many churches the neo-baroque altars which had been such a prominent expression of nineteenth- and twentieth-century ultramontanism were gouged out and put on the bonfire. Laymen and laywomen were encouraged to take prominent roles in the new vernacular masses. Many of the old triumphalist hymns were banned, being replaced by ones less likely to impede the cause of ecumenism, or by "folk hymns" . . . There was, in short, a systematic dismantling of the devotional aesthetic of the Counter-Reformation, a deliberate dispersal of the mysterious opacity and the evocation of the supernatural with which Catholicism had designedly surrounded herself. . . . the absolute distinction between priest and layman, which the church had maintained throughout the Dark and Middle Ages, and indeed reinforced in the Tridentine reforms, was now obscured . . . the demotic began to infringe upon the hieratic. The combined result of all these changes was to banish the reverential awe with which Catholics had always regarded the machinery of their church and the men who worked it.

P.J., P. 53

VERSAILLES, TREATY OF

The armistice was aptly named: the war was inconclusive. The Germans rightly claimed that the Versailles Treaty did not accurately reflect the military balance in November 1918. As Mussolini remarked (it is his only remark worth recording), the Allies should either have taken Berlin or imposed a far less onerous settlement. The first was beyond their strength, the second beyond their wisdom. Hence the resumption of the conflict was inevitable. The Second World War took place not so much because no one won the First, but because Versailles did not acknowledge this truth.

H.E., P. 380

The Versailles Treaty, in seeking to embody the principles of self-determination, actually created more, not fewer, minorities, and much angrier ones (many were German or Hungarian), armed with far more genuine grievances. The new nationalist regimes thought they could afford to be far less tolerant than the old empires. And, since the changes damaged the economic infrastructure (especially in Silesia, South Poland, Austria, Hungary and North Yugoslavia), everyone tended to be poorer than before.

M.T., P. 38

VICTORIANS

I don't know how the notion got about that the Victorians were beastly to their children. Quite the contrary: they were the first to treat children as human beings in their own right, not just inferior adults, and to give them a special status.

P.P.J., P. 266

VIETNAM

There was . . . a bitter irony in the accusations of genocide hurled at the Americans. . . . all the charges made against U.S. forces at the 1967 Stockholm "International War Crimes tribunal" were baseless. Evacuation of civilians from war zones to create "free fire" fields not only saved civilian lives but was actually required by the 1949 Geneva Convention. The heavy incidence of combat in civilian areas was the direct result of Vietcong tactics in converting villages into fortified strongholds, itself a violation of the Geneva agreement.

M.T., P. 635

In general, American public opinion strongly backed the war, which was throughout more popular than the Korean War. . . . far more Americans were critical of Johnson for doing too little than for doing too much. The notion of a great swing away from the war in public opinion, and above all the axiom that the young opposed it, was an invention. In fact support for withdrawal was never over 20 per cent until after the November 1968 election, by which time the decision to get out had already been taken. . . . It was not the American people which lost its stomach for the kind of sacrifices Kennedy had demanded in his Inaugural. It was the American leadership.

M.T., P. 637

VIOLENCE

Murder is always wrong. Thus anyone who tries to justify political violence, the greatest single evil of our age, must automatically be suspect as an enemy of our society. In fact the theories which attempt to legitimize killing in the pursuit of political objectives are, without exception, founded on false premises, illogical or rest on deliberate linguistic conjuring. Hence there is a natural presumption that anyone seeking to circumvent the common opinion that violence is wicked is an intellectual crook; as John Rawls puts it in *A Theory of Justice*: "On a subject as ancient and much discussed . .. we may probably assume that a novel, and hence interesting, view of violence is likely to be false." Moreover, a propagandist or pedagogue who is wrong about violence is almost certainly wrong about all his other claims to truth.

E.S., PP. 255–56

VIOLENCE (POLITICAL)

The virtue we should cherish most is the courage to resist violence, especially if this involves flying in the face of a public opinion which, in its fear, and in its anxiety for peace, is willing to appease the violators. Above all, violence should never be allowed to pay, or be seen to pay.

E.S., PP. 255–56

VOLK CULTURE

The modern German nation was, in one sense, the creation of Prussian militarism. In another, it was the national expression of the German romantic movement, with its stress upon the *Volk*, its mythology and its natural setting in the German landscape, especially its dark, mysterious forests. The German *Volk* movement dated from Napoleonic times and was burning "alien" and "foreign" books, which corrupted *"Volk* culture," as early as 1817. Indeed it was from the *Volk* movement that Marx took his concept of "alienation" in industrial capitalism. A *Volk* had a soul, which was derived from its natural habitat. . . . If the landscape was destroyed, or the *Volk* divorced from it, the soul dies. The Jews were not a *Volk* because they had lost their soul: they lacked "rootedness." . . . The true basis of the *Volk* was the peasant. There should of course be workers, but they had to be "artisans," organized in local guilds. The proletariat, on the other hand, was the creation of the Jews. Having no landscape of their own, they destroyed that of others, causing millions of people to be uprooted and herded into giant cities . . . moreover, the big cities would link hands across the world, forming . . . a "world proletariat" conspiring to destroy everything that had a soul, was "natural," [and] especially the German landscape and its peasantry.

M.T., P. 118

VOTING

Men and women are most sincere when they vote not with their ballot-papers but with their feet.

M.T., P. 612

W

War

War breeds revolutions, and breeding revolutions is a very old form of warfare.

M.T., P. 49

. . . war is about waste; war *is* waste.

M.T., P. 409

Christian teaching on war rests on eight principles. Going to war requires three conditions: a legitimate command, a just cause (including self-defence) and a right intention. Waging war requires two: discrimination and proportion. Both declaring and waging war are subject to the sixth and seventh principles of moral necessity and choosing the lesser evil. The eighth is the exercise of what Aquinas classified as the first of the cardinal virtues, prudential judgement. Prudence is a virtue peculiarly relevant to secular issues of public policy: it counsels us to examine history, to learn from human error, and to calculate probabilities.

P.P.J., P. 162

"War on Poverty"

As living standards rose, the definition of poverty changed, and the poor "felt" just as poor as before, though their real incomes had risen. The danger of the kind of welfare state Johnson was creating was that it pushed people out of the productive economy permanently and made them dependents of the state. Poverty increased when families split up, either by old people living apart or by divorce, with consequent divisions of income. Legislation often promoted these processes.

M.T., P. 640

WATERGATE

This was the first media *Putsch* in history, as ruthless and anti-democratic as any military coup by bemedaled generals with their sashes and sabers. It is obvious that Nixon, a responsible and experienced statesman preoccupied with the international problems of the early 1970's, not least the appalling Middle East crisis of autumn 1973 and its disastrous economic aftermath, consistently underestimated the unscrupulousness of his media enemies and their willingness to sacrifice the national interest in the pursuit of their institutional vendetta.

C., OCTOBER 1988

Nixon was tried by the media, and Kennedy and Johnson by nobody. . . . As it was, the success of the media-Democratic vendetta against Nixon, and its tragic aftermath, led to a vacuum of power in Washington and a hiatus in the exercise of American authority in the world, with disastrous consequences both for the U.S. and its allies; not until the Reagan presidency was it possible to begin the restoration of America's self-confidence and global prestige. In my view, without the absurdities of Watergate, the collapse of Soviet Communism would have begun to occur in the late 1970's rather than the 1980's.

C., DECEMBER 1991

America seems peculiarly prone to these spasms of self-righteous political emotion in which all sense of perspective and the national interest is lost. The outbreak of xenophobia in 1918–20 was the work of right-wing Democrats. The anti-Communist scare of the late 1940s and early 1950s was largely directed by conservative Republicans. The Watergate witch-hunt, by contrast, was run by

[391]

liberals in the media. In their eyes Nixon's real offence was popularity. Though he won narrowly in 1968, he successfully appealed, as president, over the heads of opinion-formers and a Democratic Congress, to unfashionable, inarticulate "middle Americans," family-loving, church-going, patriotic, industrious and anti-liberal.

M.T., P. 649

WAUGH, EVELYN

Evelyn Waugh, that superbly gifted but curmudgeonly and occasionally malevolent writer who sometimes inflicted pain by his words, was once asked a hard question by a brave woman: "Mr. Waugh, how can you behave as you do, and still remain a Christian?" He replied with grim sincerity, "Madam, I may be as bad as you say, but believe me, were it not for my religion, I would scarcely be a human being."

R.D., JUNE 1985

WEALTH CREATION

Next to the development of credit itself, the invention and still more the popularization of paper securities were probably the biggest single contribution the Jews made to the wealth-creation process. Jews hastened the use of securities just as much in areas where they felt safe as in areas where they were vulnerable, for they saw the entire world as a single market. Here, too, the global perspective which the diaspora gave them turned them into pioneers. For a race without a country, the world was a home. The further the market stretched, the greater were the opportunities.

H.J., P. 283

WEALTH, DISTRIBUTION OF

. . . the urge to distribute wealth equally, and still more the belief that it can be brought about by political action, is the most dangerous of all popular emotions. It is the legitimation of envy, of all the deadly sins the one which a stable society based on consensus should fear the most. The monster state is a source of many evils; but it is, above all, an engine of envy.

R.F., P. 9

WEEKLY

After the endless political shouting of television and the din of the dailies, the weekly provides the wearied reader with, as it were, a knob to switch off, so that as he opens its pages a blissful silence descends and he is in a calm, unhurried atmosphere of clear thinking, elegant syntax and civilised values.

S., JULY 9, 1988

WEIMAR CULTURE

There was, in fact, a modernistic cultural paramountcy in Weimar Germany. . . . [The Easterners] called it *Kulturbolschewismus*. Throughout the war the German ultra-patriotic press had warned that defeat would bring the triumph of Western "decadent" art, literature and philosophy, as though Lloyd George and Clemenceau could not wait to get to Berlin to ram Cubism down German throats. Now it had actually happened! Weimar was the great battleground in which modernism . . . fought for supremacy in Europe and the world, because in Weimar the new had the institutions . . . on its side. . . . the Weimar censorship law, though still strict, was probably the least repressive in Europe. . . . Stage and night-club shows in Berlin were the least inhibited of any major capital. Plays, novels and even paintings touched on such themes as homosexuality, sadomasochism, transvestism and incest; and it was in Germany that Freud's writings were most fully absorbed by the intelligentsia and penetrated the widest range of artistic expression.

M.T., P. 114

There is nothing more galling than a cultural tyranny, real or imaginary, and in Weimar culture "they" could plausibly be identified with the Jews . . . it is undoubtedly true to say that Weimar culture would have been quite different, and infinitely poorer, without its Jewish element, and there was certainly enough evidence to make a theory of Jewish cultural conspiracy seem plausible. . . . This was the principal reason why anti-Semitism made such astonishing headway in Weimar Germany.

M.T., PP. 116–17

THE WEST

The argument that the West was somehow to blame for world poverty was itself a Western invention. Like decolonization, it was a product of guilt, that prime dissolvent of order and justice. It reflected the same tendency to categorize people morally not as individuals but as members of classes which was the fundamental fallacy of Marxism.

M.T., P. 691

THE WEST AND FREEDOM

The 1960s, during which most Western nations doubled, and in some cases trebled, their university places, did not reinforce democratic freedoms, or enlarge the GNP or strengthen the free enterprise system. They produced the students' revolts, beginning in Paris in 1968; they detonated the Northern Ireland conflict, which is still harassing Britain. They produced the Baader-Meinhof gang in West Germany, the Red Brigades in Italy, the Left Fascist terrorism of Japan. They produced an enormous explosion of Marxist studies, centered around the social sciences, and especially sociology, and a new generation of university teachers and schoolteachers, dedicated by faith and by a sort of perverted religious piety, to the spread of Marxist ideas. It is true, of course, that student unrest, as such, has quietened down. But the steady diffusion of ideas hostile to our free system continues remorselessly.

R.F., P. 161

WHIG

The truth is that Whiggism could be illustrated but not defined; it was a shadowy ectoplasm generated by the vague ideal of *noblesse oblige*. A true Whig could not tell how he would act or think until something happened; then he knew instinctively. To men like Disraeli, Gladstone or Chamberlain, this was infuriating, even immoral—the "negation of principle." The Whigs did, however, possess one working axiom: that power should go with property. The country should be run by men with a stake in it.

S.N., P. 181

[They] despised the middle class, [and] they ignored the workers completely. . . . The Whigs . . . assumed, fatalistically, that workers—as opposed to middle-class shopkeepers—could never be converted to moderate courses. Thereby they missed a vital trick, which the Tories scooped up gratefully. For the great merit of Disraeli and Lord Randolph Churchill was to perceive that brutal economic self-interest need not necessarily be the decisive factor in determining how men vote; that even the poorest have conservative instincts.

S.N., P. 183

WILL (INDIVIDUAL)

Having watched the power of will at work . . . in my own lifetime, pushing on the hinge of history and turning the door against the apparent pressure of events, I have no doubt that it is a major factor in determining the destiny of nations, and that historians must allow for its importance—as of course the good ones have always done. Naturally willpower alone is not enough. There must be a miminal physical basis of power from which it can operate. . . . To be effective in history, the human will must be combined with judgment and realism.

A.S., JULY 1988

. . . when the moral restraints of religion and tradition, hierarchy and precedent, are removed, the power to suspend or unleash catastrophic events does not devolve on the impersonal benevolence of the masses but falls into the hands of men who are isolated by the very totality of their evil natures.

M.T., P. 376

WILSON, EDMUND

. . . between 1946 and 1955 he did not file any income-tax returns, a serious offence in the United States as in most other countries. . . . What about the Marxist tag, which he endorsed: "From each according to his ability, to each according to his need"? Or did he think that applied to others but not to himself? . . . Wilson's attitude was in fact a striking example of the intellectual who, while telling the world how to run its business, in tones of considerable moral authority, thinks the practical consequences of such advice have nothing to do with those like himself—they are for "ordinary people."

I., PP. 266–67

WOMEN

It has often struck me that when women are polled on what they value most in a man, "sense of humour" invariably comes top of the list. This is because women's lives are harder and sadder than men's and they need more laughs, though they don't, alas, always get them. It is significant that men at a strip-tease show sit in solemn silence whereas women watching a male strip laugh all the time. For women pleasure and laughter are inseparable.

S., AUGUST 6, 1988

WOMEN'S LIB

The age of ideology, of women's lib and bra-burning and all that
nonsense, is dead and forgotten. It was never of much consequence,
for women tend to be practical people who put little trust in abstract
formulations. We are now in the age of action. What women want
are results—real women in actual jobs—and they want them now.
I believe women have moved through the phase where they were
content to wait for a gradualist process to mature over decades. They
have lost patience.

s., NOVEMBER 9, 1991

WOMEN (TOPLESS)

Fanatical nudists are furious at the topless cult, which they denounce
as obscene. Call-girls hate it. Striptease dancers fear (needlessly, I
should have thought) that it will put them out of business, and
when one of their number in Australia actually wore one, she
was beaten up by her colleagues and fired. Whores and pimps—
anyone in fact who makes money out of the frustrations imposed by
conventional morality—have a vested interest in keeping the sex-
barriers high. At all costs the public must not get its sexual enjoy-
ment free. Throughout history the puritan and the professional
dispenser of sex have joined in unholy and unacknowledged wedlock.

S.N., P. 51

WORDS

Words can kill, they can transmit evil. This was a point made by
Erasmus, from whom we derive many of our modern ideas of tolerance. Deploring the unbridled polemics of the theological con-
troversialists, he warned: "The long war of words and writings will
lead to blows"—as indeed happened: books eventually produced the
Wars of Religion. It is precisely because words are so powerful that,

[397]

like money or physical force, they must be subject to the restraints of law.

s., march 4, 1989

WORDSWORTH, WILLIAM

Many of Wordsworth's fellow poets and writers criticized his identification with the Lowther interest because they did not understand or care about the localism that lay at the center of his art. Wordsworth was, and felt himself to be, a creature of the fells and their valleys, almost a part of the soil, linked to its people by countless relationships stretching back generations and by memories from earliest childhood. . . . Other writers, by contrast, had cut themselves off from their roots and had become cosmopolitan wanderers, owing allegiance more to their caste as intellectuals than to any particular place. . . . As for the critics, they had turned themselves into men from nowhere.

b.m., p. 409

WORKING CLASS

The older I get, and the more I study history, the more I find the whole concept of a "working class" mysterious. All kinds of people claim they know what the workers are thinking—Labour politicians who have inevitably changed their status by adopting a middle-class profession, academics, sociologists, pollsters, and not least tabloid editors with daughters in jodhpurs. . . . The truth is that by the time a person becomes conscious there is such a thing as a "working class," he has already lost touch with it and has ceased to be a credible authority on its characteristics.

s., may 26, 1990

WORLD WAR I

. . . the war . . . drew attention to the superficial hold Christianity appeared to possess over the passions of multitudes or the actions of their governments. . . . All the participants claimed they were killing in the name of moral principle. All in fact pursued purely secular aims. Religious beliefs and affiliations played no part whatever in the alignments. On one side were ranged Protestant Germany, Catholic Austria, Orthodox Bulgaria and Moslem Turkey. On the other were Protestant Britain, Catholic France and Italy, and Orthodox Russia.

H.C., P. 477

Had Britain stayed out of the conflict, France would have fought a wholly defensive war, the Germans would have attempted the grand offensive, found the casualties unacceptable, and chosen a political compromise as an alternative to a costly military stalemate. An uncommitted Britain would, of course, have assisted in ensuring that the compromise was fair and workable. The great Continental powers would have learned a salutary lesson, and the outcome would have been a more stable, and chastened, Europe.

H.E., P. 379

WORLD WAR I AND ENGLISH LIBERALISM

The essence of English liberalism was the moral and practical virtue of freedom: free the individual from artificial restraints, and he will realise the full potentialities of mind, body and soul. But how do you fight a total war on these principles? The tragedy is that Asquith and his colleagues tried to do it. English individualism died the hard way, in the Flanders mud. The English had always taken it for granted that men should be hired to fight wars (especially abroad), as they were hired to sail ships, drive coaches, build roads. It was a job for the poor or the professional, to perform for wages. . . . military service as a function of citizenship had never worked in England, and when it reappeared at the end of the nineteenth century it was seen as a foreign institution, advocated by the militarists and

[399]

the extreme Right; it was anathema to the Liberals and the budding Labour Party. If more men were needed, they would of course volunteer: that was the true Liberal way to fight a war, if indeed there was a Liberal way to fight a war.

H.E., P. 380

World War II

. . . predator-states practised Realpolitik in different ways and at different speeds. Stalin's Russia was the most Bismarckian, content to seize opportunity merely when it offered and patient enough to move according to geological time-scales, convinced all would be hers in the end. Germany was the most dynamic, with an imminent eschatology which Hitler felt must be realized in his lifetime. Mussolini's Italy was the jackal, following in the wake of the larger beasts and snatching any morsel left unguarded. Japan was the most unstable, haunted by the vision of actual mass-starvation.

M.T., P. 311

It is a matter of argument whether the British or the Germans first began the systematic bombing of civilian targets. Hitler (like Lenin and Stalin) had from the very first practised and defended the use of terror to obtain any or all of his objectives. What is clear is that, long before the end of 1940 . . . British bombers were being used on a great and increasing scale to kill and frighten the German civilian population . . . The policy, initiated by Churchill, approved in cabinet, endorsed by parliament and, so far as can be judged, enthusiastically backed by the bulk of the British people—thus fulfilling all the conditions of the process of consent in a democracy under law—marked a critical stage in the moral declension of humanity in our times.

M.T., P. 370

WORLD WAR II GUILT

Isn't it about time we began to treat the second world war and the Nazi epoch as history, instead of as part of current affairs? By this I mean we should begin to judge what happened 40 and 50 years ago objectively, dispassionately and without allowing our emotions to cloud our analysis of the facts. These perpetual anniversary celebrations and memorial services I suspect do more harm than good. They keep open the old sores and hatreds, rather than promote reconciliation.

S., APRIL 27, 1985

WRITER

. . . it is a curious fact that writers, the least organized in their own lives, instinctively support planning in the public realm.

M.T., P. 248

. . . writers themselves appreciate a paper where, within wide limits, they are free to express themselves and are united by a bond of talent rather than creed—and give of their best accordingly.

S., JULY 9, 1988

There is nothing that writers like better than a good shop-window, where they can display their wares to best advantage in the knowledge that they will be examined by an elite clientele in a relaxed manner.

S., JULY 9, 1988

It is a curious fact that when writers huddle together, especially over what they see as a "moral issue," they invariably talk less sense than even the most foolish of them does individually.

S., JANUARY 4, 1989

It cannot be emphasised too strongly that balanced, well-adjusted, stable and secure people do not, on the whole, make good writers, including good journalists. To illustrate the point you have only to think of a few of those who have been both good writers *and* good journalists—Swift, Samuel Johnson, Coleridge, Hazlitt, Dickens, Marx, Hemingway, Camus, Waugh, just to begin with.

s., FEBRUARY 24, 1990

WRITING

All writing is hard. Creative writing is intellectual drudgery of the hardest kind. Creative innovation, particularly on a fundamental scale, requires a still more exceptional degree of concentration and energy. To spend one's entire working life continually advancing the creative frontiers in one's art implies a level of self-discipline and intellectual industry which few writers have ever possessed.

I., P. 82

Most people when they write, including most professional writers, tend to slip into seeing events through the eyes of others because they inherit stale expressions and combinations of words, threadbare metaphors, clichés and literary conceits. This is particularly true of journalists, covering at speed occasions which are often repetitive and banal.

I., PP. 148–49

I fear it is true that in the perennial battle between writers and editors, it always pays to be difficult.

P.P.J., P. 213

Writing is a dusty business, all things considered: lonely and often depressing, more likely to end in failure and neglect than in triumph. Most authors are doomed to live in the shadows rather than in the limelight.

s., AUGUST 26, 1989

Y

YAHWEH AND THE JEWS

In exile, the Jewish faithful tried to differentiate themselves as much as possible from the pagan Babylonians: indeed, the period seemed to make Yahweh more powerful and his relationship with the Jews more exclusive, for Yahweh was behind everything that had happened in the great convulsion of Near Eastern history, and had used the mighty Assyrian and Babylonian empires as the rod of his anger, to execute his judgment against his chosen people. As Yahweh became more powerful in Jewish eyes, so he became more attached to his people, and the Israelites struggled to preserve their special identity in a hostile world striving to annihilate them.

C.H.L., PP. 74–75

YIDDISH

Yiddish was a rich, living language, the chattering tongue of an urban tribe. It had the limitations of its origins. There were very few Yiddish words for animals or birds. It had virtually no military vocabulary. Such defects were made up from German, Polish, Russian. Yiddish was particularly good at borrowing: from Arabic, from Hebrew-Aramaic, from anything which came its way. On the other hand it contributed: to Hebrew, to English-American. Its chief virtue, however, lay in its internal subtlety, particularly in its characterization of human types and emotions. It was the language of street wisdom, of the clever underdog; of pathos, resignation, suffering, which it palliated by humour, intense irony and superstition.

[403]

Isaac Bashevis Singer, its greatest practitioner, pointed out that it is the only language never spoken by men in power.

H.J., PP. 338–39

YOUTH

Young people, whether children or adolescents, tend to reject the conventional wisdom of their instructors, when they perceive it to constitute a monolithic orthodoxy. This applies whether such wisdom is radical or conservative, idealist of materialist.

P.P.J., P. 190

The one form of change we can always count on is the violent oscillation of intellectual fashion among the young.

N.Y.T.M., MARCH 22, 1984

The growing public approval of anti-culture is itself, I think, a reflection of the new cult of youth. Bewildered by a rapidly changing society, excessively fearful of becoming out of date, our leaders are increasingly turning to young people as guides and mentors—or, to vary the metaphor, as geiger-counters to guard them against the perils of mental obsolescence. If youth likes jazz, then it must be good, and clever men must rationalize this preference in intellectually respectable language. Indeed, whatever youth likes must be good: the supreme crime, in politics and culture alike, is not to be "with it."

S.N., PP. 46–47

If the Beatles and their like were in fact what the youth of Britain wanted, one might well despair. I refuse to believe it—and so I think will any other intelligent person who casts his or her mind back far enough. What were we doing at sixteen? . . . It is a marvellous age, an age of intense mental energy and discovery. Almost every week one found a fresh idol—Milton, Wagner, Debussy, Matisse, El Greco, Proust—some, indeed, to be subsequently toppled from the pantheon, but all springing from the mainstream of European culture. At sixteen, I and my friends heard our first

[404]

performance of Beethoven's Ninth Symphony; I can remember the excitement even today. We would not have wasted 30 seconds of our precious time on the Beatles and their ilk.

S.N., P. 48

Are teenagers different today? Of course not. Those who flock round the Beatles, who scream themselves into hysteria, whose vacant faces flicker over the TV screen, are the least fortunate of their generation, the dull, the idle, the failures: their existence, in such large numbers, far from being a cause for ministerial congratulation, is a fearful indictment of our education system, which in ten years of schooling can scarcely raise them to literacy. . . . [But] the boys and girls who will be the real leaders and creators of society tomorrow—never go near a pop concert. They are, to put it simply, too busy. They are educating themselves. They are in the process of inheriting the culture which, despite Beatlism or any other mass-produced mental opiate, will continue to shape our civilization.

S.N., PP. 48–49

Z

ZIONISM

. . . the Jews had grasped that the civilized world, however defined, could not be trusted. The overwhelming lesson the Jews learned from the Holocaust was the imperative need to secure for themselves a permanent, self-contained and above all sovereign refuge where if necessary the whole of world Jewry could find safety from its enemies. The First World War made the Zionist state possible. The Second World War made it essential.

H.J., P. 517

Zionism had no place for God as such. For Zionists, Judaism was just a convenient source of national energy and culture, the Bible no more than a State Book. That was why from the start most religious Jews regarded Zionism with suspicion or outright hostility and some . . . believed it was the work of Satan.

H.J., P. 547

Bibliography of Paul Johnson Works
Cited with Symbols

BOOKS

B.M.   *Birth of the Modern* (New York: HarperCollins, 1991)
C.H.L.   *Civilizations of the Holy Land* (New York: Atheneum, 1979)
E.   *Elizabeth I* (New York: Holt, Rinehart and Winston, 1974)
E.S.   *Enemies of Society* (New York: Atheneum, 1977)
H.C.   *A History of Christianity* (New York: Atheneum, 1983)
H.E.   *A History of the English People* (London: Weidenfeld, 1972)
H.J.   *A History of the Jews* (New York: Harper & Row, 1987)
I.   *Intellectuals* (New York: Harper & Row, 1988)
Id.   *Ireland* (Illinois: Academy Chicago Publishers, 1984)
M.T.   *Modern Times: The World from the Twenties to the Nineties* (New York: HarperCollins, 1992)
P.J.   *Pope John Paul II and the Catholic Restoration* (New York: St. Martin's Press, 1981)
P.P.J.   *The Pick of Paul Johnson* (London: Harrap, 1985)
R.F.   *The Recovery of Freedom* (Oxford: Blackwell, 1980)
S.N.   *Statesman and Nation* (London: Sidgwick and Jackson, 1971)

PERIODICALS

A.S.   *The American Spectator*
C.   *Commentary*
F.A.   *Foreign Affairs*
N.R.   *National Review*
N.Y.T.B.R.   *The New York Times Book Review*
N.Y.T.M.   *The New York Times Magazine*
S.   *The Spectator*
R.D.   *Reader's Digest*
U.S.N.   *U.S. News & World Report*
W.P.R.   *World Press Review*

Index of Topics

This index includes only those topics in an excerpt other than the topic under which that excerpt is listed in the text.

Marxism, 43, 55, 65, 96, 121, 126, 151, 319, 330
Marxist regimes, 112
materialism, 154
Medawar, Peter, 49
media, 57, 102, 127, 165, 186, 204, 226–31, 391
medical education, 90
mercy, 224
Messiah, 171
Mill, John Stuart, 63
monasticism, 55
moral absolutes, 146
moral law, 97
moral order, 214
moral relativism, 91
morals, 197
Moslems, 101
Muggeridge, Malcolm, 32, 86
Mussolini, Benito, 75, 80, 126, 203

Nagasaki, 136
Napoleon III, 80
nationalism, 118
National Socialism, 247, 248, 249
national spirit, 214
natural law, 3
Nazis, 17, 21, 59
Newman, John Henry, Cardinal, 5, 268
newspapers, 205
newspeak, 200
New Yorkers, 12
Nixon, Richard M., 165, 391
novels, 16

oligarchy, 281
Opium Wars, 28
Oppenheimer, Robert, 21
Ortega y Gasset, José, 377
Orwell's *Nineteen Eighty-Four*, 107

Palmer, Mitchell, 8, 11
Paris, 120
Parker, Charlie, 170
Pascal, Blaise, 180
Paul, St., 51, 52, 134, 196, 271
pedagogues, 4
Pentagon Papers, 230
Peter the Great, 135
political creed, 69
political process, 211, 280
politicians, 281, 282, 283
politics, 47, 310, 355, 364
Pol Pot, 75
pop culture, 72
Pope, Alexander, 347
Popper, Karl, 78, 274
popularity, 46
positivism, 69
post office, 113
press, 225, 284–87
pride, 110
private sector, 125
Prometheus, 221
Protestantism, 249
Protestants, 8, 163, 164
prudence, 390
public, the, 291
public spirit, 325
Puritans, 10

race, 118
racism, 65, 123
rationalism, 100
rationality, 333
Rauschning, Hermann, 21
Reagan, Ronald, 106
realpolitik, 110
reason, 333
Reformation, 24
relativism, 236, 242
religion, 99, 203, 249